The Economic Crisis and its Aftermath in the Nordic and Baltic Countries

The Nordic-Baltic region has become highly integrated. The Nordic countries have been successful in balancing competitiveness and economic growth with social inclusiveness, while the Baltic States have grown economically but remain vulnerable with weak social systems and highly unequal income distribution. European Union (EU) membership and inter-linkages with the continental Nordic banking systems appear to have affected the 2008/09 crisis response of the Baltic States.

In spite of their strengths, including their social systems, continental Nordic states are faced with a challenging mix of large, cross-border banks and highly indebted households at a time of rather weak global growth. The Baltic States are challenged by slow economic growth post-crisis, security concerns, and large-scale outward migration of the youngest and most highly educated people.

It is now a decade since the Baltic States were hit by the global crisis. It is time to take stock of their progress and assess their relations with other countries in the region and with the EU. This book focuses on the Baltics and their Nordic partners pre- and post-crisis: successes, failures, lessons learned, and future challenges, examining and comparing the crisis response of these various small states that enjoy different income levels, operate different welfare and tax systems, and seek different levels of integration with the EU.

Hilmar Þór Hilmarsson is a Professor at the University of Akureyri, School of Business and Science, Iceland, where he teaches courses on international business and macroeconomics. He received his degree in economics from the University of Iceland in 1987, an MA in economics from New York University in 1989, and a PhD in public administration and economic development from the American University in Washington, DC in 1992. He served as a Specialist and Co-ordinator with the World Bank Group in Washington, DC from 1990 to 1995, at the World Bank office in Riga, Latvia from 1999 to 2003 and the World Bank office in Hanoi, Viet Nam from 2003 to 2006. From 1995 to 1999 he served as a Special Advisor to the Minister for Foreign Affairs in Iceland.

Europa Economic Perspectives

Providing in-depth analysis with a global reach, this series from Europa examines a wide range of contemporary economic issues from areas around the world. Intended to complement the *Europa Regional Surveys of the World* series, *Europa Economic Perspectives* will be a valuable resource for academics, students, researchers, policymakers, business people and anyone with an interest in current world economic affairs.

While the *Europa World Year Book* and its associated *Regional Surveys* inform on and analyse contemporary economic, political and social developments, the Editors considered the need for more in-depth volumes written and/or edited by specialists in their field, in order to delve into a country's or a region's particular economic situation, or to examine economic theories in the context of current global economic affairs. Volumes in the series are not constrained by any particular template, but may explore any aspect of a country's recent economic issues in order to increase knowledge.

International Monetary Reform
A Specific Set of Proposals
John Williamson

Small States and the European Union
Economic Perspectives
Edited by Lino Briguglio

Advances in Geoeconomics
Edited by J. Mark Munoz

The Economic Crisis and its Aftermath in the Nordic and Baltic Countries
Do As We Say and Not As We Do
Hilmar Þór Hilmarsson

The Economic Crisis and its Aftermath in the Nordic and Baltic Countries

Do As We Say and Not As We Do

Hilmar Þór Hilmarsson

Routledge
Taylor & Francis Group
LONDON AND NEW YORK

First published 2019
by Routledge
2 Park Square, Milton Park, Abingdon, Oxon OX14 4RN

and by Routledge
605 Third Avenue, New York, NY 10017

First issued in paperback 2020

Routledge is an imprint of the Taylor & Francis Group, an informa business

Europa Commissioning Editor: Cathy Hartley
Editorial Assistant: Eleanor Simmons

British Library Cataloguing in Publication Data
A catalogue record for this book is available from the British Library

Library of Congress Cataloging in Publication Data
Names: Hilmarsson, Hilmar þór, author.
Title: The economic crisis and its aftermath in the Nordic and Baltic countries : do as we say and not as we do / Hilmar þór Hilmarsson.
Description: First Edition. | New York : Routledge, 2018. | Series: Europa economic perspectives
Identifiers: LCCN 2018018364 (print) | LCCN 2018034198 (ebook) | ISBN 9781351046831 (master) | ISBN 9781857439649 (hardback) | ISBN 9781351046831 (ebk)
Subjects: LCSH: Scandinavia–Economic conditions–21st century. | Baltic States–Economic conditions–21st century. | Scandinavia–Foreign economic relations–Baltic States–21st century. | Baltic States–Foreign economic relations–Scandinavia–21st century.
Classification: LCC HC345 (ebook) | LCC HC345 .H55 2018 (print) | DDC 330.948–dc23
LC record available at https://lccn.loc.gov/2018018364

ISBN 13: 978-0-367-90126-4 (pbk)
ISBN 13: 978-1-85743-964-9 (hbk)

Typeset in Times New Roman
by Taylor & Francis Books

Contents

Illustrations

Figures

Tables

Boxes

The Author

Hilmar Þór Hilmarsson is a Professor at the University of Akureyri, School of Business and Science, Iceland, where he teaches courses on international business and macroeconomics. He received his cand. oecon. degree in economics from the University of Iceland in 1987, an MA in economics from New York University in 1989, and a PhD in public administration and economic development from the American University in Washington, DC in 1992. He served as a Specialist and Co-ordinator with the World Bank Group in Washington, DC from 1990 to 1995, at the World Bank office in Riga, Latvia from 1999 to 2003 and the World Bank office in Hanoi, Viet Nam from 2003 to 2006. From 1995 to 1999 he served as a Special Advisor to the Minister for Foreign Affairs in Iceland. Dr Hilmarsson has published over 70 scholarly articles and book chapters and has lectured and made presentations at more than 30 universities in Europe and the USA, including the American University in Washington, DC, Aalborg University, Cornell University, Georgetown University, the Stockholm School of Economics, the University of California, Berkeley, the University of California, Los Angeles, the University of Latvia, the University of Mauritius, the University of Porto, the University of Tartu, the University of Washington, Vytautas Magnus University, the University of York, and Yale University. He has travelled to about 60 countries.

Professor Hilmarsson has held visiting appointments at several top universities in the USA and Europe. He was a Visiting Professor at the Stockholm School of Economics during the fall semester 2013, a Visiting Scholar at the University of Washington in Seattle in the spring semester 2014, a Visiting Professor at Cornell University during the fall semester 2015, a Visiting Scholar at the University of California, Berkeley during the fall semester 2016 and a Visiting Scholar at the University of Cambridge during the fall semester 2017.

Acknowledgements

I formally started work on this book while a Visiting Scholar at the University of California, Berkeley (UC Berkeley) during the fall semester 2016. My office was at the UC Berkeley Institute of European Studies and I was living in International House at UC Berkeley and benefited from speaking to great scholars from all over the world at both places. During the fall semester 2017 I was a Visiting Scholar at the University of Cambridge based at the Cambridge Centre for Economic and Public Policy, Department of Land Economy, where I continued and completed the first draft of the manuscript. My thinking about the Baltic States and their relations with the Nordic countries goes much further back in time, to when I served as a Special Advisor to the Minister for Foreign Affairs in Iceland from 1995 to 1999, a time when the Baltics were increasingly becoming integrated into Nordic co-operation as well as into international affairs. Subsequently I was privileged to work with many excellent professionals at the World Bank's Riga Office from 1999 to 2003 as well as with colleagues in other multilateral and bilateral institutions assisting with Latvia's transition at the time, and I also travelled extensively throughout the Baltics and met with many people. I also benefited from communication with many distinguished scholars, including during my appointments as a Visiting Professor at the Stockholm School of Economics in Riga (fall 2013), Visiting Scholar at University of Washington in Seattle (spring 2014) and Visiting Professor at Cornell University in Ithaca (fall 2015).

Since joining the University of Akureyri in 2006 I have greatly benefited from visiting and interacting with many students and faculty members at the following universities while teaching, giving seminars or speaking at conferences: Aalborg University (Denmark), the American University in Washington, DC (USA), Bifröst University (Iceland), Bucharest University of Economic Studies (Romania), Copenhagen Business Academy (Denmark), Cornell University (USA), Georgetown University (USA), Haaga-Helia University of Applied Sciences (Finland), Kaunas University of Applied Sciences (Lithuania), Klaipeda University (Lithuania), Pacific Lutheran University (USA), Riga Stradiņš University (Latvia), Stockholm School of Economics (Latvia and Sweden), Södertörn University (Sweden), Tallinn University of

Technology (Estonia), the University of Akureyri (Iceland), the University of the Basque Country (Spain), the University of Iceland, the University of Illinois at Chicago (USA), the University of Latvia, the University of Mauritius, the University of Porto (Portugal), the University of Tartu (Estonia), the University of Washington (USA), UC Berkeley (USA), the University of California, Los Angeles (UCLA) (USA), the University of York (UK), Vytautas Magnus University (Lithuania) and Yale University (USA). The Erasmus programme funded many of my visits to the Baltic States and I also received grants from EkoTekNord and the Nord Plus programme to visit the Nordic countries and the Baltic States. The University of Akureyri Research Fund also provided financial support for the book.

I cannot list all the lectures I have given or all the presentations made on Nordic-Baltic issues during the last ten years since I joined academia, but among recent seminars and conferences where I presented my ideas were the 12th Conference on Baltic Studies in Europe entitled: 'The Baltic states at 99: Past, Present and Future', at the University of Latvia in Riga, Latvia, in June 2017. When I was about to finish my assignment at UC Berkeley in November 2016, I gave a public presentation entitled: 'Do as we say and not as we do: Crisis response and post crisis results in the Nordic and Baltic Countries'. This presentation was co-sponsored by the Institute of European Studies; the Clausen Center for International Business and Policy; the Institute of Slavic, East European and Eurasian Studies; the EU Centre and Nordic Studies Programme. This was a great opportunity to introduce my book project and solicit questions and comments from colleagues at Berkeley. I made earlier presentations in California, both at UC Berkeley and UCLA, in May 2014. This earlier presentation at Berkeley was entitled: 'Iceland in an Era of Shadow Banking: A Model for Crash and Recovery?' This presentation was co-sponsored by the European Union Centre of Excellence; the Institute of European Studies; and the Institute of Slavic, East European and Eurasian Studies. The presentation at UCLA was entitled: 'Small States and Big Banks: What lessons can be learned from Iceland?' I also made presentations at Cornell University and Yale University in March 2014. The presentation at Cornell was sponsored by the Global Finance Initiative and entitled: 'The Banking Crisis in Iceland: Did the Government Pretend That Facts from Reality Were Other Than They Were?' At Yale I talked about Iceland and Latvia in a presentation entitled: 'Latvia and Iceland during a Global Crisis: Did They 'Own' Their Reform Programs?' In 2012 I gave a presentation at the University of Illinois at Chicago entitled: 'How Can the Baltic States Increase the Impact of their International Development Cooperation?' And in 2011 at the ninth Baltic Conference in Europe, held at Södertörn University in Sweden, my presentation was entitled: 'The Baltic States and their transition from being recipient countries to becoming donor countries'. I greatly benefited from discussions and comments received at those seminars and conferences as well as others, but the complete list of all the events in which I participated would be too long.

Naming all the individuals I interacted with while writing this book would also take too long, but I would like to name a few. While at UC Berkeley during fall 2016 I greatly benefited from discussions with Barry Eichengreen, the George C. Pardee and Helen N. Pardee Professor of Economics and Political Science. I also benefited from discussions with John Zysman, Professor of Political Science and his doctoral students Elsa Massoc and Brian Judge. I would like to thank my host, Jeroen Dewulf, Director of the Institute of European Studies and Gia White, Administrative Director, for their support in the early stages of writing on this book.

At the University of Cambridge, I benefited especially from discussions with Philip Arestis, a professor in the Department of Land Economy, and his student Christopher Day. I also discussed various parts of my work with Professor Ha-Joon Chang in the Economics Department. In October 2017 I visited the London School of Economics and interviewed Professor Paul De Grauwe, the John Paulson Chair in European Political Economy and a leading authority on the euro. I also benefited from discussions with Dr Yiannis Kitromilides at the Cambridge Centre for Economic and Public Policy, who has published on the euro crisis, including the crisis in Greece, and on Brexit. While visiting the University of Cambridge I also was a Visiting Scholar at Corpus Christi College. I want to thank the College Master, Stuart Laing, for his kind support and hospitality.

Earlier I benefited from communicating with scholars specializing in Nordic studies, including Professor Christine Ingebritsen, Director, Center for West European Studies, the University of Washington, USA; Arne Lunde, Associate Professor and Section Head, Scandinavian Section, who hosted my visit to UCLA in May 2014, and Dr Elisabeth Ida Ward, Director, Scandinavian Cultural Center, Pacific Lutheran University, USA.

In the Baltic States I have enjoyed long co-operation with many distinguished scholars, including Professor Erika Sumilo, Head of the Department of International Economics and Business, University of Latvia, Professor Ligita Šimanskienė, Klaipėda University, Lithuania and Professor Maaja Vadi at the University of Tartu in Estonia. I have participated in conferences organized by their universities and met hundreds of their students.

I would like to thank Hirokazu Miyazaki, Professor and Director of the Global Finance Initiative, for hosting my visit to Cornell University in March 2014. In October 2015, Professor Robert O. Keohane invited me to Princeton University, during which I had discussions with him and met with a group of doctoral students and faculty members. While a Visiting Professor at Cornell University during the fall semester 2015, I interacted with Professor Peter J. Katzenstein, a leading scholar of small-state issues. I also had the privilege to discuss the 2008 crisis in Iceland in his class and interact with his students. At Cornell I also met with Ravi Kanbur, who had a long and distinguished career at the World Bank Group before taking an academic position at Cornell. I also benefited from talking to my student Trung Quang Dinh, who completed his master's thesis at the University of Akureyri under my supervision and later went to Germany to pursue a doctoral degree as a Deutscher Akademischer Austauschdienst (DAAD) scholar. Professor Michael Czinkota invited me to Georgetown University to discuss the 2008 crisis in Iceland. I greatly enjoyed meeting with him and his students and gave a presentation to his international business class.

In June 2015, when writing a book chapter for Routledge on Iceland, I met with Francisco Ramon-Ballester, an economist at the European Central Bank in Frankfurt. I also met with Högni Kristjánsson, Ambassador Director General at the Ministry for Foreign Affairs in Iceland. In July 2015 I met with Marius Vahl, Senior Officer at the European Economic Area (EEA) Co-ordination Division, European Free Trade Association (EFTA), and Morten Jung, Head of Unit at the European Commission in Brussels. All these officials provided valuable comments and information.

In July 2016, before starting work on this book at UC Berkeley, I met with staff of the International Monetary Fund (IMF) to discuss my research. A follow-up meeting took place in December 2016. I especially benefited from discussions with Thomas Dorsey, Rimtautas Bartkus and Guðrún Sóley Gunnarsdóttir. Much of the data used in this book comes from IMF databases, as they provide datasets that can be compared across the countries discussed in this book.

In March 2017 I met with Uldis Rutkaste, Head of the Monetary Policy Department, and Juris Kravalis, Head of the International Relations Department at the Bank of Latvia.

In April 2017 I met with Mr Ričardas Kasperavičius, Senior Adviser in the Ministry of Finance, Vilnius, Lithuania, Professor Zenonas Norkus, Vice-Dean for Research and Strategic Planning, Faculty of Philosophy, Vilnius University and Professor Algirdas Miškinis, Vice-Dean of the Faculty of Economics, Vilnius University, Vilnius, Lithuania.

I would like to thank some of my Icelandic colleagues whom I talked to during my research. These include Ásgeir Brynjar Torfason, who had recently completed his doctoral studies in Sweden specializing in banking, and Baldur Þórhallsson, a professor and leading scholar of small state studies at the University of Iceland. I also want to thank Þráinn Eggertsson, Professor of Economics, University of Iceland and at the Hertie School of Governance, Berlin, Germany for constructive discussions and good advice over the last three decades.

I want to thank Routledge staff, especially Cathy Hartley, Europa Commissioning Editor, Eleanor Simmons, Editorial Assistant, Vera Chapman Browne, Copy Editor for the book and Dominic Corti, Senior Production Editor. Finally, I would like to thank my language editor Christopher Goddard for a careful review and excellent editing of the text.

Preface

I formally began working on this book when a Visiting Scholar at the Institute of European Studies (IES) at the University of California, Berkeley (UC Berkeley) during the fall semester 2016. Barry Eichengreen[1], Professor of Economics and Political Science at UC Berkeley, endorsed my application to visit IES. I met him and his colleagues at UC Berkeley in May 2014 when I was a Visiting Scholar at the University of Washington and gave a presentation on how the 2008 crisis severely affected my home country, Iceland.

Barry suggested that the title of this book should include: 'Do as we say and not as we do', reflecting my view of how the Nordic countries, particularly Sweden, influenced the Baltic response to the 2008/09 crisis and arguably pushed them, especially Latvia, in directions in which the Nordic countries, most notably Finland and Sweden, did not go themselves during their own banking crisis in the 1990s. The Baltics could not devalue their currencies during the 2008/09 crisis but during the crisis in the 1990s both Finland and Sweden did. The title thus became *The Economic Crisis and its Aftermath in the Nordic and Baltic Countries: Do As We Say and Not As We Do*. The crisis in the title refers mainly to the global economic and financial crisis that hit in the latter part of 2008, but other crises are also discussed for comparison, including an earlier crisis that hit Finland and Sweden in the early 1990s. I myself am from Iceland, the smallest—and sometimes forgotten—member of the Nordic group, which also includes Denmark, Finland, Norway and Sweden. Three of those Nordic countries—Denmark, Norway, and Swede—are also referred to as the Scandinavian countries; the continental Nordics then also include Finland. Iceland, which is surrounded by the Atlantic Ocean, of course does not qualify as a continental Nordic country.

My opinion was, and still is, that the ownership of the banking systems in the Baltics— Estonia, Latvia, and Lithuania—greatly influenced their crisis response and that the consequences continue post-crisis. The Baltics kept fixed exchange rates and implemented austerity programmes that could hardly have been implemented in any of the Nordic welfare democracies and perhaps not in any of the pre-2004 member countries of the European Union (EU) without serious civil unrest. Foreign banks, mainly continental Nordic banks, may also have influenced the actions of Nordic governments, the EU itself and the larger EU member states. Those interlinkages are discussed in this book. One can even ask whether sovereign countries such as the Baltics can be regarded as financially sovereign when their banking systems are primarily owned by a single country—in this case Sweden. This is not to say that Sweden had bad intentions when expanding its banking operations cross-border to the Baltic States. Foreign banks operating in transition countries such as the Baltics can help with modernization and increase competition, resulting in greater efficiency, better services, and so on. But a very high level of ownership concentration can be dangerous for both home and host countries. Perhaps Sweden, and even the EU as well as the larger EU member states, must do as their banks say? Keeping a fixed exchange rate became an EU condition for allowing the Baltics to enter the euro area against the advice of the International Monetary Fund (IMF), at least in the case of Latvia, the only Baltic State requesting and receiving IMF assistance during the 2008/09 crisis.

The Baltic States have historical ties with the Nordic countries and are in close geographical proximity to the continental Nordics, especially Finland, Sweden and Denmark. When the Baltics joined the World Bank Group as full member states, they also joined its Nordic Constituency, which now became the Nordic Baltic Constituency. This meant that at the World Bank Group the Baltic States shared a common board member, called the executive director, with the Nordic countries, and the Baltic staff that would become advisors at the Nordic Baltic office. The same arrangement would be used at the IMF. The Nordic countries and the Baltics would also cooperate at the European Bank for Reconstruction and Development (EBRD). This would also mean even closer ties and co-operation between the Nordic countries and the Baltic States during the latter's political and economic transition from Soviet central planning to a market economy. The Nordic countries were then, as they still are, donor countries, whereas the Baltic States were recipient countries of foreign aid, but have in recent years begun the transition to become donor countries in international organizations and also operate their own bilateral development programmes. The contribution of the Baltic States to international development cooperation remains small even taking into account the small size of their economies. Like Iceland, they tend to limit their international involvement to activities that are in their own economic, political and security interests. Now the Baltics are also members of the Nordic Investment Bank, based in Helsinki, Finland.

Iceland, the smallest member of the Nordic group, made the political decision in 1991 to become the first country in the world to recognize the independence of the Baltic States. Discussion on the Baltics and their future prospects received much attention in Iceland at the time. This decision was not without risks for Iceland, as trade with the Soviet Union had been important for decades. In fact, Iceland was then dependent on the Soviet Union for oil and gas. But Iceland took the initiative and the continental Nordics—Denmark, Finland, Norway and Sweden—would soon follow and open embassies in the Baltic States. Later they would also provide critical assistance to support the transition and modernization of the Baltic States. In addition to official development assistance, the private sector in the Nordic countries also engaged in the Baltics. Iceland's decision to recognize the Baltic States broke the ice and it remains uncertain if and when the other Nordic countries would have taken this initiative without a broader multilateral consensus, including within organizations such as the North Atlantic Treaty Organization (NATO) and the EU. On this issue Iceland made a unilateral move without consulting multilateral channels or the larger EU member states.

In my capacity as Political Advisor to the Icelandic Minister for Foreign Affairs, I visited the Baltic capitals several times and was, among other things, involved in integrating them into Nordic-Baltic World Bank Group co-ordination, especially when meetings for the constituency, which I also happened to chair, took place in Iceland. I took the initiative to invite the Baltic States for the first time to those meetings when they took place in Reykjavík. Not all the Nordic countries welcomed this initiative and felt that the Nordic countries should meet separately and speak 'Scandinavian'[2]. The fact of the matter, though, was that the Baltic States could not as independent states be excluded and they would eventually have to be integrated fully into the group.

Co-ordination between the Nordic countries and the Baltic States was especially intensive when the Icelandic Minister of Foreign Affairs represented all the Nordic and Baltic States at World Bank Group annual meetings as well as on the joint World Bank Group/IMF Development Committee. As could be expected, the Baltic States were initially occupied with their own development and transition as they, unlike the Nordic countries, were receiving assistance from the World Bank.

While the Baltic States are in geographical proximity to the Nordic Countries and their people are in many ways like-minded, they are also different. The Nordic countries managed to retain their independence after the Second World War. They have also managed to achieve status as among the highest-income countries in the world, and are classified as welfare states. Indeed, the Nordic welfare model is known internationally. They enjoy high status in the international arena and are often proactive in international organizations. The Baltic States, on the other hand, were occupied during and after the Second World War, were annexed by the Soviet Union and suffered from Soviet dominance and central planning.

Since independence in 1991, the Baltic States are increasingly integrating into the global system, but it is not clear where they are heading. Their current economic and social policies are neoliberal, with highly unequal income distribution, and their international approach focuses on their own narrow self-interest. Ethnic divisions, economic hardship and political strain still challenge democracy in the Baltics.

The integration of the Baltic States into global and European structures is driven both by their economic transition and by security concerns. They became members of the EU in 2004 and subsequently adopted the euro[3].

They have also all become member states of NATO. The Baltic States enjoyed strong economic growth after independence, but were severely hit by the 2008/09 global crisis, from which they are still recovering. This included social and economic sacrifices during the crisis with severe cuts in income and their still fragile, now almost non-existent, welfare programmes. Among the consequences has been outward migration on a large scale, especially among young people.

The fact that the Baltics are ethnically divided adds to the complexity of their transition. About 25% of the Estonian population is of Russian origin[4]. Even more complicated is the situation in Latvia, where close to 30% of the population is of Russian origin, as is about half the population of Riga. Ethnic divisions are a less serious issue in Lithuania. The presence of a large Russian population in the Baltics and proximity to the Russian Federation still creates tensions and security concerns. Many Russians born in the Baltics consider the Baltics as their home.

When transitioning to a market economy, the Baltic States have not emphasized welfare capitalism like the Nordic countries. In this regard the Baltics resemble the neoliberal Anglo-Saxon countries rather than the Nordic welfare states. Questions remain as to where they are heading in the short, medium, and long term. The Baltic States are closely connected with the continental Nordic countries via trade and investment links, but especially via the financial sector. The willingness of the Baltic States to make sacrifices and implement austerity programmes under pressure from larger nations and international organizations, most notably the EU, raises questions about their motives. A large share of their populations want close integration with Europe, and in particular the Nordic countries. EU membership represents a quest to achieve prosperity with the high standards of living enjoyed by prosperous Europe. Euro area membership has probably improved the security profile of the Baltics, but the economic costs have also been high as the euro area has experienced a prolonged crisis. NATO membership represents a quest for security and stability, but it also has been an irritant for Russia. The Russian minority undoubtedly also values relations with Russia. These divisions and security concerns, in addition to economic and welfare issues, also affect the behaviour and political economy of the Baltic States.

As victims during the 2008 global crisis, the Baltic States made painful transitions with high human costs, losing some of the youngest and most talented people to migration. Their response was undoubtedly influenced by the actions taken by continental Nordic countries to protect their own interests, and by pressures from the EU as well as from global institutions such as the IMF. Most notable were continental Nordic/Swedish banking interests. However, we should also bear in mind that income and wealth distribution within the Baltics is uneven, so that the preferences of the élite[5] in those countries are likely to differ from those of poorer members of the population. The austerity programmes implemented in the Baltics could scarcely have been implemented in any of the Nordic countries, where they are likely to have resulted in civil unrest on a large scale. Yet, this book will argue, Nordic banking owners, supported by their governments and the EU, protected their interests at the cost of the Baltic peoples' fragile welfare systems. Foreign banks in the region were bailed out. Ethnic divisions as well as proximity to Russia also played a role in the response by the Baltics, which wanted to remain a part of Europe, having only regained independence from Russia some 17 years earlier. It is also notable that the only countries in the Nordic-Baltic group adopting the euro, i.e. Finland and the Baltics, all share a border with Russia. Security seems as much a factor as possible economic benefits in the decision to adopt a common currency. What would have happened if the Swedes had decided to sell their banking interests in the Baltics? Potentially Russian or Chinese interests could have entered the frame, which might have given rise to further uncertainty.

The Baltics regained their independence a quarter of a century ago and it is now a decade since they were hit by the global crisis. It is time to take stock of their progress and assess their relations with other countries and with the EU. This includes the benefits and challenges associated with European economic integration. This book will focus on the Baltics and their Nordic partners pre- and post-crisis: successes, failures, lessons learned, and future challenges.

Notes

1 Barry Eichengreen is the George C. Pardee and Helen N. Pardee Professor of Economics and Political Science, see further https://eml.berkeley.edu/~eichengr/.
2 Danes, Norwegians and Swedes can understand each other's languages reasonably well but Icelandic remains the original Nordic language and is much less influenced by continental Europe than those three languages. For an interesting article on the Icelandic language, see 'An old tongue's new tricks: a language both ancient and modern' in *The Economist*, 23 Dec 2017, pp. 61–63, available at www.economist.com/news/christmas-specials/21732691-language-both-ancient-and-modern-strange-reinvention-icelandic. Finnish is from an entirely different language family.
3 Estonia adopted the euro in 2011, Latvia in 2014 and Lithuania in 2015.
4 **Important note for readers**: When encountering the terms 'Russians', 'Russian-speaking minority', 'of Russian origin' and similar expressions, the reader should exercise caution and bear in mind that ethnicity is a highly complex topic beyond the scope of this book, a focus of research in its own right, in which perceptions and politics may play as important a role as facts. In geopolitical terms, especially in the context of this book, the definition of 'Russians' is highly sensitive. With that in mind, the terms "Russians", "Russian-speakers", and so on are here very broadly applied to individuals, both Russian and non-Russian e.g. Ukrainians (see www.onlatvia.com/ukrainians-196) , Belarusians (see www.onlatvia.com/belarusians-194), Poles (see www.onlatvia.com/poles-7) and others from former Soviet republics and elsewhere present in the Baltics and who may speak Russian either as a mother tongue, or as a main means of communication or as a second/common language and who may have links to, or roots/family in, the former Soviet Union or its offspring—the Russian Federation (which contains many non-Russian minorities, such as Chuvash and Tartars) see e.g. www.newworldencyclopedia.org/entry/Russian_Federation and a plethora of Soviet successor states, such as Turkmenistan and

Georgia, not to mention the Commonwealth of Independent States (CIS), see http://www.cisstat.com/eng/cis.htm. These individuals form a significant minority (notably in Riga and Daugavpils in Latvia, see http://minorityrights.org/minorities/russians-4/ and Narva in Estonia, see www2.ohchr.org/english/bodies/hrc/docs/ngos/LIC_Estonia99.pdf) *passim,* also http://minorityrights.org/country/estonia/ and http://worldpopulationreview.com/countries/latvia-population/ Moreover, and perhaps surprisingly to those familiar with Riga, the absence of ethnicities from demographic figures sits somewhat strangely with the presence e.g. in Riga of restaurants and/or community associations from these countries in addition to 'Russian' ones (e.g. Armenians http://asbarez.com/45350/armenian-community-of-riga-marked-1700th-anniversary/ and Georgians, http://diaspora.gov.ge/?p=8490). In addition, some of Riga's thriving Jewish community may identify as Russian: see e.g. www.jewishvirtuallibrary.org/latvia-virtual-jewish-history-tour while Latvia also has a population of Roma—see https://ec.europa.eu/info/publications/national-roma-integration-strategies-annual-reports_en.

5 This book follows the definition at https://en.oxforddictionaries.com/definition/ 'Elite, a group or class of people seen as having the greatest power and influence within a society, especially because of their wealth or privilege.

Abbreviations and Acronyms

(The) Baltics	the Baltic States (Estonia, Latvia, Lithuania)
BIS	Bank for International Settlements
BRICS	Brazil, Russia, India, China, South Africa
CBI	Central Bank of Iceland
CEE	Central and Eastern Europe
EBRD	European Bank for Reconstruction and Development
ECB	European Central Bank
ECU	European Currency Unit
EEA	European Economic Area
EEC	European Economic Community
EEE	Eastern European economies
EFTA	European Free Trade Association
EIB	European Investment Bank
EMS	European Monetary System
EMU	Economic and Monetary Union
ERM	Exchange Rate Mechanism
EU	European Union
EU-15	the member states of the EU prior to 1 May 2004 (Austria, Belgium, Denmark, Finland, France, Germany, Greece, Ireland, Italy, Luxembourg, the Netherlands, Portugal, Spain, Sweden and the United Kingdom)
FDI	foreign direct investment
FX	foreign exchange
GDP	gross domestic product
GNI	gross national income
IMF	International Monetary Fund
NATO	North Atlantic Treaty Organization
NB8	the five Nordic countries plus the three Baltic countries (Nordic-Baltic Eight)
NIB	Nordic Investment Bank
(The) Nordics	the Nordic countries (Denmark, Finland, Iceland, Norway, Sweden)
OECD	Organisation for Economic Co-operation and Development

OSCE	Organization for Security and Co-operation in Europe
PIIGS	Portugal, Italy, Ireland, Greece, Spain
PSAL	programmatic structural adjustment loan
SDR	Special Drawing Rights
SGP	Stability and Growth Pact
SIC	Special Investigation Commission
UC	University of California (e.g. UC Berkeley)
UCLA	University of California Los Angeles
UK	United Kingdom
UN	United Nations
US(A)	United States (of America)
USSR	Union of Soviet Socialist Republics

Introduction

This book focuses on a group of small states: the Nordic-Baltic countries, comprising the five Nordic countries (Denmark, Finland, Iceland, Norway and Sweden) and the three Baltic States (Estonia, Latvia and Lithuania), their response to the crisis of 2008/09 and the post-crisis consequences. Sometimes they are collectively referred to as the Nordic-Baltic Eight (NB8). The analysis will have both a regional and an international focus, as regional institutions such as the European Union (EU) and global institutions such as the International Monetary Fund (IMF) affect the environment in which these countries operate and can influence their policy choices.

This is especially true of the Baltics, which are not as wealthy as the Nordics and may thus be more dependent on regional or international assistance, especially during times of crisis. States within the Nordic-Baltic group may also affect policy decisions within the group—most notably, larger, wealthier states may influence policy choice in smaller states. This book's subtitle, 'Do as we say and not as we do', refers mainly to a comparison between how Nordic countries may want the Baltic States to respond to crisis as compared to how they would respond themselves in comparable situations. For example, we can compare how Finland and Sweden responded to the banking crisis they experienced in the 1990s with how the Baltic States responded to the 2008/09 global economic and financial crisis, arguably under Nordic (mainly Swedish) influence. All those countries are then influenced by regional and global institutions, as will be discussed.

Contradictions can occur in the way in which countries respond to challenges and the way in which they expect other countries to respond, even in similar circumstances. This can have intended and unintended consequences, with economic, political, social and security implications. While the discussion in this book focuses on the five Nordic countries and the three Baltic States, it can also be of interest to anyone studying the challenges faced by small states and their behaviour, including their interactions with larger states, with banks that are large compared to the size of their economies, as well as with regional and global organizations. All these players influence and are influenced by consequences for small states. Larger states and international organizations can become a shelter for small states during times of crisis, but smaller, weaker states can also be vulnerable if conflicts of interest exist. The private sector also plays a role here, including banks that may seek to influence the behaviour of governments and, regional and international organizations.

The Nordic countries have linkages with the Baltic States due to geographical proximity, but also because of a shared history that dates back centuries. Hence it is reasonable to assume that the Nordic countries feel a certain degree of responsibility for the fate of the Baltic States, which have suffered a turbulent history. Independent and co-operative Baltic States are also of importance for the Nordic countries for economic and for security reasons. Prior to the establishment of the Soviet Union, the Baltic States had strong business ties with the Nordic countries stretching all the way back to the Middle Ages.

After the Second World War the three Baltic States were under Soviet occupation as component republics of the Union of Soviet Socialist Republics (USSR)[1]. The fall of the Soviet Union was an opportunity for the Baltic States to re-establish their independence. One can even argue that the Nordic countries have served as mentors for the Baltic States in the post-Soviet period, which already spans a quarter of a century, and played a crucial role in their transition from being Soviet republics to modern independent states. Nevertheless, the Baltic relationship with Russia still remains important because of shared borders, transport, trade and investment linkages, and because of the presence of a large number of Russians[2] who live in the Baltics, especially in Estonia and Latvia, and who consider them as their home country. A stable Russia is thus important for the Baltic States. The behaviour of the Baltic States, most notably a strong desire for close European integration, cannot be fully understood without taking into account their proximity to Russia, the borders[3] and the presence of a large population residing in the Baltic States that is of Russian origin. A stable and democratic Russia would certainly help the Baltics in their transition as well as in regional and global integration.

Iceland was the first country in the world to recognize the independence of the Baltic States when the Soviet Union fell in 1991. One could sense some irritation among the Nordic countries, as well as among EU and North Atlantic Treaty Organization (NATO) member states, when Iceland, the smallest country among the Nordics, took this initiative at a time when others emphasized caution in destabilizing the Soviet Union and did not want to disrupt the partnership with the reformist Soviet leader Gorbachev. The other Nordic countries soon followed the Icelandic initiative and became involved in their transition, opening embassies and initiating bilateral assistance programmes. Iceland, the smallest of the Nordic countries and the furthest away from the Baltics, did not have a capacity for such engagement, but nonetheless remained a strong supporter of Baltic independence internationally, including within international organizations. Business ties also developed in various sectors, becoming especially strong in the financial sector, where

Sweden became a dominant player. Trade between the Baltics and the Nordics grew—especially between Estonia on the one hand and Finland and Sweden on the other. Foreign direct investment was important in all the Baltic States, especially from Sweden as well as between Finland and Estonia[4].

In 1994 Carl Bildt, then Prime Minister of Sweden, wrote an article entitled: 'The Baltic Litmus Test'. In the article he comments as follows:

> Following the lead of Sweden and the Nordic countries, the European Union recently concluded free trade agreements with the Baltic countries, paving the way for European agreements similar to those concluded with the Central European Countries. More significantly, the EU has committed itself to having Estonia, Latvia and Lithuania eventually become members.
>
> (Bildt 1994, p. 82)

European integration was thus seen as of crucial importance for the Baltic States. The Nordic countries, especially those that were already members of the EU[5], would advocate Baltic membership. Integration into European systems and institutions was seen as critical for the economic transition of the Baltics, but also for political and security reasons, given their shared borders with Russia. In fact, the process of bringing the Baltic States into the institutions of European co-operation was seen as a way to contribute not only to their own security, but to the security of the whole northern European region, including the Nordic countries.

According to Bildt's article, the risk of Russia again becoming a threat to the international system was, as it still is, a key concern. After the fall of the Soviet Union, Russia only bordered the EU in the Nordic-Baltic region. Soon the Baltic States would also apply for NATO[6] membership and the role of the USA as the backbone of NATO would become crucially important for their independence and security. Russia continues to be a concern for the Baltics; indeed, the annexation of the Ukrainian territory of Crimea by Russia in 2014 has heightened the Baltic States' risk profile. Questions about the commitment of the administration of Donald J. Trump in the USA to NATO present a further concern for the Baltics and Nordic NATO member states—and undoubtedly also for the Nordic non-NATO member states, Finland and Sweden. The USA has become unpredictable, with President Trump arguing one day that NATO is obsolete and another day saying it is not, and its commitment and intentions have come under question in Europe.

The Nordic countries and the Baltic States have pursued quite different levels of European integration, including different monetary regimes. Iceland and Norway are the least integrated into European structures, staying out of the EU, but both are members of the European Free Trade Association with its access to the EU single market via the European Economic Area Agreement in 1994. Both countries have their own currency, the Icelandic króna and the Norwegian krone. Denmark and Sweden are more integrated as EU member states. Both countries have their own currency, but the Danish krone is pegged to the euro while the Swedish krona is floating. Finland and the Baltic States have the highest level of integration as EU member states which are also members of the euro area. All the Nordic countries and Baltic States are members of the Schengen Area.

One could perhaps argue that their different approaches to integration weaken this group of countries within the EU, with no obvious pathways common to the whole group. The EU has failed to deal decisively with the aftermath of the 2008/09 crisis. For the 'hardcore' euro area member states in the Nordic-Baltic group, (that is, Finland and the Baltics), structural flaws in the monetary union remain a concern that can result in increased uncertainty and disintegration.

In addition to participation in European integration, albeit at different levels, the Nordic countries and the Baltic States co-operate in several international and regional organizations. Examples of co-operation in global organizations are the Bretton Woods institutions, i.e. the World Bank Group and the IMF. In both institutions the Nordic and Baltic representatives share executive offices and a common board member, called the executive director. The board member rotates and each country will have a representative who might be the executive director, the alternate executive director or an advisor. Co-operation in regional institutions extends to the European Bank for Reconstruction and Development, and the Nordic Investment Bank is also important.

While the Nordic countries and the Baltic States are linked via European institutional structures, co-operate in global and regional institutions, have a shared history and are in close geographic proximity, as discussed above, they are also in many aspects quite different from one another. When the global financial and economic crisis hit in 2008, their situations shared some similarities, but there were also differences. Among those differences was the fact that the Nordic countries are all high-income countries and have strong social 'safety nets'. The Nordics are classified as welfare states and the Nordic welfare model is well known internationally. By international standards they have a relatively even income distribution (according to the Gini index) and they generally have a favourable business and investment climate on a global scale (see Table I.1). By contrast, the Baltic States have reached high income levels according to World Bank Group classifications, but their income is still much lower than that enjoyed by the Nordic countries. Moreover, their income is less evenly distributed among their citizens and their governments have not attempted to establish welfare systems that resemble those in the Nordic countries. In fact, this book will argue that their welfare system resembles the Anglo-Saxon model more closely than the Nordic welfare model. Their business and investment climate, as measured by the World Bank's *Doing Business* report, is considered favourable on a global scale (see Table I.1).

Table I.1 The Nordic-Baltic region—Some key indicators

Country	*Size of economy 2016 (US$ million)*	*World ranking of economy 2016*	*Relative share of total Nordic and Baltic economies 2016 (%)*	*Gross national income per capita 2016 (US$)*	*Gini coefficient[7] 2015*	*World Bank Ease of Doing Business rank (June 2017)*	*Population at June 2017 (million)*	*Land area (sq km)*
Nordics								
Denmark	295,164	37	19.5	61,310	27.4	3	5.73	42,430
Finland	229,810	44	15.2	47,380	25.2	10	5.49	303,890
Iceland	16,598	113	1.1	47,640	23.6	19	0.33	100,250
Norway	388,315	28	25.7	103,050	23.9	9	5.23	365,245
Sweden	492,618	22	32.5	61,600	26.7	8	9.90	407,340
Baltics								
Estonia	22,691	105	1.5	18,530	34.8	16	1.32	42,390
Latvia	27,035	102	1.8	15,660	35.4	22	1.96	62,190
Lithuania	41,244	88	2.7	15,380	37.9	20	2.87	62,675

Sources: World Bank (2016a and 2016b), World Bank (2017), Eurostat (2017) and Statistics Iceland (2015).

The Baltics have emerged from their Soviet communist past to become orthodox free market societies, perhaps hoping that this approach would become a driver of strong future growth arising from vibrant business, both domestic and foreign. Indeed, the Baltic States need high growth in gross domestic product (GDP) to converge with the Nordic countries in terms of income and welfare for their citizens. However, as will be discussed, the results of their economic policy—especially during the crisis, but also in its aftermath—are disappointing, exhibiting rather slow growth, high unemployment and uneven income distribution. Grounds for optimism about convergence with the rich Nordics or EU-15[8] member states have, after 25 years of independence, become somewhat illusory.

In addition to official institutional links between the Nordic countries and the Baltic States, personal and private sector links between those countries also exist. The Nordics had enjoyed close political and cultural ties for decades, long before the Baltics reclaimed their independence in 1991. The Nordics maintained a passport union that allowed their citizens visa-free travel between member states. Citizens of the Nordic countries have often sought jobs and education outside their own country and, to a large extent, within the Nordic region. Soviet occupation of the Baltic States disrupted interaction between them and the Nordic countries for decades. EU membership has since 2004 enabled access by Baltic citizens to the common EU internal market, including in the Nordic countries[9]. In fact, after the fall of the Soviet Union and with full EU membership, including free flow of labour, goods, services and capital, things have changed dramatically. People move freely across Nordic and Baltic borders for business, as tourists, for jobs, seeking education, and so on. Now extensive trade and investment flows occur between the Nordic countries and the Baltic States.

Like many countries in Central and Eastern Europe, the Baltic States had no modern banking systems at independence. This resulted in a banking system that was mostly imported from other countries. For the Baltics, the banking systems came across borders from the Nordic countries, especially Sweden. These foreign banks with their highly concentrated ownership helped modernize the Baltics and provided the financial services needed to rebuild these countries after the devastation left by the Soviet Union. However, cross-border trade, investment and financial sector links can bring not only benefits but also challenges. This became clearly evident during the crisis that hit in 2008. The banking interlinkages between the continental Nordic countries and the Baltic States were a challenge for both groups of countries. Indeed, those links can yield unexpected and unintended outcomes for the players involved in both home and host countries.

The crisis and post-crisis developments in the Baltic States have received much less international attention than in the Southern European countries: Greece, Italy, Portugal, and Spain. The plight of Greece has been widely covered, and continues to be hotly debated. One reason for this is that the Southern European countries are all much larger than the Baltic States in terms of either the size of their economy or the size of their population. The combined GDP of the Baltic States accounts for slightly less than half of the economy of Greece[10]. Because of their relative size, the Southern European countries pose a more serious threat to the EU and euro area stability than do the Baltics. The other reason is that the Baltics appear to be more willing to do what they are told by stronger outside forces, yielding to the demands of larger states as well as regional and international organizations. Instead of shielding the Baltics, outside forces oppress them. To a degree, the Baltics are victims of circumstances and geography.

Internally the Baltics have made progress and are now modern states. However, ethnic divisions persist, along with economic hardship, highly unequal income and wealth distribution and political tensions. Government policies that would have resulted in civil unrest in other countries could be implemented in the Baltics without much resistance, given that extreme austerity did not lead to serious or long-lasting riots in the Baltics. Instead, the result would be mass exit from the Baltics, mainly to richer countries that can offer Baltic citizens a better income and more generous welfare benefits.

The EU has attempted to praise the Baltics as examples of how countries should respond to crisis via a fixed exchange rate and austerity programmes—policies that the EU may have wished to see applied in Southern Europe. The architect of austerity in Latvia, Valdis Dombrovskis—then the country's prime minister—was appointed to a position on the European Commission after his resignation in 2014, becoming Vice-President for the Euro and Social Dialogue[11]. It will be argued in this book that implementing extreme austerity in a relatively poor country led, in Latvia's case, to the loss of human capital as a consequence of long-term unemployment, as well as migration resulting from the austerity programme. It is our contention that the programme will slow long-term growth in the Baltics and indeed in the EU overall.

When preparing a proposal for this book the following questions came to mind:

- How did the Nordic countries and the Baltic States respond to the 2008/09 global crisis, and what are the economic and social post-crisis consequences?
- How did banking, investment and trade linkages affect the crisis response in the Nordic-Baltic region?
- How did the Baltic States respond to the 2008/09 crisis, compared to the crisis response in Finland and Sweden in the 1990s?
- How have the welfare and tax systems in the Baltic States developed in recent years compared to the Nordic welfare and tax systems?
- How are the austerity programmes implemented in the Baltic States, and the associated human costs, likely to affect long-term growth potential in the Baltic States?
- What are the opportunities and challenges of economic integration in the Nordic-Baltic region, given the different levels of involvement of those

countries in EU institutions and systems, including financial sector integration?

These questions relate to crisis response and post-crisis consequences in the Nordic and Baltic region. They also highlight the possible effects of interlinkages between the Nordic countries and the Baltic States and how they affect policy decisions, and, eventually, economic and social outcomes. It is now more than a quarter of a century since the Baltic States once again became independent and 10 years since the global crisis hit. Sufficient time has now passed to be able to see some of the medium- and long-term effects of different policy decisions. It is also interesting to take stock of the economic and social conditions in the Baltics, given the time that has passed since their independence. However, the overall purpose of this book is to compare and contrast different policies and policy outcomes as between the Nordic countries, on the one hand, and the Baltic States on the other, and to see how the interlinkages between these two groups are affecting the Baltic States in particular. When proceeding with research, even more questions and issues came to mind. Some of these are addressed in this book, while others are subjects for future research as discussed in detail at the end of the concluding chapter in this book.

Although this book is not intended to be a list of questions and answers, the chapters have been framed in the following way to respond to the questions and issues raised above.

Chapter 1 Theories employed and methodology applied in this book.
Chapter 2 Pre-crisis and post-crisis economic and social performance of the Nordic countries and the Baltic States: an overview.
Chapter 3 The Nordic countries and the Baltic States—small states and multilateralism.
Chapter 4 European Union integration and the Nordic-Baltic region, Schengen and NATO.
Chapter 5 Exchange rate policy: fixed or floating?
Chapter 6 The challenges of euro area membership: Economic benefits versus security concerns, and the euro area versus NATO.
Chapter 7 Nordic-Baltic banking interconnectedness and its consequences.
Chapter 8 International organizations as economic policy advisors for small states: the Baltics as victims?
Chapter 9 The Nordic welfare model[12] and the Baltic States' Anglo-Saxon bias.
Chapter 10 Fragile Baltic democracy and the challenges posed by outbound migration.
Chapter 11 The extreme cases of Iceland and Latvia during the global economic and financial crisis.
Chapter 12 The Nordic-Baltic region: successes, failures, lessons learned and future challenges.

Chapter 13 The Nordic countries and the Baltic States: the need for further research.

Finally, a reminder for the reader: When reading the book cover to cover the reader will notice a certain amount of repetition. This is because each chapter is meant to some extent to be independent for those who prefer to dip into the book to study specific issues instead of reading the whole book in traditional 'start-to-finish' style.

Notes

1 The USSR, also called the Soviet Union in this book, is the former northern Eurasian empire (1917/22–1991) stretching from the Baltic and Black Seas to the Pacific Ocean and, in its final years, consisting of 15 Soviet Socialist Republics: Armenia, Azerbaijan, Belarus, Estonia, Georgia, Kazakhstan, Kyrgyzstan, Latvia, Lithuania, Moldova, Russia, Tajikistan, Turkmenistan, Ukraine, and Uzbekistan. The capital was Moscow, then and now the capital of Russia.
2 For more details, see endnote discussion in Preface.
3 Estonia and Latvia have eastern borders with Russia but Lithuania shares borders with the Kaliningrad exclave of Russia. Kaliningrad is sandwiched between Poland to the south and Lithuania to the north and east.
4 See the Baltic Cluster Report, Figure 3, page 10. Available at: www.imf.org/en/Publications/CR/Issues/2016/12/31/Baltic-Cluster-Report-Selected-Issues-41541.
5 Denmark, Finland and Sweden.
6 The North Atlantic Treaty Organization (NATO), also called the North Atlantic Alliance, is an intergovernmental military alliance based on the North Atlantic Treaty signed on 4 April 1949. At present, NATO has 28 members. In 1949, the 12 founding members of the Alliance were: Belgium, Canada, Denmark, France, Iceland, Italy, Luxembourg, the Netherlands, Norway, Portugal, the UK and the USA. The other member countries are: Greece and Turkey (date of joining 1952), Germany (1955), Spain (1982), the Czech Republic, Hungary and Poland (1999), Bulgaria, Estonia, Latvia, Lithuania, Romania, Slovakia, Slovenia (2004), and Albania and Croatia (2009). See www.nato.int/cps/en/natohq/topics_52044.htm.
7 The Gini index is a measurement of the income distribution of a country's residents. This number, which ranges between 0 and 1 and is based on residents' net income, helps define the gap between rich and poor, with 0 representing perfect equality and 1 representing perfect inequality. It is typically expressed as a percentage, referred to as the Gini coefficient. See www.investopedia.com/terms/g/gini-index.asp.
8 The EU-15 comprised the following 15 countries: Austria, Belgium, Denmark, Finland, France, Germany, Greece, Ireland, Italy, Luxembourg, Netherlands, Portugal, Spain, Sweden and the UK.
9 Iceland and Norway are not EU member states but have access to the EU internal market via the European Economic Area Agreement.
10 See for example: http://databank.worldbank.org/data/download/GDP.pdf.
11 See https://ec.europa.eu/commission/commissioners/2014-2019/dombrovskis_en.
12 Here the Nordic model is discussed since striking similarities exist between the principal features of this model among the Nordic countries: Denmark, Finland, Iceland, Norway and Sweden. Obviously important differences also exist between the economies and policies of the Nordic countries but these will not be discussed in this book.

References

Bildt, C. (1994). 'The Baltic Litmus Test'. *Foreign Affairs*, Vol. 73, No. 5.

Eurostat (2017). *Database.* Available at: http://ec.europa.eu/eurostat/data/database.

Statistics Iceland (2015). 'Risk of poverty and income distribution 2014'. Available at: www.statice.is/publications/publication-detail?id=55055*Statistical Series*, 5 June 2015, Vol. 100, Issue 18. (Accessed on 7 January 2018).

World Bank (2016a). 'Gross domestic product 2016'. Available at: http://databank.worldbank.org/data/download/GDP.pdf (Accessed on 7 January 2018).

World Bank (2016b). 'Land area (sq. km)'. Available at: http://data.worldbank.org/indicator/AG.LND.TOTL.K2. (Accessed on 7 January 2018).

World Bank (2017). *Doing Business 2018. Reforming to Create Jobs.* Available at: www.doingbusiness.org/reports/global-reports/doing-business-2018. (Accessed on 7 December 2017).

1 Theories employed and methodology applied in this book

The theoretical approach employed in this book is multidisciplinary. It draws on theories in economics, international trade and finance, political science, public administration, and public policy. This broad approach also reflects the author's academic training and diverse experience in economic development, international trade and finance, and public administration; working as a staff member of a global financial institution—the World Bank Group—in three different continents, as an advisor to a minister for foreign affairs, and in academia as a professor.

Definitions and theories used in the book are introduced and discussed in more detail in each chapter where they are employed. These include different definitions, some still debated, such as what constitutes a small state. This discussion is relevant for the study, because the Nordic countries and the Baltic States—upon which the book focuses—are all classified as small states in European small states literature. But what is small is relative to what one is comparing with. What is a small state in the Asian context may not be small in the European context.

Theories about the behaviour of small states in multilateral institutions are also discussed, along with how they co-operate with, influence or are influenced by larger states, as well as other small states, when participating in multilateral arrangements including regional and global institutions. For example, a small state may seek shelter by co-operating with a large state on a bilateral basis—e.g. Iceland and the USA—but also by becoming a member in international organizations, e.g. the Baltics as European Union (EU) member states. Both cases involve costs, benefits and associated risks, which will be discussed in the book. As will be seen, shelter can be both a blessing and a curse for small states.

The book also mentions theories of economic integration in the context of the Nordic countries and the Baltic States. These countries have sought different levels of economic and political integration in Europe and thus have different arrangements with the EU as member or non-member states. The different pathways chosen in the Nordic-Baltic region may complicate future co-operation. Security is also central for the survival of small states, which may want to address security concerns in co-operation with other countries. The transatlantic link with North America has been central to the security of the Nordic-Baltic region, so the book refers to academic literature in this field. The North Atlantic Treaty Organization (NATO) is discussed in the book, since six out of eight countries in the Nordic-Baltic group are members, while the two non-members (Finland and Sweden) co-operate closely with NATO.

Different approaches and theories of exchange-rate policy and optimal currency areas are discussed in the context of the euro area, which some countries in the Nordic-Baltic region have entered, while others have chosen to keep their own currency and different exchange rate regimes, floating or pegged. The economics of monetary union are discussed, focusing on the euro area, including challenges related to fiscal union, banking union and common deposit insurance, as well as other issues. The book also analyses cross-border banking interconnectedness and the benefits, costs and risks associated with financial integration in the Nordic-Baltic region and participation or non-participation in a common EU banking union.

The extreme cases of Iceland and Latvia are compared and contrasted. Both countries were exceptionally hard hit by the 2008/09 crisis but chose very different pathways in their quest for recovery. In Iceland the local currency depreciated sharply and fiscal deficits were large and long-lasting, while Latvia kept the exchange rate fixed and implemented austerity. Iceland and its interactions with international organizations are also discussed to highlight the vulnerability of small states when they are isolated from international assistance, in this case resulting in an unprecedented collapse of its financial sector over a few days.

International organizations are analysed, especially in cases where international financial institutions and the EU act as neutral advisors to member states, with emphasis on their behaviour *vis-à-vis* small states. International organizations such as the Bretton Woods institutions maintain research departments and publish analytical work. Are small states at risk, for example, when dealing with international organizations that also include larger, richer and more powerful states which have an agenda that they can potentially impose on international organizations and therefore also on other less powerful, weaker member states? Can small states benefit while working with a group of countries when they chair the group and hold an important position on behalf of other countries such as at the World Bank and the International Monetary Fund (IMF) or in the EU?

The relationship between the Nordic welfare model and the Anglo-Saxon model is analysed in the context of the Nordic countries and the Baltic States. Sharp differences exist between the welfare model that the Nordic countries have adopted compared to the current neoliberal laissez-faire approach in the Baltic States, resulting in relatively friendly business environments, but weaker welfare systems. Democracy is also discussed, employing theories on 'Exit, Voice and Loyalty' (Hirschman 1970) to explain the different behaviour of individuals in the Nordic region versus the emerging Baltic region and how it may affect those countries. The focus here is mainly on the Baltic States, whose democracy is evolving and may still be fragile. The challenge of outward migration from the Baltic States is analysed as well as their social performance, using indicators measured by Eurostat such as: the Gini coefficient, the income quintile share ratio, the at-risk-of-poverty rate and, finally, the proportion of people at risk of poverty or social exclusion.

The methodology used in the book is the case study method, i.e., multiple case studies and comparative analysis. Compared to other research methods, a case study enables the researcher to examine the issues involved in greater depth. Among the sources of evidence used for analysis in the book are secondary data, including reports[1] and scholarly literature such as articles and books. The author also conducted interviews and exchanged emails with many scholars, mainly in the field of economics, international finance, political science, and public administration. This consultation also included interviews at the European Central Bank in June 2015, the EU and the European Free Trade Association in July 2015, the IMF in July and December 2016, in Latvia and Lithuania in February and April 2017, at the University of Cambridge in August and September 2017 and at the London School of Economics in October 2017.

The author made an open presentation at the University of California, Berkeley on 10 November 2016 and benefited greatly from the discussion[2]. The author also made a presentation on this topic at an international conference in Riga in June 2017 followed by a lively debate. The author has also engaged in discussion and dialogue with students and scholars from many universities[3] over the last 10 years, as recognized in the acknowledgements section.

Direct observation also plays a role in this book, as the author draws on his experience and observations while living in Iceland prior to and during the 2008/09 economic and financial crisis. The author also worked for the World Bank office in Riga, Latvia, for four years, from 1999 to 2003 and travelled extensively throughout the Baltic States during this period. Since 2006 he has lectured as a professor at many universities in all three Baltic States. In addition, he has lectured at universities in Denmark and Finland and was a visiting scholar at the Stockholm School of Economics in Riga during the fall semester of 2013. He was also a Special Advisor to the Icelandic Minister for Foreign Affairs from 1995 and 1999 and was Iceland's representative in the Nordic-Baltic World Bank co-ordination group, which, among other issues, discussed Scandinavia's response to its 1990s crisis and lessons learned.

Case studies, such as those that appear in this book, can hardly present results that can be evaluated on the basis of statistical significance. Therefore, caution is called for before generalizing or projecting the findings of one case study onto another case or situation (see for example Yin 2009). However, the study will refer to empirical studies by other researchers in academic institutions, as well as at institutions such as the IMF, the World Bank Group and the EU. Data from these and other institutions are used in tables and graphs to make sure that they can be compared across the countries discussed.

Some lessons from this book could have wider relevance than for the Nordic countries and the Baltic States only. This is especially true of small countries with a large cross-border banking sector with limited fiscal space to support banks during a financial crisis.

The case study method has been used before in analysing crisis and post-crisis issues. For example, Stiglitz (2016) claims, in his book *The Euro—How a Common Currency Threatens the Future of Europe:* 'This book is about economics and economic ideologies and their interactions with politics: it is a case study of how, even with the best of intentions, when new institutions and policies are created on the basis of oversimplified views of how economies function, the results can be not only disappointing, but even disastrous' (Stiglitz 2016, p. 7). Similar statements could also be made concerning the Baltic States and their move to orthodox free market policies, as well as the nature of Swedish cross-border engagement, not only within the continental Nordic region but even more so in the Baltics.

When attempting to explain the crisis response of the Nordic countries and the Baltic States and post-crisis results, it would be insufficient to rely on economic and financial analysis only. Focusing on typical variables of economic performance such as economic growth, unemployment, inflation, fiscal or current account balance, and debt would produce an incomplete analysis. In addition to such indicators, it is also important to consider social or welfare indicators, including those on poverty, social exclusion, income inequality and migration, to name just a few. Indicators that evaluate the business and investment environment in the Nordic-Baltic group are also referenced. Data on national accounts are mainly from the IMF's *World Economic Outlook* database, and data on social and welfare indicators from Eurostat.

It is also important to consider the political realities that have shaped these countries, with the Baltics having been part of the Soviet Union, which did not allow them freedom to protest or the possibility to migrate to other countries. These options did not re-emerge until the Baltics became EU member states, so that their citizens can again do both: criticize and/or exit across borders. In contrast, the Nordic countries are democracies and welfare states and did not suffer occupation after the Second World War.

Furthermore, we also need to consider security concerns when attempting to explain the behaviour of small states. The choice of a country to enter the euro area cannot be explained by economic integration theories only. Euro area membership is not only about belonging to a common currency area. It can also be viewed as a security alliance that comes in addition to—or perhaps to some extent replaces—the assurances that NATO provides or has provided. This is especially the case when the commitment of the largest contributor to NATO, namely the USA, has become uncertain. Given the complex economic, political and security environment which the Nordic-

Baltic region faces, the multiple theoretical and methodological approaches used in the book are thus essential for the analysis.

Notes

1 Including from institutions such as the IMF, the World Bank Group, the EU, and the European Central Bank.
2 The Institute of European Studies and the Clausen Center at UC Berkeley hosted this event, also supported by the EU Center; the Institute of Slavic, East European and Eurasian Studies; and the Nordic Studies Programme.
3 These include: Aalborg University (Denmark), the American University, Washington, DC (USA), Bifröst University (Iceland), Bucharest Academy of Economic Studies (Romania), Copenhagen Business Academy (Denmark), Cornell University (USA), Georgetown University (USA), Haaga-Helia University of Applied Sciences (Finland), Kaunas University of Applied Sciences (Lithuania), Klaipeda University (Lithuania), Odessa National Academy of Food Technologies (Ukraine), Pacific Lutheran University (USA), Riga Stradiņš University (Latvia), Stockholm School of Economics (Latvia and Sweden), Södertörn University (Sweden), Tallinn University of Technology (Estonia), the University of Akureyri (Iceland), the University of the Basque Country (Spain), the University of Iceland, the University of Illinois at Chicago (USA), the University of Latvia, the University of Mauritius, the University of Porto (Portugal), the University of Tartu (Estonia), the University of Washington (USA), the University of California, Berkeley (USA), the University of California, Los Angeles (USA), the University of York (UK), Vytautas Magnus University (Lithuania) and Yale University (USA).

References

Hirschman, A. O. (1970). *Exit, Voice and Loyalty: Responses to Decline in Firms, Organizations, and States.* Cambridge, MA and London: Harvard University Press.

Stiglitz, J. E. (2016). *The Euro—How a Common Currency Threatens the Future of Europe.* New York and London: W. W. Norton & Company.

Yin, R. K. (2009). *Case Study Research. Design and Methods* (4th ed., Vol. 5). California: SAGE Inc.

2 Pre-crisis and post-crisis economic and social performance of the Nordic countries and the Baltic States: an overview

The purpose of this chapter is to provide an overview of the pre- and post-crisis economic performance of the Nordic countries and the Baltic States. The period covered is 2005 to 2016. This can be a useful background for the chapters that follow, which will provide a greater in-depth analysis of the issues involved. Among the questions asked in the introduction to the book were the following:

- How did the Nordic countries and the Baltic States respond to the 2008/09 global crisis and what are the economic and social post-crisis consequences?
- How did banking, investment and trade linkages affect crisis response in the Nordic-Baltic region?
- How did the Baltic States respond to the 2008/09 crisis compared to the crisis response in Finland and Sweden in the 1990s?
- How have the welfare and tax systems in the Baltic States developed in recent years as compared to the Nordic welfare and tax systems?
- How are the austerity programmes implemented in the Baltic States, and the associated human costs, likely to affect long-term growth potential in the Baltic States?
- What are the opportunities and challenges of economic integration in the Nordic-Baltic region, given the different levels of involvement of those countries in EU institutions and systems, including financial sector integration?

This chapter will touch upon these questions but, as we shall see, the following chapters will analyse them in more detail until conclusions are reached in the final chapter of the book.

Crisis response and the economic and social post-crisis consequences

The economic and financial crisis that hit in the fall of 2008 was a global crisis affecting every corner of the world. All the Nordic countries (Denmark, Finland, Iceland, Norway and Sweden) and the Baltic States (Estonia, Latvia and Lithuania) faced negative growth rates in gross domestic product (GDP) the following year, in 2009. The drop in GDP and the increase in unemployment were larger in the Baltic States and Iceland than in any of the continental Nordic countries[1], (see Tables 2.1 and 2.2).

Their policy response was different, at least partially because of different levels of economic integration with the EU, as well as different aspirations for euro area membership[2]. This included different exchange rate regimes, floating and fixed, as will be discussed later in this book. At the time of the crisis in 2008/09, policy outcomes resulting from the different policy regimes were unknown for obvious reasons. Sufficient time has now passed to be able to see the short-, medium- and maybe some long-term economic consequences, perhaps even learning and drawing lessons from them. This chapter provides an overview of some key economic indicators during the years leading up to the crisis from 2005 to when the crisis hit in the fall of 2008, and the following years, 2009 to 2016.

While similarities can be found across the countries discussed in this book, we must also remember that these eight countries had different initial conditions and different experiences in the crisis. We should therefore be careful before generalizing across all of them, especially when comparing the Baltic States with the Nordic countries. We should keep in mind that these countries are at different levels of development. The five Nordic countries are all high-income countries, with a GDP per capita[3] in 2008 ranging from US $53,785 (Finland) to $96,500 (Norway). The Baltic States are at a lower income level, with a GDP per capita in 2008 ranging from $15,102 (Lithuania) to $18,144 (Estonia). The Nordic countries, as Nordic welfare states, have established themselves as among the richest countries in the world in per capita income terms, while the Baltic States, while classified as high-income countries by the World Bank, are still emerging countries in transition and have a more neo-liberal policy stance. In terms of economic and welfare policies the Baltics, post-Soviet Union, have chosen a very different path from the Nordics.

The Baltic States had extremely large and unsustainable imbalances in 2007, with current account deficits of 15% of GDP in Estonia and Lithuania, and 21% in Latvia, (see Table 2.3). Iceland had an even more extreme current account imbalance during the crisis (23% in 2008), driven by its cross-border banking activities.

Other indicators in the Baltics tell a similar story. Annual GDP growth rates were at or near 10% throughout the 2005–2007 period, and exceeded 10% at least once in all three Baltic States during this period. Unemployment fell sharply in all three countries to levels that some, including the IMF, would consider below structural unemployment and below levels seen before or since. In fact, none of the Baltic States has yet returned to pre-crisis unemployment rates.

This boom was not driven by fiscal imbalances; Estonia was in surplus from 2005–07, while Latvia and Lithuania were near balance (see Table 2.4).

Table 2.1 Nordic countries, Baltic States and euro area: Gross domestic product, constant prices 2005–16 (% change)

	2005	*2006*	*2007*	*2008*	*2009*	*2010*	*2011*	*2012*	*2013*	*2014*	*2015*	*2016*
Nordics												
Denmark	*2.3*	*3.9*	*0.9*	**-0.5**	**-4.9**	1.9	1.3	0.2	0.9	1.7	1.6	1.7
Finland	*2.8*	*4.1*	*5.2*	**0.7**	**-8.3**	3.0	2.6	-1.4	-0.8	-0.6	0.0	1.9
Iceland	*6.7*	*5.0.*	*9.4*	**1.5**	**-6.9**	-3.6	2.0	1.2	4.4	1.9	4.1	7.2
Norway	*2.6*	*2.4*	*2.9*	**0.4**	**-1.6**	0.6	1.0	2.7	1.0	1.9	1.6	1.1
Sweden	*2.8*	*4.7*	*3.4*	**-0.6**	**-5.2**	6.0	2.7	-0.3	1.2	2.6	4.1	3.2
Baltics												
Estonia	*9.4*	*10.3*	*7.7*	**-5.4**	**-14.7**	2.3	7.6	4.3	1.9	2.9	1.7	2.1
Latvia	*10.7*	*11.9*	*9.9*	**-3.6**	**-14.3**	-3.8	6.4	4.0	2.6	2.1	2.7	2.0
Lithuania	*7.7*	*7.4*	*11.1*	**2.6**	**-14.8**	1.6	6.0	3.8	3.5	3.5	1.8	2.3
Euro area	*1.7*	*3.2*	*3.0*	**0.4**	**-4.5**	2.1	1.6	-0.9	-0.3	1.3	2.0	1.8

Source: International Monetary Fund (2017).

Table 2.2 Nordic countries, Baltic States and euro area: Unemployment rate 2005–16 (% of total labour force)

	2005	*2006*	*2007*	*2008*	*2009*	*2010*	*2011*	*2012*	*2013*	*2014*	*2015*	*2016*
Nordics												
Denmark	*4.8*	*3.9*	*3.8*	**3.5**	**6.0**	7.5	7.6	7.5	7.0	6.5	6.2	6.2
Finland	*8.5*	*7.8*	*7.0*	**6.4**	**8.3**	8.5	7.8	7.7	8.2	8.7	9.4	8.8
Iceland	*2.6*	*2.9*	*2.3*	**3.0**	**7.2**	7.6	7.1	6.0	5.4	5.0	4.0	3.0
Norway	*4.6*	*3.4*	*2.5*	**2.6**	**3.2**	3.6	3.3	3.2	3.5	3.5	4.4	4.7
Sweden	*7.6*	*7.0*	*6.1*	**6.2**	**8.3**	8.6	7.8	8.0	8.0	7.9	7.4	6.9
Baltics												
Estonia	*8.0*	*5.9*	*4.6*	**5.5**	**13.5**	16.7	12.3	10.0	8.6	7.4	6.2	6.8
Latvia	*10.1*	*7.0*	*6.1*	**7.7**	**17.6**	19.5	16.2	15.0	11.9	10.8	9.9	9.6
Lithuania	*8.3*	*5.8*	*4.2*	**5.8**	**13.8**	17.8	15.4	13.4	11.8	10.7	9.1	7.9
Euro area	*9.1*	*8.4*	*7.5*	**7.6**	**9.6**	10.2	10.2	11.4	12.0	11.6	10.9	10.0

Source: International Monetary Fund (2017).

Table 2.3 Nordic countries and Baltic States: Current account balance 2005–16 (% of GDP)

	2005	*2006*	*2007*	*2008*	*2009*	*2010*	*2011*	*2012*	*2013*	*2014*	*2015*	*2016*
Nordics												
Denmark	*4.2*	*3.3*	*1.4*	**2.9**	**3.5**	6.6	6.6	6.3	7.8	8.9	9.2	7.9
Finland	*3.2*	*3.8*	*3.8*	**2.2**	**1.9**	1.2	-1.8	-1.9	-1.6	-1.3	-0.6	-1.1
Iceland	*-15.9*	*-23.3*	*-14.0*	**-22.6**	**-9.6**	-6.6	-5.3	-4.0	6.0	4.0	5.4	7.9
Norway	*16.2*	*16.1*	*12.2*	**15.7**	**10.6**	10.9	12.4	12.4	10.2	11.0	8.7	5.0
Sweden	*6.1*	*8.2*	*8.2*	**7.9**	**6.0**	6.0	5.5	5.6	5.3	4.6	4.7	4.5
Baltics												
Estonia	*-8.7*	*-15.0*	*-15.0*	**-8.7**	**2.5**	1.8	1.3	-2.4	-0.1	1.0	2.3	1.9
Latvia	*-11.8*	*-20.9*	*-20.8*	**-12.4**	**7.8**	2.0	-3.2	-3.6	-2.7	-2.0	-0.8	1.5
Lithuania	*-7.3*	*-10.6*	*-15.1*	**-13.3**	**2.1**	-0.3	-3.9	-1.2	1.5	3.6	-2.3	-0.9

Source: International Monetary Fund (2017).

Table 2.4 Nordic countries and Baltic States: Fiscal (headline) deficit 2005–16 (% of GDP)

	2005	*2006*	*2007*	*2008*	*2009*	*2010*	*2011*	*2012*	*2013*	*2014*	*2015*	*2016*
Nordics												
Denmark	*5.0*	*5.0*	*5.0*	**3.2**	**-2.8**	-2.7	-2.1	-3.5	-1.0	1.1	-1.8	-0.6
Finland	*2.6*	*3.9*	*5.1*	**4.2**	**-2.5**	-2.6	-1.0	-2.2	-2.6	-3.2	-2.7	-1.9
Iceland	*4.5*	*5.9*	*4.9*	**-13.0**	**-9.7**	-9.8	-5.6	-3.7	-1.8	-0.1	-0.8	12.4
Norway	*14.9*	*18.0*	*17.0*	**18.5**	**10.3**	10.9	13.2	13.5	10.5	8.5	5.9	3.1
Sweden	*1.8*	*2.2*	*3.3*	**1.9**	**-0.7**	-0.1	-0.2	-1.0	-1.4	-1.6	0.2	0.9
Baltics												
Estonia	*1.6*	*2.4*	*2.4*	**-2.9**	**-1.9**	0.1	1.1	-0.3	-0.2	0.7	0.1	0.3
Latvia	*-1.0*	*-0.5*	*0.6*	**-3.2**	**-7.0**	-6.5	-3.2	0.2	-0.6	-1.7	-1.5	-0.4
Lithuania	*-0.5*	*-0.4*	*-1.0*	**-3.3**	**-9.3**	-6.9	-8.9	-3.1	-2.6	-0.7	-0.2	0.3

Source: International Monetary Fund (2017).

Among the Nordics, only Iceland had a serious fiscal imbalance, of 13% in 2008.

In the Baltics this boom was driven by consumption and investment fuelled by both foreign lenders and domestic misperceptions. Most notable was the flow of private-sector loans from Sweden to the Baltics.

General government gross debt was low in the Baltics in 2007: in Estonia it was 3.7% of GDP, reaching 7.2% and 16.6% in Latvia and Lithuania, respectively, for the same year. In contrast, general government gross debt as a percentage of GDP reached 64.9% in the euro area and 57.9% in the EU in that year. This debt then grew dramatically in the Baltic States, where foreign banks had to be bailed out and the governments ran deficits in the following years (International Monetary Fund 2017), (see Table 2.5).

Private sector consolidated debt grew dramatically in all three Baltic States from the time they entered the EU in 2004 until 2009. In Estonia private debt as a percentage of GDP grew from 85.4% in 2004 to 153.2% when it peaked in 2009. The numbers for Latvia were 64% in 2004 but reached 134.0% when they peaked in 2010. In Lithuania, private debt as a percentage of GDP grew from 40.4% in 2004 to 83.3% when it peaked in 2009 (Eurostat 2017) (see Table 2.6). Cross-border private-sector lending from the continental Nordics had thus been fuelling imbalances in the Baltics for years before the crisis hit, as will be discussed in more detail later in this book.

Iceland, which is at a higher income level, with GDP per capita in 2008 of US $55,572, had similarly unsustainable imbalances, with a current account deficit of 23% of GDP in 2006 and 14% in 2007. Iceland's GDP growth rate reached 9% in 2007, while unemployment was below 3% throughout 2005 to 2007. During this period there was a fiscal surplus of about 5%. In Iceland the imbalances were to a large extent driven by an unsustainable cross-border expansion of domestically-owned banks. General government debt in Iceland as a percentage of GDP grew from 27.3% in 2007 and peaked at 95.1% in 2011 (see Table 2.7).

The situation was different among the continental Nordics. Current accounts were slightly in surplus in Denmark and Finland, with larger surpluses in Norway and Sweden. Unemployment was low relative to structural and historical unemployment. GDP growth was good, but not extraordinarily high. Denmark is set apart by its housing boom and bust, the latter beginning before the crisis hit. Both general government debt and private sector consolidated debt as a percentage of GDP were higher in Denmark, Finland and Sweden pre-crisis than in the Baltics, but neither grew as dramatically during the crisis as in the Baltics and Iceland. In Norway, general government debt as a percentage of GDP was on the decline after 2007 (International Monetary Fund 2017 and Eurostat 2017), (see Tables 2.7 and 2.8).

With or without a global crisis, adjustments in consumption were arguably inevitable in the Baltic States and Iceland. Many households were spending well above their income levels, and the private sector as a whole was borrowing unsustainable amounts from abroad (see Table 2.6). It was not even a

Table 2.5 Baltic States, euro area and EU: General government gross debt 2007–16 (% of GDP)

	2007	*2008*	*2009*	*2010*	*2011*	*2012*	*2013*	*2014*	*2015*	*2016*
Country										
Estonia	*3.7*	**4.7**	**7.0**	6.5	6.1	9.7	10.2	10.7	10.1	9.5
Latvia	*7.2*	**16.1**	**32.5**	40.3	37.5	36.7	35.8	38.5	34.8	34.3
Lithuania	*16.6*	**15.3**	**29.0**	36.3	37.3	39.8	38.7	40.5	42.5	40.0
Euro area	*64.9*	**68.6**	**78.4**	84.0	86.8	91.4	93.7	94.4	92.6	91.3
EU	*57.9*	**62.3**	**72.6**	78.5	81.3	85.3	87.2	88.1	86.7	85.8

Source: International Monetary Fund (2017).

Table 2.6 Baltic States: Private sector consolidated debt 2004–15 (% of GDP)

	2004	*2005*	*2006*	*2007*	*2008*	*2009*	*2010*	*2011*	*2012*	*2013*	*2014*	*2015*
Country												
Estonia	*85.4*	*96.6*	*114.0*	*123.0*	**136.7**	**153.2**	140.4	120.4	117.8	115.6	116.6	116.0
Latvia	*64.0*	*81.1*	*97.2*	*102.6*	**104.5**	**125.4**	134.0	115.3	97.9	92.6	96.2	88.7
Lithuania	*40.4*	*50.2*	*62.4*	*74.7*	**76.7**	**83.3**	74.5	64.7	61.1	56.3	54.0	55.0

Source: Eurostat (2017).

Table 2.7 Nordic countries, euro area and EU: General government gross debt 2007–16 (% of GDP)

	2007	*2008*	*2009*	*2010*	*2011*	*2012*	*2013*	*2014*	*2015*	*2016*
Country										
Denmark	*27.3*	**33.3**	**40.2**	42.6	46.1	44.9	44.0	43.9	39.5	39.9
Finland	*33.9*	**32.6**	**41.7**	47.1	48.5	53.9	56.4	60.2	63.6	63.6
Iceland	*27.3*	**67.1**	**82.6**	88.1	95.1	92.5	84.7	82.4	68.0	53.2
Norway	*49.2*	**47.3**	**41.9**	42.4	28.9	30.1	30.6	28.2	33.2	33.2
Sweden	*38.1*	**36.7**	**40.2**	37.6	36.9	37.2	39.8	44.6	42.9	41.6
Euro area	*64.9*	**68.6**	**78.4**	84.0	86.8	91.4	93.7	94.4	92.6	91.3
EU	*57.9*	**62.3**	**72.6**	78.5	81.3	85.3	87.2	88.1	86.7	85.8

Source: International Monetary Fund (2017).

Table 2.8 Nordic countries: Private sector consolidated debt 2004–16 (% of GDP)

	2004	*2005*	*2006*	*2007*	*2008*	*2009*	*2010*	*2011*	*2012*	*2013*	*2014*	*2015*	*2016*
Country													
Denmark	*173.0*	*187.7*	*200.0*	*208.5*	**222.3**	**232.2**	220.6	221.0	224.0	216.1	214.1	207.6	210.7
Finland	*107.6*	*115.9*	*119.2*	*123.6*	**132.7**	**142.8**	148.9	145.4	148.6	147.7	149.6	152.9	149.3
Sweden	*144.4*	*151.9*	*154.1*	*167.9*	**189.1**	**201.5**	189.1	190.8	192.3	194.5	193.9	188.4	188.5

Source: Eurostat (2017).

question of repaying foreign funding or borrowing from domestic banks, even if they were branches or subsidiaries as in the Baltic States. Simply adjusting to a new steady state under the assumption that existing claims by foreigners on the economy would be rolled over indefinitely would have implied a large downward adjustment in domestic demand.

For the continental Nordics, the crisis was more of a typical advanced economy downturn. Benchmarked against the USA and the United Kingdom, Norway experienced a somewhat milder recession than either the USA or the UK, while the other three Nordics experienced larger declines in output. Unemployment increased by less in all of the continental Nordics than in either the USA or the UK.

General government total expenditure was at different levels in the Nordic countries than in the Baltic States before the crisis. In Denmark and Sweden, it was about 50% of GDP from 2005 to 2007, in Finland about 48% and in Norway and Iceland about 40%[4]. General government expenditure in the Baltic States, while significantly lower than in the Nordics, was remarkably similar over the same period, at about 34% for all three countries (see Table 2.9).

Post-crisis, the Baltic States have returned to economic growth. All three Baltic States experienced GDP growth above 6% in 2011 and close to 3% from 2012 to 2014. Currently the GDP growth rate is about 2%, similar to the euro area average. The current growth rate would be acceptable to the Nordics, which are already at very high income levels, but less acceptable for the Baltics, whose goal is to catch up with the Nordics. Unemployment, which peaked in 2010 in all three Baltic States at about 17% in Estonia, 20% in Latvia and 18% in Lithuania, has come down but remains higher than pre-crisis unemployment levels.

It will be argued in this book that banking interlinkages between the Nordic countries and the Baltic States affected the crisis response of the Baltics. Foreign banks were in favour of fixed exchange to protect their portfolio in the Baltics and the EU also made a fixed exchange rate a condition to euro area entry for the three Baltic states. In effect, the fixed exchange rate policy forced the Baltics into austerity. In contrast, the sharp depreciation that occurred in Finland and Sweden in the 1990s was critical for their recovery. Automatic stabilizers were allowed to run their course. This will be discussed in some detail later in the book.

Welfare and tax systems in the Baltic States and Nordic countries compared: the links to Baltic austerity

The welfare systems in the Baltic States are less generous than in the Nordic countries, not only in absolute terms—as can be expected in countries with much lower per capita income levels—but also in relative terms, that is, a lower portion of their smaller per capita income goes to support their welfare systems. This makes their people more vulnerable during a crisis.

Table 2.9 Nordic countries and the Baltic States: General government total expenditure 2005–16 (% of GDP)

	2005	*2006*	*2007*	*2008*	*2009*	*2010*	*2011*	*2012*	*2013*	*2014*	*2015*	*2016*
Nordics												
Denmark	*51.2*	*49.8*	*49.6*	**50.5**	**56.8**	57.1	56.8	58.3	56.5	55.3	54.8	53.5
Finland	*49.3*	*48.3*	*46.8*	**48.3**	**54.8**	54.8	54.4	56.1	57.4	58.1	57.0	55.7
Iceland	*41.5*	*41.1*	*41.0*	**55.7**	**48.5**	49.4	45.7	45.4	44.0	45.3	42.9	46.1
Norway	*41.0*	*39.3*	*39.5*	**38.9**	**45.0**	44.1	43.0	42.2	43.3	45.1	48.0	50.2
Sweden	*51.7*	*50.4*	*48.7*	**49.3**	**52.0**	51.0	50.4	51.5	52.2	50.5	49.3	48.6
Baltics												
Estonia	*33.4*	*33.3*	*33.6*	**39.0**	**44.2**	40.4	37.4	39.1	38.3	38.4	40.2	40.1
Latvia	*34.5*	*33.9*	*33.2*	**36.7**	**42.8**	43.1	38.8	37.4	37.4	37.8	37.7	36.7
Lithuania	*33.4*	*33.7*	*34.4*	**37.0**	**43.7**	41.2	41.5	35.2	34.7	34.0	34.4	33.5

Source: International Monetary Fund (2017).

Looking at human indicators, such as the proportion of people at risk of poverty or social exclusion, and the at-risk-of-poverty rate, as measured by Eurostat, the Baltic States do not perform well. This is not only in comparison with the Nordics, but also compared to countries in Europe with a similar income level, such as the Czech Republic, Slovakia and Slovenia, as will be discussed in detail later in the book. If we consider income inequality measured by Eurostat using the quintile share ratio or the Gini index, the Baltic States are among the countries with the most unequal income distribution in Europe; indeed, they come close to countries like Bulgaria and Romania, with their much lower income levels and less advanced economies. The Nordic countries, on the other hand, feature among the countries with the most equal income distribution in Europe and worldwide. Table 2.10 below shows some selected social indicators for the Nordics and the Baltics, but more countries will be included in the analysis in a later chapter in the book.

As for the social and economic costs of the crisis, the question arises whether we can speak of austerity in a macroeconomic sense. Arguably, the countries that went through a serious crisis (the Baltics and Iceland) produced a textbook fiscal response to it. Expenditure-to-GDP ratios rose sharply in almost all countries between 2008 and 2009 (see Table 2.9), receding substantially thereafter. In 2009, general government expenditure in Estonia and Lithuania represented about 44% of GDP, and in Latvia about 43%.

However, if we consider absolute numbers, the picture is different. While general government total expenditure ratios as a percentage of GDP

Table 2.10 Selected social indicators in the Nordic and Baltic countries in 2016

	Proportion of population at risk of poverty or social exclusion (%)	*At-risk-of-poverty rate (%)*	*Gini coefficient*	*Income quintile share ratio*[5]
Nordics				
Denmark	16.7	11.9	27.7	4.1
Finland	16.6	11.6	25.4	3.6
Iceland	13.0	9.6	23.6	3.4
Norway	15.3	12.2	25.0	3.7
Sweden	18.3	16.2	27.6	4.3
Baltics				
Estonia	24.4	21.7	32.7	5.6
Latvia	28.5	21.8	34.5	6.2
Lithuania	30.1	21.9	37.0	7.1

Source: Statistics Iceland (2017) and Eurostat (2017).

Note: Data for Iceland refer to 2015.

increased in the Baltics from 2007 to 2009 (2010 in Lithuania) a sharp reduction occurred in general government total expenditure between 2008 and 2010, especially in Latvia, which perhaps implemented the most aggressive austerity programme, (see Table 2.11 below).

When reviewing the increase in government total-expenditure-to-GDP ratios in the Baltics from 2008 to 2009, we need to keep in mind that GDP in the Baltics dropped severely during the crisis. GDP dropped even further because of the fixed exchange-rate policies that these countries implemented, and also because of their austerity programmes, which had the opposite effect to what a fiscal stimulus would have had, resulting in GDP contraction instead of recovery.

The picture is more complicated in the other Nordics. In Denmark, the expenditure ratio rose by about seven percentage points but then did not fall in any meaningful way until 2015. In Finland, a similar pattern occurred up to 2009, after which the ratio kept on gradually rising. However, both countries experienced a second recession in 2012–2013. Denmark has just recently begun a weak recovery, while Finland has arguably not yet started on a clear path to recovery.

Norway barely had a recession and expenditure has continued to rise. In Sweden, the pattern was a more subdued rise and fall in the expenditure ratio, similar to that in the Baltics and Iceland, but more subdued than those countries, and even more so in comparison with the UK and the USA.

The welfare and tax systems in the Baltic States resemble the USA and the UK more than the Nordics. Instead of the progressive taxes that tend to characterize the Nordic countries, the Baltics have preferred a flat tax on income. The tax burden is thus disproportionately borne by the poor, contributing to the unequal income distribution discussed above.

If we consider ratios for the incidence of material deprivation in the Baltics, these tended to reduce pre-crisis as government expenditure grew. After 2008 the portion of people suffering from material deprivation in the Baltics grew again as a consequence of the austerity programmes imposed (Table 2.12).

Not surprisingly, the ratio for the incidence of material deprivation in the Nordics is much lower, both because those countries have higher per capita income and because they spend a higher portion of their income on public welfare programmes. In contrast to the Baltics, the incidence of material deprivation in the Nordics tended to be lower after the crisis hit in 2008 than during the years prior to the crisis (Table 2.13).

Austerity programmes in the Baltic States, human costs and long-term growth

Some would argue that, rather than austerity, what happened in the countries suffering crises was a rebalancing in the private sector to unwind unsustainable overspending. People and businesses were existing beyond their means, and had to adjust once the credit to finance their overspending was

Table 2.11 Baltic States: General government total expenditure, current prices 2004–16 ('000 million units of national currency)

	2004	*2005*	*2006*	*2007*	*2008*	*2009*	*2010*	*2011*	*2012*	*2013*	*2014*	*2015*	*2016*
Country													
Estonia	*3.29*	*3.76*	*4.50*	*5.46*	**6.44**	**6.26**	5.96	6.24	7.05	7.28	7.59	8.17	8.45
Latvia	*3.69*	*4.69*	*5.79*	*7.48*	**8.92**	**8.06**	7.72	7.86	8.15	8.51	8.93	9.19	9.17
Lithuania	*6.04*	*7.02*	*8.12*	*10.00*	**12.11**	**11.76**	11.55	12.98	11.74	12.14	12.44	12.84	13.26

Source: International Monetary Fund (2017).

Table 2.12 Baltic States: Incidence of material deprivation 2004–16 (% of population)[6]

	2004	*2005*	*2006*	*2007*	*2008*	*2009*	*2010*	*2011*	*2012*	*2013*	*2014*	*2015*	*2016*
Country													
Estonia	*21.3*	*26.6*	*17.7*	*15.4*	**12.4**	**17.1**	22.3	21.5	21.3	19.4	15.7	12.8	11.7
Latvia	-	*56.8*	*50.8*	*42.9*	**35.7**	**40.2**	46.6	49.0	44.6	40.4	34.6	29.7	26.4
Lithuania	-	*51.7*	*41.4*	*29.6*	**23.0**	**27.4**	36.3	35.1	34.4	31.7	28.3	27.3	26.1

Source: Statistics Iceland (2017) and Eurostat (2017).

Table 2.13 Nordic countries: Incidence of material deprivation 2004–16 (% of population)[7]

	2004	*2005*	*2006*	*2007*	*2008*	*2009*	*2010*	*2011*	*2012*	*2013*	*2014*	*2015*	*2016*
Country													
Denmark	*6.5*	*7.6*	*7.8*	*7.0*	**5.4**	**6.0**	6.0	6.2	6.9	8.8	7.7	8.0	6.5
Finland	*10.6*	*10.8*	*9.9*	*9.4*	**9.1**	**8.2**	8.4	8.4	8.9	8.5	7.9	7.7	8.3
Iceland	8.0	*8.0*	*7.0*	*7.4*	**2.5**	**3.4**	6.5	6.9	6.8	6.6	5.5	5.0	-
Norway	6.0	*7.8*	*6.2*	*5.1*	**4.6**	**5.2**	5.3	5.3	4.5	4.8	3.3	4.1	4.1
Sweden	6.9	*5.7*	*6.2*	*5.8*	**4.6**	**4.8**	3.9	4.2	4.4	4.3	3.2	4.0	3.7

Source: Statistics Iceland (2017) and Eurostat (2017).

withdrawn. Focusing on social consequences, a sharp rise in unemployment occurred in the Baltics and Iceland when the bubble burst. Unemployment went from unsustainably low levels in 2006–07 to much-higher-than-structural unemployment levels during the recession. Unemployment remained high thereafter, in spite of massive migration from the Baltics. In Iceland, however, unemployment is lower and the migration of people is more circular.

In contrast to the Baltics, Iceland ran larger fiscal deficits for a longer period. Its approach was more Keynesian[8] (see Table 2.4). Iceland is a welfare state that resembles the continental Nordics, so that automatic stabilizers have a more powerful effect than in the Baltics and, if allowed to run their course, cause larger deficits. As it was not (and is not) an EU member state, Iceland had no need when the crisis struck to take into consideration the Stability and Growth Pact fiscal deficit target of 3% of GDP, nor the corresponding debt level target of 60% of GDP, both of which the Baltic States had to consider.

Iceland was also not aiming for euro area membership, and its policy response included not only temporary large fiscal deficits but also a devaluation of its currency. The Baltics, with their fixed exchange rate policies and smaller deficits over a shorter period of time, had to cut their social programmes much more, including within the already underfunded health and education sectors. As will be argued in this book, the austerity programmes of the Baltics could not have been implemented in the Nordics as they would have resulted in social unrest. Income and wealth inequality tolerated in the Baltics would not sit well in the Nordics.

Banking, investment and trade linkages in the Nordic and Baltic region

The Nordic countries and Baltic States are closely linked via their banking sectors, with the exception of Iceland. Trade links vary, being reasonably close among the continental Nordics and Estonia, but less close with Iceland, Latvia, and Lithuania. Investment links are largely similar to trade links. These links probably affected crisis transmission (including links with the euro area) more than they affected crisis response. As argued in this book, cross-border banking interlinkages between Sweden and the Baltics restricted their ability to respond to the 2008/09 crisis.

Similarities are discernible between the Finnish and Swedish (and Norwegian) crises in the 1990s and the crisis that hit in 2008, in that a financial system that had been deregulated some years earlier overheated due to lax lending standards. Arguably, regulators and bankers were not sufficiently experienced to respond to overheating in a timely way. This, however, is not an entirely satisfactory explanation, given that the Baltic banks were branches and subsidiaries of Nordic banks, which should have been able to draw on recent painful memories.

Both opportunities and challenges arise from economic integration in the Nordic-Baltic region, including financial sector integration. 'Ever closer union' seems to be going through a rough patch in general. The Nordic banks seem to be doing their best to opt out of the banking union. Nordea, for example, is turning all of its subsidiaries into branches. Denmark and Sweden are showing no apparent interest in the banking union, and the Norwegian authorities view participation in the banking union as unconstitutional.

Given that all of the major banks are headquartered in Denmark, Norway, or Sweden, the Nordic links seem likely to prove more important than the banking union. Of course, as EU or European Economic Area members, current levels of trade investment and banking links with the EU are likely to be maintained. Iceland is its own special case, of course, with little in the way of banking links, and little intention of joining the EU any time soon.

Notes

1 Iceland belongs to the Nordic group of countries but not the continental Nordic group.
2 Only Finland had adopted the euro when the crisis hit.
3 GDP per capita for all countries is at current prices.
4 The lower levels of general government expenditure in Iceland and Norway can perhaps partly be explained by a very high per capita GDP level in Norway and the absence of military expenditure in Iceland.
5 The ratio of total income received by the 20% of the population with the highest income (top quintile) to that received by the 20% of the population with the lowest income (lowest quintile). Income must be understood as equivalized disposable income.
6 See further: http://ec.europa.eu/eurostat/tgm/table.do?tab=table&init=1&language=en&pcode=tessi082&plugin=1.
7 See further: http://ec.europa.eu/eurostat/tgm/table.do?tab=table&init=1&language=en&pcode=tessi082&plugin=1.
8 See discussion at: www.imf.org/external/pubs/ft/fandd/2014/09/basics.htm.

References

Eurostat (2017). *Database*. Available at: http://ec.europa.eu/eurostat/data/database.
International Monetary Fund (2017). *World Economic Outlook Database*. Available at: www.imf.org/external/pubs/ft/weo/2017/02/weodata/index.aspx.
Statistics Iceland (2017). Available at: www.statice.is/.

3 The Nordic countries and the Baltic States—small states and multilateralism

The Nordic countries and the Baltic States are all considered to be small states in the European small-states academic literature. Naturally the question arises: what exactly is a small state? Many academic authors have addressed this question (see, for example, Crowards 2002, Thorhallsson 2006, and Maass 2009), but no consensus has been reached on a single definition. This question will probably never be settled once and for all, and some researchers have queried whether there can, or should, be a single and universal definition of what constitutes a small state.

Definitions of 'small states'

One criterion for determining whether a country is small is to look at the size of its population, its land area, its productive capacity (the size of the economy as measured by gross domestic product—GDP) and military capacity (the size of the military) (East 1975, p. 160). More recently, some scholars have introduced additional variables to determine whether or not countries should be classified as small (see, for example, the comprehensive analysis by Thorhallsson 2006).

Countries can also be considered small in one sense but not small if viewed in another context. Sweden, the largest country in the Nordic group, may be classified as a small state in Europe on the basis of its population, but Sweden is large in Europe on the basis of its geographical size, while, according to World Bank data, its economy is the 22nd largest in the world (see Table I.1). Smallness is relative and can also be viewed differently in different regions of the world. The Republic of Korea (South Korea), a high-income economy with a population of over 50m. and a strong military, regards itself as a small state (Maass 2009, p. 79). Viet Nam, with a population larger than that of Germany, the most populous country in Europe, may consider itself a small state given its proximity to the People's Republic of China, with the largest population in the world and vast land territory. A small state in Asia as compared to China or India might not be considered a small state in Europe, Africa or Latin America, so definitions will vary across geographic regions.

Small states can also be large in certain activities. For example, the Scandinavian countries—Denmark, Norway and Sweden—are all considered small in the European small-states literature. However, these countries are not small in terms of their absolute contributions to international development co-operation. This is because they are relatively rich and contribute a larger share of their gross national income to international development co-operation than any state that is considered large in Europe—or globally, for that matter. This gives those countries a special status in the international arena and makes them more influential in global affairs. Those continental Nordic states are known for maintaining a high profile within international organizations.

Small states can also possess special knowledge and experience that is valuable globally, thus making them important even as small states. The Baltic States (Estonia, Latvia and Lithuania) are small actors in international development co-operation on the basis of their financial contributions, both in absolute and per capita terms (Hilmarsson 2011). But they have made a transition from being republics within the USSR to becoming modern states in a relatively short time. They have also applied for, and implemented, accession to become European Union (EU) and euro area member states, requiring them to make a challenging transition. This transition experience can be important and valuable when shared with other, more fragile states in Europe and Central Asia, such as Ukraine, Georgia and Moldova, which share a similar history. This transition experience need not necessarily be based on success stories only: lessons learned from mistakes committed can be equally important.

Iceland is a small state, but it has extensive experience in the generation of clean energy—utilizing both geothermal and hydroelectric power—which has received international attention. Its geothermal plants have been outstandingly successful. This experience is valuable globally during a time when many nations want to make the transition to clean energy for environmental reasons, and forms part of the global fight against climate change. Iceland also has valuable experience in the management of its fisheries resources. Small states can thus possess experience that can be beneficial for other countries, large and small, and can potentially have both regional and global implications.

Among EU member states, only six countries—France, Germany, Italy, Poland, Spain and the UK—have traditionally been classified as large states, while the remaining 22 EU member states are classified as small. According to these criteria, countries such as Iceland (a non-EU member) and the Baltic States, discussed in this book, are all small states. The Scandinavian countries, with their larger populations and GDP, are also considered small states here in line with European small-states literature.

Small states as a group

A final issue to mention is that small states can be more influential if they successfully co-operate in groups with other like-minded countries. One example is how the Baltic States and the Nordic countries[1] co-operate in the Bretton Woods institutions, i.e. the World Bank and the International Monetary Fund (IMF). Arguably these countries are more influential in the World Bank Group than their size would suggest, because some countries in this group are, as already noted, more generous in their support for international development co-operation than large states, while some countries in this group have unique transition experience. But this means that these small countries must have a common goal and share similar interests, which is not always the case.

Weaker states can be vulnerable in such groups if conflicts of interest arise. During the global crisis in 2008/09, the continental Nordic countries and the Baltic States, for example, did not share the same interests. The Scandinavian countries, mainly Sweden, the largest owner of the banking systems in the Baltic States, and the largest member of the Nordic group, sought to protect their banking sectors, while the interest of the Baltic States may have lain in protecting the welfare of their people and human capital to preserve long-term economic growth. The Baltic States thus became vulnerable and could be expected to pay a high price to prevent Swedish banks from exiting the Baltics, and potentially being sold to purchasers from outside the European region (from Russia or China, for example), which could have serious implications, in both economic and security terms. Small states can seek shelter from relatively larger states and benefit from this co-operation, as the Baltics did by using Nordic banks to modernize their financial sector. But when crisis hits and the interests of those nations diverge, the smaller weaker states can become vulnerable rather than sheltered, and the consequences can be dramatic.

The Nordic countries and the Baltic States have also sought different levels of European economic integration and have different arrangements *vis-à-vis* the EU, all the way from being European Free Trade Association (EFTA) or European Economic Area (EEA) members (least integrated) to being EU/euro area members (most integrated). This will be discussed in some detail in the following chapter. One can argue that those diverse arrangements complicate their regional co-operation, but views on the EU and the euro vary greatly within the Nordic-Baltic group so that these countries cannot be considered like-minded on the benefits of ever closer EU integration. Common pathways in the future for the Nordic-Baltic group can thus be hard to find.

Small states and multilateralism

The issues discussed in this book centre around the 2008/09 global economic and financial crisis, crisis response and post-crisis economic and social consequences in the eight countries of the Nordic-Baltic Region. It is also notable that at the time of writing about a quarter of a century has passed since the Baltic States regained their independence. Among concerns with small states are governance issues, including vulnerabilities in small states with small institutions and limited human and administrative capacity. This is especially true of very small countries such as Iceland and transition countries such as the Baltic States, but is less of a concern with the continental Nordic countries.

Small states often rely heavily on external trade and depend on larger states because their population only permits a limited variety of production; they also rely on open market access supported by global or regional trade regimes. Key issues in this regard relate to how small countries work with international organizations and how they can manage their relationships with large multilateral powers and bureaucracies. Small states may seek shelter within an international organization, but it would be naïve to assume that international organizations are neutral and without an agenda and are not affected by other institutions as well as governments, especially those of large, powerful states. It is also important to consider how small states co-operate with other countries multilaterally.

How are small states such as the Baltic States and Iceland affected when dealing with other small states that are richer and more powerful, such as the larger Scandinavian countries or large EU member states during a crisis? Those more powerful states may also seek to influence multilateral institutions such as the EU, the IMF and the North Atlantic Treaty Organization (NATO). How do small states maximize their benefits or engage in damage control when dealing with more powerful states and international organizations? This will also be discussed in some detail in later chapters of this book in a chapter focusing on Iceland and Latvia, two small states that became extremely vulnerable during the 2008/09 economic and financial crisis, where larger, more powerful states interfered, sometimes very aggressively, seeking to influence international organizations such as the EU and the IMF.

From a theoretical perspective, multilateralism can be viewed as the international governance of the many. It can open up the possibility for small states, along with larger, more powerful states, to participate in international decision-making. According to Thorhallsson, the small-states literature generally claims that it is beneficial for small states to concentrate on multilateral relations within international organizations (Thorhallsson 2005). In addition to seeking shelter bilaterally with support from larger states, small states can be sheltered by multilateral institutions such as the World Bank, the IMF, the World Trade Organization, and the EU. Shelter within multilateral organizations (e.g. the Baltics in the EU) has perhaps become more common than bilateral shelter (of the type Iceland obtained from the USA during the Cold War, for example).

When discussing multilateralism, Kahler notes that '[s]maller, weaker states were believed to be disadvantaged by bilateralism…' and '[i]n their formal institutional design at least, most post-war multilateral institutions incorporated a larger role in decision making for states that were not great powers and could not aspire to be' (Kahler 1992, p. 681). An example of this today is the EU, where one could argue that small states can punch above their weight as a result of digressive proportionality in the European Parliament and representation in the European Commission. But the counter-argument is that in reality the largest states make all the most important decisions. When discussing the role of small states as aid donors, Hoadley predicts high levels of participation by small states in multilateral agencies (Hoadley 1980, p. 129). A current example of this is the continental Nordics, but not the Baltics. More recently, Evans and Newnham argue that small states are said to show limited involvement in international affairs, favour international governmental organizations, are strong advocates of international law, shy away from the use of military force and in general have limited, mostly regional, foreign policy priorities (Evans and Newnham 1998, pp. 500–501). Here the Baltic States can provide a current example: their involvement in international affairs at this stage of their development is focused on participation that helps them in their economic transition and their quest for security, for survival in the shadow of a large state, Russia, which undermines their sovereignty. Finally, Maass states that '[m]embership and participation in international governmental organizations is not only a frequent priority of small states, but it has also been discussed as an indicator of independence, and as such as a secondary definitional requirement for small states in particular' (Maass 2009, p. 69). According to all those theories, small states would be more likely to want to engage in multilateral decision-making than to deal with larger states on a bilateral basis. This is understandable, as small states may be disadvantaged in their dealings with larger states in bilateral negotiations, for example because their human resources and institutions are more restricted. Small states may thus choose to form alliances.

As Ingebritsen (2006) argues when discussing the Scandinavian countries, a group of small states can be influential and 'these states exercise collective authority beyond their borders that exceed their military or economic might' (Ingebritsen 2006, p. 1). She also argues that the Scandinavian states are likely to be found in groups that seek to strengthen international institutions. The Scandinavian countries are rather homogenous in terms of their populations and have a similar culture, emphasizing, for example, equality for all their inhabitants. They may thus perhaps be more likely to be able to form a common policy agenda than some other countries.

If, on the other hand, we consider the Baltic States, the picture is different. They are still in economic transition, with lower per capita incomes than the Scandinavian countries. Currently, the Baltic States have weak welfare systems with highly uneven income distribution among their citizens, even compared to transition countries with similar income levels. In fact, the Baltics have the highest level of income inequality, not only within the EU but also within the EEA, according to Eurostat data. Estonia and Latvia also have large Russian minorities, which are presumably less likely to favour EU and euro area membership than those more numerous members of their populations who are not of Russian origin. Due to their similar development levels, the Baltic States are more likely to be able to form a common agenda with each other than with the Nordics. For example, this is likely to be the case on economic policy and social issues, where the Nordics remain welfare states but the Baltics can be viewed as more neoliberal and Anglo-Saxon. Because of the uneven income and wealth distribution within the Baltics, the élites in those countries are likely to have different preferences from the poorer segments of the population, resulting in more divided societies than the Nordics. Nevertheless, the Baltics are now modern states and have an opportunity to reform, thereby becoming wealthier, and more inclusive and egalitarian.

A group of small states such as the Nordic countries and the Baltic States can attempt to exercise some collective authority as long as they share a common policy agenda. This might apply, for example, in security policy, since all the countries are either members of NATO or (in the cases of Finland and Sweden) are non-members which nevertheless co-operate closely with NATO. However, this becomes more complicated if conflicts of interest arise within the group, as happened when the 2008 financial crisis unfolded in the Nordic-Baltic region. Since the Nordic countries were the owners of the Baltic banking systems, continental Nordic interests were not the same as Baltic interests.

Regional interests also came into play here, as the EU desperately struggled with protecting its banking systems and sought to protect foreign banking interests in the Baltic States, even if doing so necessitated the introduction of programmes of extreme austerity in those countries, which remained relatively poor compared with other EU member states.

The EU joined forces with the continental Nordic countries against the advice of a global institution, namely the IMF. What was good for the Nordic countries during the global crisis in 2008/09 was not good for the Baltic States. Banking interlinkages within Scandinavia that extended to the Baltic States affected the behaviour of the Scandinavian countries. In such cases there is a danger that the relatively larger states in a group will dominate its smaller and weaker members. A larger Nordic country (in this case, Sweden), forms an alliance with an international body (the EU), which the smaller states (the Baltics) do not necessarily consider in their interest and which the IMF opposed.

Similarly, Iceland became vulnerable when disputes arose in connection with the collapse in 2008 of the Icelandic-owned online savings brand Icesave, which had offered cross-border high interest deposit accounts in the UK and the Netherlands. The EU backed attempts by its two member states to compel the Icelandic Government to repay compensation that the UK and Dutch authorities had paid to cover savers' losses; however, the EFTA Court subsequently ruled that Iceland had no legal obligation to do so[2].

System-determining, -influencing, -affecting or -ineffectual

Princeton professor Robert O. Keohane (1969) differentiated between four systemic roles that modern states may be considered by their leaders to play, in terms of their impact on the international community. These are as follows: (i) *System-determining*, when a state plays a critical role in shaping the international system; (ii) *System-influencing*—states that cannot expect individually to dominate the international system, but that may be able to influence it through unilateral or multilateral action; (iii) *System-affecting*—states that cannot affect the international system if acting alone but that can exert significant impact on the system if working through small groups or alliances or through universal or regional international organizations; and (iv) *System-ineffectual*—states that can do little to influence the system-wide forces that affect them, except in groups which are so large that each state has minimal influence (Keohane 1969, pp. 295–296).

The USA clearly assumed the role of a system-determining state at the Bretton Woods conference in 1944, when its economy represented about 50 % of global GDP. Although the USA could still be considered system-determining today, its influence has reduced in relative terms, since its GDP is now equivalent to about 25 % of the world economy. This is not because the US economy has not grown in output terms: rather, it is attributable to the rebuilding of the European and Japanese economies from the ruins of the Second World War and the rise of new emerging powers, most notably the BRICS[3] nations. In today's world the USA could in some cases be classified as system-influencing, rather than system-determining. This implies that the USA cannot expect individually to dominate the international system but may be able to influence it through unilateral or multilateral action—if it is to achieve the latter, it must participate actively in multilateral institutions such as the World Bank and the IMF—both of which are based in Washington, DC and were established under US dominance at the Bretton Woods conference—and in the New York-based United Nations. In recent years the USA has opted not to participate in two newly established multilateral organizations, both of which could be seen as 'challengers' to the Bretton Woods institutions—the New Development Bank (formerly the BRICS Development Bank), launched in Shanghai, China, in 2015, and the Chinese-led Asian Infrastructure Investment Bank, established in 2016 and headquartered in Beijing.

If we consider the EU, the distinction between the Union and its member states is crucial. Larger countries would naturally be expected to wield more influence in the system than small countries. It would hardly be possible to talk about any single country that is system-determining within the EU. Nevertheless, countries such as Germany and France might be seen as system-influencing states within the Union, particularly when acting together. It has been argued that the most influential actors in the EU during the 2008/09 crisis turned out to be the heads of state of government and the foreign ministers of Germany and France—not the President of the Council, the

President of the Commission, nor the High Representative, none of whom exercised the same influence (see Howorth 2017). Arguably, the power of France and Germany to play a critical role in shaping the EU system has been reinforced in the light of the forthcoming exit of Britain from the EU, otherwise known as Brexit. Germany and France may also be considered system-affecting within the global system, if they speak with one voice.

How can this categorization contribute to the behaviour of small states in international organizations? As Keohane observes, '...a major function of international organizations—perceived by many small and middle powers—is to allow these states acting collectively to help shape developing international attitudes, dogmas and codes of proper behaviour' (Keohane 1969, p. 297). The Nordic countries and the Baltic States could perhaps be system-affecting within the Bretton Woods institutions if they share, and push for, a common agenda. The Baltic States would, on the other hand, be system-ineffectual if acting there alone, due to their small size and small contributions to those institutions. Indeed, the Baltics would probably also be system-ineffectual within the EU if they were not supported by other countries, such as the Nordic EU member states—Denmark, Finland and Sweden. The Baltic States and Iceland, acting alone or even in partnership with a very large number of other countries, such as the 31 member states of the EEA, are likely to have little impact on system-wide forces and would be classified as system-ineffectual. However, situations do exist, including the international development co-operation arena, where small countries that work in partnership—examples include the Nordic-Baltic groups in the World Bank and the IMF—can become system-affecting. This is because the Nordic countries, especially Denmark, Norway and Sweden, are leaders in international development co-operation and can, as a group, exert a significant impact globally. For a group of small states to exert a significant impact by working through small groups or alliances or through universal or regional international organizations, they must share a common interest and a common view on development or economic policy, as in the Bretton Woods institutions mentioned above.

When considering the countries in the Nordic-Baltic group that are EU member states, those countries (and especially the Baltic States) can exercise increased authority when their representatives hold important positions within the EU, such as that of a member of the European Commission with an important portfolio. Another example is the presidency of the Council, which rotates among the EU member states every six months. During this six-month period, the presidency chairs meetings at every level in the Council, helping to ensure the continuity of the EU's work in the Council[4]. While the rotating presidency system cannot be expected to allow small states to push issues of national interest against the will of other EU member states, it nevertheless gives countries holding the presidency higher status in the international arena. This can be important for small states, especially emerging countries like the Baltics, but is also a great challenge for them given their relatively small institutions.

Aside from the possibility of small states forming an alliance, a large country and a small state may also co-operate closely. An example of this is the bilateral defence agreement between Iceland and the USA. This relationship dates back to 1944, during the Second World War, when Iceland declared its independence from Germany-occupied Denmark, in a move supported by the USA. The resultant bilateral defence agreement with the USA was beneficial to Iceland's international influence in the post-war period and especially during the Cold War, when the USA maintained a sizeable military presence in Iceland. The political relationship with the USA also benefited Iceland in its dispute with the UK during the so-called 'Cod Wars', when Iceland expanded its fishery limits in the North Atlantic.

The Baltic States, which share borders with Russia, have viewed the USA as a guarantor of security in the Baltic region, and are all members of NATO. In return for an alliance with a larger nation, small states may decide to participate in activities that are favoured by its ally, including military or peacekeeping operations in distant regions. However, the election of Donald J. Trump as President of the USA in November 2016 has lessened the certainty surrounding this relationship, since the new president has questioned not only the relevance of NATO but also the USA's very commitment to the alliance.

Although it is useful to review the small-states literature to better understand the behaviour of those states, we must keep in mind that no universal formula explains how small states act in regional or international organizations. This varies depending on many issues, including how these institutions are organized, what the issues are, and other factors. (For example, the World Bank Group consists of five institutions, each with its own structure and instruments.) Small states in Europe can also respond to international events differently from small states in Asia or Africa; they may also behave differently from other small states in Europe owing to other circumstances. The deployment by the relatively rich Scandinavian countries of strong welfare systems for their citizens is one characteristic which differentiates them from other European small states. In the chapters that follow we shall continue to consider the influence that states have on one another, and how they interact and respond in different circumstances.

Notes

1 Denmark, Finland, Iceland, Norway and Sweden. Reference is also made in this chapter to the Scandinavian countries, which are: Denmark, Norway and Sweden.
2 See www.eftacourt.int/.
3 BRICS is an acronym for an association of five major emerging market economies: Brazil, Russia, India, China and South Africa.
4 See further: www.consilium.europa.eu/en/council-eu/presidency-council-eu/.

References

Crowards, T. (2002). 'Defining the category of "small" states'. *Journal of International Development, 14*(2), pp. 143–179. Available at: http://onlinelibrary.wiley.com/doi/10.1002/jid.860/abstract (Accessed on 2 April 2017).

East, M. A. (1975). 'Size and Foreign Policy Behavior: A Test of Two Models'. In: C. W. Kegley, Jr. et al. (eds) *International Events and the Comparative Analysis of Foreign Policy.* Columbia, SC: University of South Carolina Press.

Evans, G. and Newnham, J. (1998). *The Penguin Dictionary of International Relations.* London: Penguin Books.

Hoadley, J. S. (1980). 'Small states as aid donors', *International Organizations* 31, 1, Winter 1980 1980, pp. 121–137. Available at: www.jstor.org/stable/2706619 (Accessed on 1 April 2016).

Howorth, J. (2017). '"Stability on the Borders": The Ukraine Crisis and the EU's Constrained Policy Towards the Eastern Neighborhood', *Journal of Common Market Studies*, Volume 55, Number 1. pp. 121–136. Available at: http://onlinelibrary.wiley.com/doi/10.1111/jcms.12448/pdf (Accessed on 15 December 2017).

Hilmarsson, H. (2011). 'How can the Baltic States as Non-DAC donors best contribute to international development cooperation?' *Baltic Journal of Economics*, Vol. 112, pp. 27–40.

Ingebritsen, C. (2006). *Scandinavia in World Politics.* Lanham, MD and Oxford: Rowman & Littlefield.

Kahler, M. (1992). 'Multilateralism with small and large numbers'. *International Organizations,* Vol. 46, No. 3 (Summer 1992 1992), pp. 681–708. Available at: www.jstor.org/stable/2706992 (Accessed on 1 April 2017).

Keohane, R. O. (1969) 'Lilliputians' Dilemmas: Small States in International Politics'. *International Organizations*, Vol. 23, No. 2 (Spring 1969 1969), pp. 291–310.

Maass, M. (2009). 'The elusive definition of the small state'. *International Politics, 46* (1), pp. 65–83. Available at: www.palgrave-journals.com/ip/journal/v46/n1/abs/ip200837a.html (Accessed on 2 April 2017).

Thorhallsson, B. (2005). 'What features determine small states' activities in the international arena? Iceland's approach to foreign relations until the mid-1990s'. *Stjórnmál og stjórnsýsla—Veftímarit, Stofnun stjórnmála og stjórnsýslu, Háskóli Íslands.* 1:1, pp. 107–140. Available at: www.irpa.is/article/view/861/pdf_4 (Accessed on 1 April 2017).

Thorhallsson, B. (2006). 'The size of states in the European Union: Theoretical and conceptual perspectives'. *European Integration*, 28(1), pp. 7–31. Available at: www.tandfonline.com/doi/abs/10.1080/07036330500480490#.UzuCFqJkUm8 (Accessed on 2 April 2017).

4 European integration and the Nordic-Baltic region, Schengen and NATO

The five Nordic countries and the three Baltic States are now closely interlinked via trade, investment, the mobility of people, and finance. They are sometimes referred to as the Nordic-Baltic region (5+3) or the Nordic-Baltic Eight (NB8). The countries in this group have pursued varying forms of integration with the European Union (EU)[1], according to their different economic and political priorities, and security concerns. Countries in the Nordic-Baltic region are affected by their relations and ties among themselves, relations with the EU, and with individual EU member states. They are also influenced by non-EU member states in Europe: most notably, five countries in this group share borders with Russia[2]. In fact, the Nordic-Baltic region is the only part of the EU that borders Russia. Countries in distant regions can also be an important influence, especially the USA because of its role as security guarantor in Europe via its participation in the North Atlantic Treaty Organization (NATO)[3] and its leadership within that alliance—although developments since the 2016 presidential elections have raised concerns about a weakening US commitment (see Chapter 3). Iceland, for its part, has a bilateral defence agreement with the USA. While the focus of this chapter is mainly on the EU and NATO, it should be noted that those countries also co-operate in other institutions such as the Bretton Woods institutions discussed before, as well as the European Bank for Reconstruction and Development, the Council of Europe, the Organization for Security and Co-operation in Europe and the United Nations, amongst others.

From an economic point of view, European integration is important for the Nordic countries and the Baltic States, as their economies largely—albeit to varying degrees—depend upon trade of goods and services with EU member states, and thus upon access to the EU internal market. Dependence on trade with other nations is typical of small states such as the countries of the NB8, which have relatively small domestic markets, produce a limited variety of goods and need to rely on cross-border trade to achieve economies of scale[4] in their production. Cross-border capital flows within the EU are also important to the eight countries. This is especially true of the Baltic States, which are still in transition, catching up with richer EU member states. Access to the common labour market can be beneficial, especially if the flows of people are circular—that is, where people migrate to other countries and return with more experience and education. Nevertheless, this can be a challenge for the lower-income Baltic States, where young people may not have an incentive to return once settled in higher-income countries with better living conditions, including more advanced welfare systems. The austerity programmes in the Baltics have made them particularly vulnerable in recent decades. Security issues also constitute an important incentive to participate in European integration, and defence alliances are particularly important for small states that can be, and often have been, threatened by larger, more powerful neighbours. Iceland, located in the Atlantic Ocean and isolated from continental Europe, is notable in this regard. The absence of borders with powerful countries has also sometimes made Iceland more secure.

Because of their strategic locations, the Nordic countries were the targets of conquest or control during the Second World War. Denmark and Norway were occupied by Germany, while Finland fought against the Soviet Union. Iceland was under British, and later US, occupation. Only Sweden managed to remain neutral. All the Nordics regained their independence after the war. In contrast, all three Baltic States were under occupation for decades during the Soviet era, until 1991.

Despite their differing levels of European integration, all the Nordic countries and the Baltic States are participants in both the European Economic Area (EEA)[5] and the Schengen Area[6]. Six out of the eight countries are EU member states and two (Iceland and Norway) are European Free Trade Association (EFTA)[7] member states. Four of the Nordic-Baltic EU member states are also euro area member states and have thus adopted the euro[8] (see Figure 4.1 below).

Among the NB8 countries, Iceland and Norway have the lowest level of economic integration, being members of EFTA and parties to the EEA Agreement since 1994. While they are not EU member states, this arrangement provides them with access to the EU internal market, which is critical for their export sectors. Denmark and Sweden are full EU member states. While neither country has chosen to enter the euro area and adopt the euro as their legal tender, Denmark has pegged its krone to the euro[9]. Sweden, on the other hand, maintains a floating exchange rate regime with an inflation target (Gylfason et al. 2010, p. 167). Finland and the Baltic States have the highest level of EU integration among the NB8, being member states of both the EU and the euro area.

All eight Baltic and Nordic countries participate in the Schengen agreement, along with 18 other European countries, enabling free movement of their citizens within the Schengen Area[10]. In addition to economic and security benefits from European integration, all the Nordic countries and Baltic States except Finland and Sweden are members of NATO[11]. It is notable, but perhaps not surprising given their history and security concerns, that the Baltic States are the most internationally integrated countries in the Nordic-Baltic group. For the Baltics, EU membership was to provide long

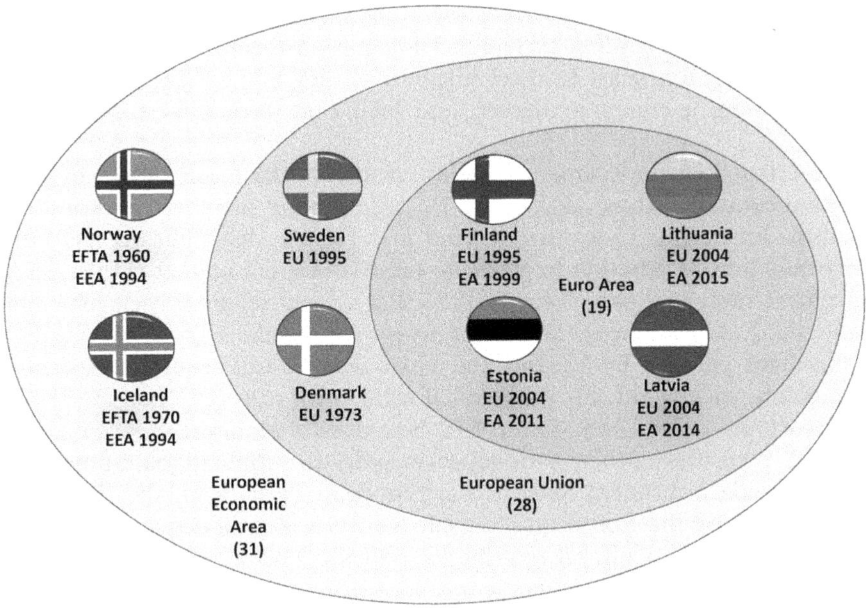

Figure 4.1 Different levels of European integration within the Nordic-Baltic region
Legend: European Area (EA), European Economic Area (EEA) and European Union (EU)
Source: Constructed by the author; EFTA 2014 and European Commission 2018b.

term prosperity, with NATO membership providing military protection and security. They have sought the closest possible links with the West, including the older EU-15 member states (i.e. the member states before the 2004 and 2007 enlargements)[12], as well as with the USA.

Free trade theories and economic integration

For the Nordic countries and the Baltic States, free trade among themselves and within the EU internal market is critical: arguably the internal market is the EU's greatest asset. Classical economic theory documents gain from international trade, demonstrating that nations can improve the welfare of their populations by engaging in cross-border trade with other nations. Trade between nations can, at least in theory, result in a positive sum game, meaning that the trading countries are all better off, benefiting from their gains from trade[13]. To this day this is one of the fundamental principles underlying arguments for all countries to strive to expand and to promote free world trade (e.g. Czinkota et al. 2009). The efficiencies derived from economies of scale also constitute a key argument in favour of economic integration[14]: the creation of a common market allowing larger production and trading volumes and benefiting all participating countries. The EU pursues regional integration, where those who have access to its common market can benefit as described above. According to regional integration theory, the level of integration varies. From least to most integrative, they are: a free trade area, a customs union, a common market, and finally, an economic and political union.

EFTA is a free trade area, and thus represents the loosest form of economic integration, where all barriers to trade among member countries are removed. This is the route that Iceland and Norway have chosen and currently maintain, in addition to access to the EU internal market via the EEA Agreement that came into force in 1994. Both countries have been reluctant to join the EU and have so far chosen to stay out of the Union. The current arrangement pursued by Iceland and Norway does not require a common trade policy, such as a common external tariff, with respect to non-members, as do customs unions such as the EU. Nor does it require the surrender of numerous measures of their national sovereignty to supranational authorities in Union-wide institutions such as the European Parliament, the European Commission and the European Council. Nor, too, does it require participation in common agricultural or fisheries policies. Furthermore, Iceland and Norway do not take part in European Central Bank activities as they are not part of the monetary union and have their own currencies.

The Nordic countries of Denmark, Norway and Sweden were among the founding members of EFTA in 1960. The two remaining Nordic countries under consideration here, Iceland and Finland, joined EFTA in 1970 and 1986, respectively. As at 2018 the only Nordic countries that remain members of EFTA are Iceland and Norway. Denmark left in 1973 to join the European Economic Community (EEC), while Finland and Sweden left in 1995 to join the EU (see Table 4.2 below). Those Nordic countries were willing to surrender some of their national sovereignty to supranational authorities in Union-wide institutions and possibly hoped that they, as a like-minded group on many issues, would be able to influence the EU, that is, by being 'system-affecting' in the sense suggested by Keohane (see Keohane 1969 and Chapter 3).

Currently EFTA has four member states: Iceland, Liechtenstein, Norway and Switzerland. EFTA has three core tasks: the first is the liberalization of intra-EFTA trade. Second, the EFTA states have built networks of preferential trade relations throughout the world, currently consisting of 25 free trade agreements with 35 partners[15]. Third, three of the four EFTA states—Iceland, Liechtenstein and Norway—are parties to the EEA Agreement[16], which ensures their participation in the Internal Market of the EU (EFTA 2014)[17]. Switzerland, also an EFTA member state, does not participate in the EEA Agreement, but has a bilateral agreement with the EU[18].

As EFTA/EEA member states, Norway and Iceland have no formal influence on EU decision-making. They cannot directly affect EU laws and regulations governing the EU internal market that they are part of. However, EFTA/EEA member states can participate in what is called 'decision-shaping'. This means that in the phase of preparatory work undertaken by the

European Commission in drawing up new legislative proposals, the EEA Agreement contains provisions for input from the EEA/EFTA side at various stages before new legislation is adopted (see Figure 4.2 below)[19].

Given how small the EFTA/EEA member states are compared to the EU, it is questionable whether they can be classified as system-affecting in the EU context. The reality is that Iceland and Norway receive the rules and laws governing the single European market via email, without being able to directly influence the process of making them. In this regard, we can speak of sovereignty infringement. Since Iceland and Norway can only comment on those laws and regulations at an early stage of preparation at an expert level, they are not part of the final decision-making process and must adopt whatever decision is made finally by EU member states. This is the cost of enjoying access to the single market. So far the benefits have been assessed as higher than the costs.

As Table 4.1 shows, EFTA has lost most of its original members: these, which included Denmark, Finland and Sweden, chose closer economic integration by joining the EEC, and later the EU. The Baltics never joined EFTA, instead seeking full EU membership immediately following the re-establishment of their independence in 1991.

The EU has been moving towards an economic and political union. This involves not only the abolition of tariffs and quotas among members—as in the case of a free trade area such as EFTA—but also a common tariff and

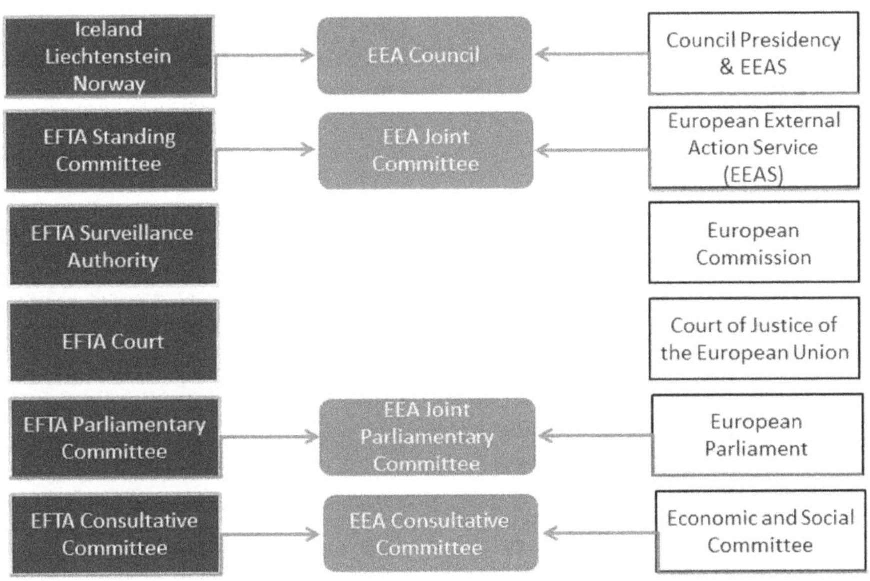

Figure 4.2 Decision Shaping: EEA/EFTA participation in the preparation of new EU law

Source: Hilmarsson (2016)

Table 4.1 European Free Trade Association (EFTA) membership gains/losses 1960–1995

1960	*Austria, Denmark, Norway, Portugal, Sweden, Switzerland and the UK establish EFTA*
1970	*Iceland* becomes a member of EFTA
1973	*Denmark* and the UK leave EFTA to join the EEC
1985	Portugal leaves EFTA to become a member of the EEC
1986	*Finland* becomes a full member of EFTA
1991	Liechtenstein becomes a member of EFTA
1995	Austria, *Finland and Sweden* leave EFTA to join the EU

Source: EFTA 2014; Constructed by the author.

Legend: NB8 countries in italics.

quota system, abolition of restrictions of factor movements, and the harmonization and unification of economic policies and institutions. While EFTA has lost membership, the EU has expanded its membership, to 28 countries as at 2018, to include six of the NB8 countries. Denmark joined (the then EEC) in 1973, Sweden and Finland joined the EU in 1995, and the Baltics—Estonia, Latvia and Lithuania—in 2004 (see Table 4.2 below). Norway rejected EEC membership in a referendum in 1973 and rejected EU membership in a referendum in 1994. Iceland applied for EU membership in 2009, but in 2013 the Icelandic government requested that 'Iceland should not be regarded as a candidate country for EU membership' (see Table 4.2 below). This decision was made without a public referendum, but by a cabinet coalition formed in 2013. There are no signs of change and the new cabinet formed in 2017 is unlikely to seek EU membership.

Table 4.2 The EU and the Nordic-Baltic Region 1962–2013

1962	*Norway, the UK, Denmark and Ireland apply for membership in the EEC*
1973	*Denmark,* Ireland and the UK become members of the EEC. *Norway* rejected EEC membership in a popular referendum
1994	The Norwegian referendum rejects accession to the EU
1995	Austria, *Finland, and Sweden* become members of the EU
2004	*Estonia, Latvia and Lithuania* join the EU
2009	Iceland applies to join the EU
2013	The Icelandic government requests that 'Iceland should not be regarded as a candidate country for EU membership'[20]

Source: Constructed by the author. See further https://europa.eu/european-union/about-eu/countries_en.

Legend: NB8 countries in italics.

The formation of an economic union requires nations to surrender some measure of their national sovereignty to supranational authorities in union-wide institutions. Surrendering sovereignty is not controversial only in the Nordic region—where Iceland and Norway have declined to join the EU—but also in other countries, as the recent decision of the UK to leave the EU demonstrates. The forthcoming British exit (Brexit) was decided upon by means of a referendum, held on 23 June 2016. It remains to be seen how Brexit will be implemented and if other EU member states will follow the UK's example and consider their own exit. This also depends on what kind of a deal the UK manages to make with the EU. EFTA nations are closely watching EU and UK negotiations, as the final outcome could result in demands for a changed EEA agreement.

EU member states clearly have different opinions on what regional integration should include, and how far it should go. Nineteen out of 28 member states have adopted the euro as their common currency and sole legal tender (see Figure 4.1). Among the Nordics, Denmark and Sweden, both EU members, have chosen to stay out of the euro area.

The formation of a common currency area can bring economic benefits to the members of the currency union, particularly if there is a high degree of international trade among them—that is, a high level of trade integration. This is primarily because of reductions both in transaction costs in trade and in exchange-rate uncertainty. However, joining a currency union also involves costs, namely the loss of independent monetary policy and of the exchange rate as a means of macroeconomic adjustment. Among the Nordic countries, only Finland has adopted the euro. However, all the Baltic States have also so (see Table 4.3 below). Denmark and Sweden rejected euro area membership and adoption of the euro in referendums. Iceland and Norway would not be eligible for membership in the euro area unless they first joined the EU and then fulfilled the euro area convergence criteria[21] for at least two years.

Small states, as well as large states, have a choice whether to engage in bilateral negotiations and/or multilateral arrangements to address issues that cannot only be resolved within their borders. The Nordic countries have rather homogenous populations and are often considered like-minded, with a

Table 4.3 The Euro Area and the Nordic-Baltic Region 1992–2015

1992	*Denmark granted opt-outs from participating in the euro*
1999	Finland becomes a member of the euro area and adopts the euro
2003	Sweden decides not to adopt the euro for the time being in a referendum
2011	Estonia becomes a member of the euro area and adopts the euro
2014	Latvia becomes a member of the euro area and adopts the euro
2015	Lithuania becomes a member of the euro area and adopts the euro

Source: Constructed by the author. See further https://europa.eu/european-union/about-eu/countries/member-countries_en.

similar social and cultural background which has given them similar political traditions. Arguably, a Nordic group with a co-ordinated approach to European integration could have become a stronger voice within EU decision-making bodies. This might have helped to further the interests of the Nordic countries, as well as influencing the future direction of European integration efforts themselves (Gylfason et al. 2010, p. 167). On the other hand, the Baltic States share a common European integration approach but are neoliberal, with markedly different approaches from the Nordic countries in terms of both economic and social policies.

The Baltics, along with Finland, all share the same level of integration, being members of both the EU and the euro area.[22] Finland adopted the euro in 1999, Estonia in 2011, Latvia in 2014 and Lithuania in 2015. The Baltic States made huge sacrifices to ensure euro area membership by implementing austerity programmes during the 2008/09 global economic and financial crisis. Such policies would have been difficult—if not impossible—to implement without the risk of social unrest in the Nordic countries, where there appears to be a lower level of tolerance for radical government decisions. Arguably, income and wealth inequality within the Baltic States has undermined democracy in those countries, with divisions between the élite and the poor much sharper than in the Nordics.

Economic integration and security concerns

In addition to economic considerations, when joining the euro area, Finland and later the Baltic States had political motives to settle their political identities once and for all. Finland has long existed in the shadow of either the Soviet Union or Russia. The Baltic States were occupied by the Soviet Union after the end of the Second World War until regaining independence in 1991, and all four share a border with Russian territory. For those countries, EU and euro area membership are more than merely an economic integration arrangement. Security concerns are also of utmost importance for Finland and the Baltics. The EU could hardly ignore an attack on a member state without responding. Furthermore, an attack on a member of the euro area could not be tolerated by the larger EU countries, especially Germany and France—both also members of the single currency area. In addition to EU and euro area membership, the Baltic States all became members of NATO in 2004[23]. It is notable that while EU enlargement proved to be a very lengthy and complex process for new member states, including the Baltics, NATO enlargement, which proceeded in parallel, proved much simpler and faster, perhaps as a result of US support.

Of the Nordic countries, Denmark, Iceland and Norway joined NATO in 1949 and thus had been members for 55 years when the Baltic States joined the alliance (see Figure 4.3). NATO still remains the primary actor in European collective defence. The Baltics participated in a twin enlargement of the EU and NATO in 2004, driven by economic, political and security motives.

Since the occupation of the Crimean peninsula of Ukraine by pro-Russian armed groups in early 2014 the Baltics have been increasingly concerned with the emerging security threat from Russia, and have looked primarily to NATO, led by the USA, for protection. As NATO's commitment increased within Europe due to its expansion, the USA was reducing its military presence in Europe, which has weakened NATO as a guarantor of peace on the continent.

Furthermore, the extent of the US commitment to NATO came under question during the 2016 presidential campaign as a result of pronouncements by the then presidential candidate Donald J. Trump, who was subsequently elected to office. Trump had stated that NATO may be 'obsolete' and had demanded that the USA's European allies start paying their way in NATO. Regardless of Trump's views and intentions, Europeans may need to recognize that the USA may in future not be able—financially, politically or militarily—to play the role of global policeman it assumed in 1945 (see, for example, Howorth 2017). The USA is faced with many challenges, most notably in the Middle East and in the Pacific region. Its share of global GDP has declined from around 50% at the time of the Bretton Woods conference to closer to 25% in the late 2010s. As Angela Merkel stated days before Trump's inauguration in January 2017, Europe's fate is 'in our own hands' [24].

It can thus be argued that there is a need to rethink relations between the EU and NATO. This issue will be discussed further in Chapter 6, which deals with challenges within the euro area and related issues—economic benefits versus security concerns—where the argument is made that the euro area may to some extent have replaced NATO as a security alliance, backed up by Germany and France as military powers. The EU powers may also increasingly need to take over leadership of NATO as US commitment weakens, given that at the present time the relative economic power of the USA has diminished, its presence in Europe has been reduced and it has other security priorities, most notably in the Middle East and in the Pacific.

Nordic-Baltic collective influence

If all the NB8 states were EU member states and presented a united position on integration issues, they might be able to influence the other 22 EU member states to a greater degree than they can today. The same level of integration within the EU could make the Nordic countries and the Baltic States system-affecting—that is, states that cannot affect the international system if acting alone but that can exert significant impact on the system if working through small groups or alliances or through universal or regional international organizations.

In retrospect, the most effective and successful exercise of the EU in recent decades has arguably been the transformation of most Central and Eastern European states, including the Baltics, from authoritarian polities and command economies into democracies embracing market forces and the rule of

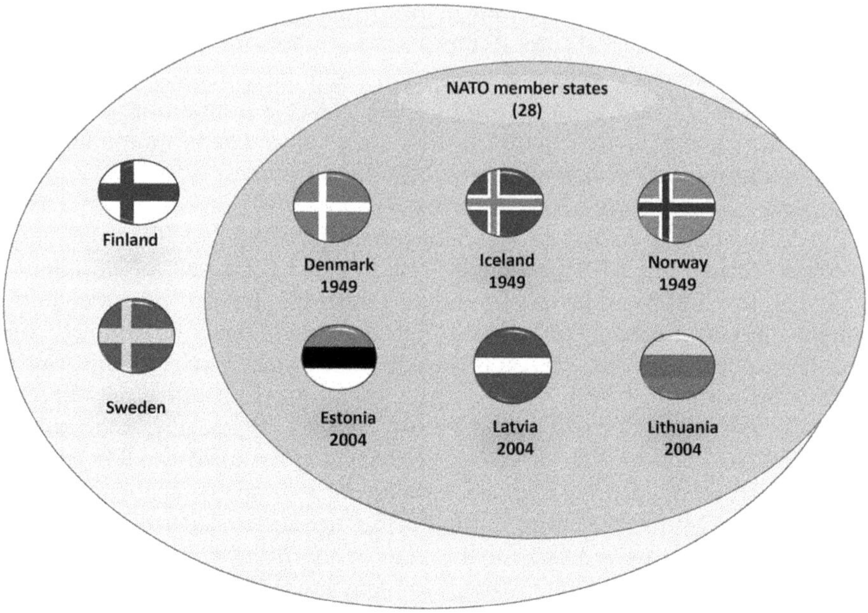

Figure 4.3 Nordic and Baltic membership in NATO
Source: Constructed by the author.

law. However, as already noted, the Nordics are rich 'welfare states', with economic and social policies that differ from the relatively poorer, neoliberal Baltics. How much benefit they could gain from co-operation is questionable, especially when the countries have different policy priorities and continue to be at very different levels of economic development.

Furthermore, the EU and the euro area have not shown impressive economic performance since the 2008/09 crisis. Economic growth remains low and unemployment remains high, especially among young people. As EU member states, Denmark and Sweden have chosen to keep their own currency, the former with an exchange rate pegged to the euro and the latter with a floating exchange rate and an inflation target. They have kept the option to manage their own exchange rate, whereas Finland and the Baltic States are locked in a fixed exchange policy via the euro. From an economic perspective, euro area membership means giving up monetary autonomy for member countries, and comes at the cost of increased macroeconomic instability should asymmetric shocks become significant.

Notes

1 The EU is an economic and political union between 28 European countries (in 2018) that was created in the aftermath of the Second World War, initially to foster economic co-operation: the idea being that countries that trade with one another

become economically interdependent and so more likely to avoid conflict, see further https://europa.eu/european-union/about-eu/eu-in-brief_en Current member states are: Austria, Belgium, Bulgaria, Croatia, Cyprus, the Czech Republic, Denmark, Estonia, Finland, France, Germany, Greece, Hungary, Ireland, Italy, Latvia, Lithuania, Luxembourg, Malta, the Netherlands, Poland, Portugal, Romania, Slovakia, Slovenia, Spain, Sweden and the UK.

2 Estonia, Finland and Latvia have eastern borders with Russia, while Lithuania borders the Russian exclave, Kaliningrad Oblast, to the west. Norway borders Russia in the north-east.

3 NATO's essential purpose is to safeguard the freedom and security of its members through political and military means: see further www.nato.int/nato-welcome/index.html Among the Nordic countries, Denmark, Iceland and Norway are NATO members, as are all three Baltic States. Finland and Sweden are not NATO member states but co-operate closely with the alliance.

4 Economies of scale mean the cost advantage that arises with increased output of a product. Average cost per unit decreases as volume increases.

5 The EEA unites the EU member states and the three EEA EFTA states (Iceland, Liechtenstein, and Norway) into an internal market governed by the same basic rules. These rules aim to enable goods, services, capital, and persons to move freely about the EEA in an open and competitive environment—a concept referred to as the 'four freedoms', see further www.efta.int/eea.

6 The free movement of persons is a fundamental right guaranteed by the EU to its citizens. It entitles every EU citizen to travel, work and live in any EU country without special formalities. Schengen co-operation enhances this freedom by enabling citizens to cross internal borders without being subjected to border checks. Non-EU countries including Iceland and Norway also participate in Schengen. See further European Commission 2018a and http://ec.europa.eu/home-affairs/what-we-do/policies/borders-and-visas/schengen_en.

7 EFTA is an intergovernmental organization set up for the promotion of free trade and economic integration for the benefit of its four member states (Iceland, Liechtenstein, Norway and Switzerland). EFTA is responsible for the management of: (i) the EFTA Convention, which forms the legal basis of the organization and governs free trade relations between the EFTA states; (ii) EFTA's worldwide network of free trade and partnership agreements; and (iii) the EEA Agreement, which enables three of the four EFTA Member States (Iceland, Liechtenstein and Norway) to participate in the EU Internal Market, see further www.efta.int/about-efta/european-free-trade-association and EFTA 2014.

8 All 28 EU member states are part of Economic and Monetary Union (EMU) and co-ordinate their economic policymaking to support the economic aims of the EU. However, a number of member states have taken a step further by replacing their national currencies with the single currency, the euro. These member states form the euro area. When the euro was first introduced in 1999—as 'book' money— the euro area was made up of 11 of the then 15 EU member states. Of the Nordic countries, only Finland became a member of the euro area, in 1999. All three of the Baltic States are members (see below). As at 2018, the euro area numbers 19 EU member states. Of the Nordic countries outside the euro area, Denmark has 'opted out' from joining (laid down in Protocols annexed to the Treaty) and Sweden has not yet qualified to be part of the euro area, see further https://ec.europa.eu/info/business-economy-euro/euro-area/what-euro-area_en.

9 A peg means that a currency is anchored to another currency or basket of currencies. Denmark has a treaty-based exception, i.e. 'opt-out' from monetary union, which is not the case for Sweden.

10 The appropriate authorities may issue a Schengen Visa—a document for visiting/travelling to and within the Schengen Area. The Schengen Area comprises 26

countries that have agreed to allow free movement of their citizens within this area. Of these, 22 are members of the EU and the other four belong to EFTA. The Schengen Area covers the majority of European countries, except for the following six EU members: Bulgaria, Romania (both of which are in the process of joining), Croatia, Cyprus, Ireland and the UK. Of non-EU states, Iceland, Liechtenstein, Norway and Switzerland belong to the Schengen area, and their citizens are guaranteed free movement. See further www.schengenvisainfo.com/.

11 NATO is always headed by a European Secretary General although the USA has dominated the alliance in military terms.

12 Austria, Belgium, Denmark, Finland, France, Germany, Greece, Ireland, Italy, Luxembourg, the Netherlands, Portugal, Spain, Sweden and the United Kingdom.

13 Without trade, countries can consume what they produce, but with trade they can consume beyond their production capabilities.

14 In addition to the economic benefits of economic integration, important political and security concerns may also drive the integration process.

15 EFTA is not a customs union.

16 The EEA Agreement does not include the following EU policies: Common Agriculture and Fisheries Policies; Customs Union; Common Trade Policy; Common Foreign and Security Policy; Justice and Home Affairs (the EFTA states are part of the Schengen area); and Economic and Monetary Union.

17 The EEA EFTA states do not have the right to participate in political decision-making within the EU institutions. The EEA Agreement does, however, enable EEA/EFTA state experts to contribute to the shaping of EU legislation (EFTA 2014).

18 More information can be found about this agreement on the European Commission website https://eeas.europa.eu/delegations/switzerland_de and on the Swiss Federal Administration website www.eda.admin.ch/dea/fr/home/bilaterale-abkommen.html?lang=en.

19 Decision-shaping is the phase of preparatory work undertaken by the European Commission to draw up new legislative proposals. The European Commission has an exclusive right to propose new legislation but is obliged to call on advice from external sources when doing so. The EEA Agreement contains provisions for input from EEA/EFTA members at various stages before new legislation is adopted. Input can take the form of participation by EEA/EFTA experts on European Commission committees or submission of EEA/EFTA comments, as well as adoption of resolutions in response to European Commission initiatives. Bearing in mind that the EEA/EFTA States have little influence on the decision-making phase on the EU side, it is all the more important for them to be actively involved in the decision-shaping process of EEA legislation. See further www.efta.int/eea/decision-shaping.

20 https://ec.europa.eu/neighbourhood-enlargement/countries/detailed-country-information/iceland_en.

21 See further: https://ec.europa.eu/info/business-economy-euro/euro-area/enlargement-euro-area/convergence-criteria-joining_en

22 The Baltic States are also NATO member states, giving them an arguably higher level of integration than that of the Nordic countries, none of which is a member of all three groupings—the EU, the euro area and NATO.

23 Estonia, Latvia and Lithuania became members of NATO on 29 March 2004. As former satellite states of the Soviet Union, they had been members of the Warsaw Pact from 1955 to its dissolution in 1991.

24 http://uk.businessinsider.com/merkel-hits-back-at-trump-europes-fate-is-in-our-own-hands-2017-1?r=US&IR=T.

References

Czinkota, M. R., Ronkainen, I. A., Moffett, M. H., Marinova, S. and Marinov, M. (2009). *International Business, European Edition*. Oxford: John Wiley & Sons.

EFTA (2014). *This is EFTA*. Available at: www.efta.int/sites/default/files/publications/this-is-efta/this-is-efta-2014.pdf (Accessed on 5 March 2017).

European Commission. (2018a). *Schengen Area*. Available at: https://ec.europa.eu/home-affairs/what-we-do/policies/borders-and-visas/schengen_en (Accessed on 15 January 2018).

European Commission. (2018b). *What is the euro area?* Available at: https://ec.europa.eu/info/business-economy-euro/euro-area/what-euro-area_en (Accessed on 6 January 2018).

Guardian. (2016). Finland says it is nearing security deal with US amid concerns over Russia. Available at: www.theguardian.com/world/2016/aug/22/finland-us-russia-military-security (Accessed on 5 January 2017).

Gylfason, Þ., Holmström, B., Korkman, S., Söderström, H. T. and Vihriälä, V. (2010). '*Nordics in Global Crisis—Vulnerability and resilience*'. Helsinki:Research Institute of the Finnish Economy (ETLA)/Taloustieto Oy. Available at: https://economics.mit.edu/files/5729 (Accessed on 15 December 2017).

Hilmarsson H. Þ. (2016). 'Iceland and the Challenge of European Integration: Is European Union Membership Feasible?' In Lino Briguglio (ed.) *Small States and the European Union. Europa Economic Perspectives.* Abingdon and New York: Routledge.

Howorth, J. (2017). '"Stability on the Borders": The Ukraine Crisis and the EU's Constrained Policy Towards the Eastern Neighborhood', *Journal of Common Market Studies*, Volume 55, Number 1. pp. 121–136. Available at: http://onlinelibrary.wiley.com/doi/10.1111/jcms.12448/pdf (Accessed on 15 December 2017).

Keohane, R. O. (1969) 'Lilliputians' Dilemmas: Small States in International Politics'. *International Organizations*, Vol. 23, No. 2 (Spring 1969 1969), pp. 291–310.

NATO (2018). *What is NATO?* Available at: www.nato.int/nato-welcome/index.html (Accessed on 18 January 2018).

5 Exchange rate policy: fixed or floating?

When the Baltic States re-established their independence in 1991, they had to make decisions on their own future economic policies, including both fiscal and monetary policies. This included future exchange-rate regimes. Before independence they had shared the rouble with the Soviet Union until its collapse. After 1991 economic stability—not least price stability—was high on the agenda in all the Baltics. They wanted to establish credible economies. Stability also turned out to be related to their quest for security and survival and eventual participation in the European Union (EU)'s Economic and Monetary Union (EMU).

Economists are divided in their views on what constitutes the best exchange regime for countries. Supporters of hard pegs[1] often argue that they result in more credibility, lower inflation and a more stable economic environment. This can encourage trade, result in lower interest rates and thus more investment and stronger growth in gross domestic product (GDP). Supporters of floating exchange rates argue that, under a flexible exchange rate, the economy has greater ability to adjust to external shocks. Adjustment is easier and results in faster growth. This had been consistent with the experience of the Nordic countries, including during their crisis in the 1990s, when both Sweden and Finland devalued their currencies sharply.

The Baltics 'go hard' with a fixed exchange rate: reasons and consequences

All three Baltic States adopted hard exchange rate pegs early on during their economic transition from the Soviet Union. Estonia introduced a currency board pegging their new local currency, the kroon, to the Deutsche Mark. Lithuania set up a US dollar-based currency board in 1994 for its new currency, the litas. In the same year Latvia pegged its currency, the lat, to the SDR[2] under a quasi-currency board arrangement, with deviations of ±1 % from the central parity allowed, and base money fully backed by foreign reserves (Belhocine et al. 2016)[3].

Exchange regimes vary greatly within emerging Europe[4]. The Baltic States became EU member states in 2004. Euro area accession economies are required to hold their exchange rates stable for at least two years as a pre-condition for acceptance into the euro area. Eventually all the Baltics adopted the euro: Estonia in 2011, Latvia in 2014 and Lithuania in 2015. Once members of the euro area, their currency is fixed as long as they remain members. Since independence in 1991, exchange rate stability appears to have become sacred in the Baltics, perhaps in the belief that this would result in more foreign investment, thriving businesses and economic growth.

This is a different approach compared to the Nordic countries such as Iceland, Norway and Sweden, whose exchange rates have been, and remain, flexible. Among the Nordics, Finland was one of the first countries to adopt the euro on 1 January 1999, while in Denmark the Danish krone is pegged to the euro, so that Denmark is not allowed to determine its monetary policy independently. To date, Finland remains the only Nordic country in the euro area using the euro as legal tender.

When discussing developments in the Southern European peripheral euro area, the PIIGS[5] (Portugal, Ireland, Italy, Greece and Spain) Maurice Obstfeld (2013), professor at UC Berkeley—and, during the time of writing, Chief Economist of the International Monetary Fund (IMF)—commented as follows:

> In my view, the euro crisis has been primarily a crisis of banking and financial markets. In the environment of copious global credit during the euro's first decade, the single currency brought institutional changes (including a big decline in currency risk) that increased the access of the peripheral euro zone borrowers (initially Greece, Ireland, Italy, Portugal, Spain) to external funding on terms virtually identical to those of Germany. The ability to run large current account deficits [...] allowed the peripheral countries to maintain high levels of consumption and investment despite postponing necessary structural reforms, such as those in labour markets and in the public finances.
>
> (Obstfeld 2013, p. 147)

The Baltic States were all EU member states when the 2008/09 crisis occurred, but, unlike the PIIGS they did not adopt the euro until after the crisis, as mentioned above. Nevertheless, their governments did maintain a fixed exchange-rate policy throughout the crisis to enable euro adoption as soon as possible post-crisis, since such a policy was a firm condition from the EU for euro adoption and was also strongly favoured by the owners of foreign banks operating in the Baltics and by their home governments. For example, during a meeting with his Latvian counterpart in Riga in 2012, Swedish Minister for Finance Anders Borg urged Latvia not to delay its goal of joining the euro area in 2014[6]. The same encouragement had also applied to Estonia before it joined the euro area in 2011 and would apply to Lithuania, which would join in 2015. This was understandable, as euro adoption would eliminate exchange rate risks for foreign banks and reduce the risk of the need for a bailout from their Nordic home governments.

Some pre-crisis similarities are evident between developments in the Baltic States and the Southern European peripheral countries, including high levels of consumption and investment. During the years prior to the crisis, the Baltic States did run large current account deficits (see Figure 5.1). Foreign capital was flowing into the Baltics from Scandinavia, mainly Sweden, increasing private sector debt, fuelling the real-estate and financial sectors and contributing to strong GDP growth. Nevertheless, the Baltic States did not run large fiscal deficits from 2005 to 2007, and public debt was low (see Figure 5.2 and Figure 6.1). The boom was thus being fuelled by external capital flows and not by government budget deficits. Given the high pre-crisis GDP growth rates, which rose close to 10% in 2005–07 (see Figure 5.3), in retrospect the Baltic States should arguably have run significant budget surpluses instead of being close to fiscal balance. This is perhaps among the most important lessons to be drawn post-crisis, as this would have given more room for much-needed fiscal stimulus when the crisis occurred.

Obstfeld argues that the '…two most robust indicators of future financial crisis, for emerging and industrial countries alike, are domestic credit expansion and real appreciation of the currency' (Obstfeld 2013, p. 146). The Baltic States had certainly been flooded with cheap credit, mainly on the part of Swedish banks which, given their lending behaviour, must have considered their Baltic clients to be low-risk borrowers. Furthermore, according to Obstfeld, 'One key element raising the vulnerability to global crisis and contagion has been the explosive growth of financial transactions with a cross-border or cross-currency component' (Obstfeld 2013, p. 147). Scandinavian banks happily provided cross-border finance to the Baltic States, fuelling increasing private sector indebtedness as well as irrationally exuberant asset-price inflation. Much as in the peripheral euro area countries, investment in the Baltic States went into non-tradable housing, making it largely unavailable to repay foreign debts. Banks in Scandinavia actually shifted their

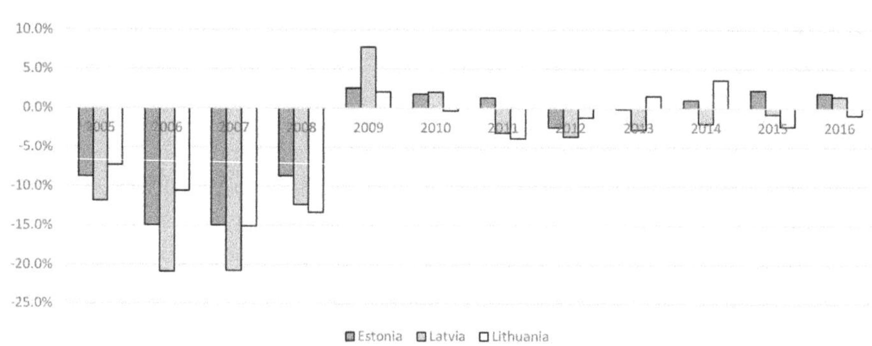

Figure 5.1 Baltic States: Current account balance 2005–16 (% of GDP)
Source: International Monetary Fund (2017).

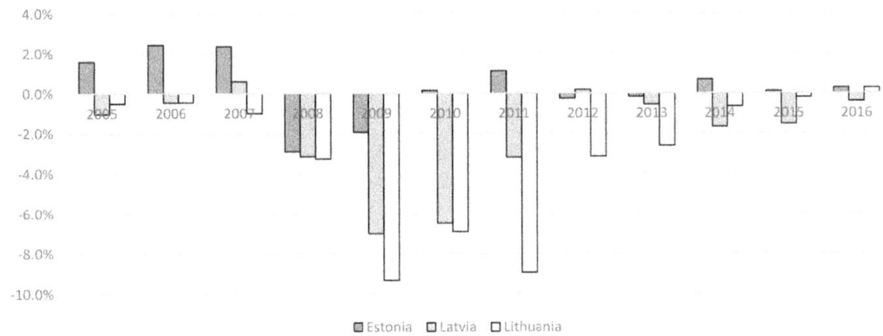

Figure 5.2 Baltic States: Fiscal (headline) deficit 2005–16 (% of GDP)
Source: International Monetary Fund (2017).

portfolio composition to favour lending to the Baltic States, and took on added leverage so as to be able to lend more, making their balance sheets both more fragile and bigger relative to the fiscal capacities of their home governments. Cross-border lending to the Baltics was not only a problem there, but also became a problem within the continental Nordic group.

Taking loans in euros became attractive in the Baltics, given the lower interest rate on euro loans compared to loans in the domestic currencies—lats, kroons and litas—but the exchange rate risk was there and would not be eliminated until the Baltics adopted the euro. As Grönn and Fredholm (2013) eloquently put it:

> It should be mentioned that there is no risk as long as the fixed exchange rate [in the Baltic States] is maintained, but can potentially imply large

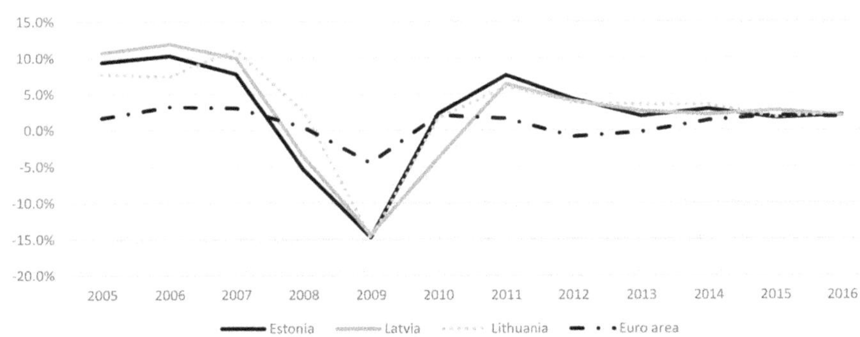

Figure 5.3 Baltic States and euro area: Gross domestic product, constant prices 2005–16 (% change)
Source: International Monetary Fund (2017).

> credit losses [for banks] if the currencies were to depreciate. Since investors had underestimated the potential risks in the Baltic countries, the Nordic parent banks were allowed continued access to cheap funding at a price corresponding to the risk of the banking groups. The consequence of the Nordic parent banks not assessing their own risk properly in turn led to the interest rate offered to the Baltic borrowers being too low. This inadequate risk management contributed to large capital flows to these countries as the Nordic banks underestimated the risks of the exposure in the Baltic countries.
>
> (Grönn and Fredholm 2013)

Clearly, Baltic borrowers took risks when borrowing in euros while receiving income in local currencies. At the same time, the Scandinavian banks took risks lending in euros to those whose primary income was in lats, kroons and litas. For this reason, devaluation was difficult. Moreover, foreign banking interests and large euro borrowers in the Baltics, mostly the Baltic élite, supported by the EU and foreign banks, insisted on fixed exchange rates in all three Baltic States. But for every irresponsible borrower there was also an irresponsible lender who should have known that, in the event of devaluation, the ability of the borrower to repay would be diminished. The foreign-owned banks in the Baltics should have known this, and the responsibility and the costs should have been better shared. The governments in the Nordic countries and Baltic States failed in their risk management.

Unfortunately, the fixed exchange-rate policy did not result in the 'tiger' performance for which the Baltic governments had hoped, with ever-rising incomes and better quality of life for the Baltic peoples. Effectively, the cost of failure was paid by the poor and most vulnerable in the Baltic States, via austerity programmes and regressive tax systems.

Does exchange rate policy matter for economic growth?

As we have seen, the decision of the Baltic States to adopt a fixed exchange-rate policy after re-establishing independence in 1991 was perhaps mainly related to their quest for economic stability and post-Soviet growth, as well as security. European integration was to bring economic prosperity, but it also involved political and security dimensions in addition to membership of the North Atlantic Treaty Organization. EU membership came in 2004, some 13 years after independence. Eventually, some 20 years after independence, the Baltics adopted the euro, thereby committing to a fixed exchange rate for the duration of their membership of the euro area. During the transition years, post-Soviet exchange rate policy was thus vital for those countries.

What does economic theory say about exchange rates and economic growth? Barry Eichengreen (2008), a leading scholar in the field of financial crisis, has argued that '[u]sing the real exchange rate to provide an incentive to shift resources into manufacturing provides a boost to national income insofar as there are conditions making for higher productivity in manufacturing than in agriculture' (Eichengreen 2008, p. 2)[7]. And in terms of evaluating what is known about the real exchange rate and economic growth, he states:

> My reading of the evidence [...] is that the real exchange rate matters. Keeping it at competitive levels and avoiding excessive volatility are important for growth. That said, the statistical evidence is not overwhelming. But this fact, in and of itself, conveys an important message. A stable and competitive real exchange rate should be thought of as a facilitating condition.
>
> (Eichengreen 2008, p. 4).

When discussing fiscal policy Eichengreen observes:

> Fiscal policy is likely to have a more sustained impact. Consider first the case where the exchange rate is pegged (or heavily managed). Increased public spending (or increased private spending in the case where the fiscal expansion takes the form of tax cuts) falls partly on traded goods, whose prices are given, and partly on nontraded goods, whose prices consequently tend to rise. The pressure of public spending can therefore cause the real exchange rate to become overvalued. It will shift resources into the production of nontraded goods. Relatively restrictive fiscal policy thus tends to be part and parcel with the maintenance of a competitive real exchange rate and encouragement of export-led growth. This is an implication of basic models of the two-sector open economy.
>
> (Eichengreen 2008, p. 5)

The Baltics had huge current account deficits prior to the crisis, but did not run large fiscal deficits (see Figures 5.2 and 5.3 above). In fact, the euro area policy of keeping fiscal deficits below a maximum of 3% of GDP (as specified under the 1997 Stability and Growth Pact) does not leave much room for fiscal stimulus, especially when crisis occurs. During the crisis in Latvia in 2008/09 the IMF suggested a 15% devaluation of the lat before the country's adoption of the euro would be considered. According to the IMF analysis, the exchange rate had become overvalued[8]. According to Eichengreen:

> If the exchange rate becomes significantly overvalued, then the right approach to fostering growth and development is to realign it. This can be accomplished by nominal depreciation, ideally in conjunction with policies of wage restraint designed to prevent the real effects from being dissipated by inflation, and appropriate adjustments of monetary and fiscal policies [...].
>
> (Eichengreen 2008, p. 15)

The Baltic States did not go for nominal depreciation as Eichengreen suggests. They opted for internal devaluation, which had become a condition for euro adoption[9].

As Eichengreen (2008) notes: 'The real exchange rate is best thought of as a facilitating condition: keeping it at competitive levels and avoiding excessive volatility facilitate efforts to capitalize on these fundamentals' (Eichengreen 2008, p. 20). And further:

> [e]ven a facilitating condition can be important. Development experience— first and foremost that of the high-growth economies of East Asia, but also **development experience generally—shows that keeping the real exchange rate at competitive levels can be critical for jump-starting growth** [emphasis added]. Experience also shows that high levels of exchange rate volatility can be disruptive to exports and investment. This is not the same as saying that real exchange rate policy can substitute for the presence of a disciplined labour force, high savings, or a foreign investment-friendly climate. **But it can help to jump-start growth by encouraging the redeployment of resources into manufacturing and reaping immediate productivity gains** [emphasis added].
>
> (Eichengreen 2008, p. 20)

And, as Eichengreen points out: '[The People's Republic of China] has utilized a low and stable real exchange rate to move resources into manufacturing' (Eichengreen 2008, p. 21). This is interesting in the Baltic context. After the Baltic States reclaimed independence, they surely enjoyed a relatively favourable business and investment climate before the 2008/09 crisis, at least according to the 'Doing Business' reports of the World Bank (World Bank 2017). Many reforms were initiated prior to their accession to the EU in 2004. Cheap capital was mainly flowing in from Scandinavia, obviating the need for large amounts of savings, and relatively cheap labour was available. But the exchange rate was fixed and became overvalued in the pre-crisis period[10]. The exchange rate was thus not a facilitating condition, but acted more like a straitjacket. All the Baltic States kept a fixed exchange rate until they adopted the euro, whereupon the fixed exchange-rate policy became irreversible. Before the 2008/09 crisis, investment was flowing into real estate and financial services, while manufacturing lagged behind. This situation has not improved greatly in the post-crisis period, with the Baltic States still possessing relatively weak export sectors.

Exchange rate regimes, the path to euro adoption and the decision to devalue

In 2012 Bas B. Bakker and Christoph Klingen edited a report for the IMF entitled: *How Emerging Europe Came Through the 2008/09 Crisis: An Account by the Staff of the IMF's European Department*[11]. The chapter on

Latvia was entitled: 'Latvia: The Domino That Did Not Fall'. Latvia was the hardest hit country among the Baltic States in terms of GDP decline during the crisis. The chapter title appears to imply a certain admiration for Latvia's response to the crisis and its persistence. This is somewhat ironic because, when the crisis hit, the IMF seemed to assume that this domino would indeed fall, i.e. that devaluation was necessary and inevitable.

In the chapter on Latvia, IMF Latvia mission chief Mark Griffiths (2012) states:

> The program's strategy was centred on maintaining Latvia's exchange rate peg. In light of Latvia's large current account deficit, **estimates of overvaluation** [emphasis added], and the difficulties in defending an exchange rate peg under an open capital account in the middle of a financial panic, exchange rate policy was hotly debated in the program discussions. The IMF wanted to make sure that all options were considered, including the possibilities of a widening of the exchange rate band to ±15 per cent or some form of accelerated euro adoption, potentially at a depreciated rate [...] However, the EU authorities firmly ruled out immediate euro adoption as inconsistent with the Maastricht Treaty. The Latvian authorities were unequivocally committed to keeping the exchange rate peg, since it had been the linchpin of economic stability since the early days of transition. Moreover, devaluation would have had severe balance sheet effects, since most private sector debt was denominated in euros and rollover of external debt might have become even more difficult. However, the decision to leave the exchange rate unchanged increased demands on the rest of the program.
>
> (Griffiths 2012, p. 115)

Not everyone agrees on the scenario of unequivocally committed Latvian authorities keeping the exchange rate peg. For example, Aldis Austers (2014) states:

> [t]he scale and depth of the recent crisis is related to a disagreement between the Bank of Latvia and the government over macroeconomic strategy prior to the crisis. The Bank of Latvia had focused on the fixed exchange rate, but the government was not willing to sacrifice the speed of growth to the fiscal austerity required by a fixed exchange rate. Besides, the Latvian authorities had greatly encouraged the widespread euroisation of the economy (up to 80 per cent of mortgages were issued in euros in 2008), which ultimately limited the scope of action during the recession.
>
> (Austers 2014, p. 231)

Thus, according to Austers (2014) there were different views within the government on the merits of the fixed exchange-rate policy, and some debate took place. As Griffiths (2012), cited above, noted: 'exchange-rate policy was hotly debated in the program discussions'. The fact that the IMF prepared a box entitled 'Alternative Exchange Rate Options' in its Country Report of January 2009 suggests that devaluation was at some point discussed between the IMF and the Government of Latvia. The devaluation scenario presented by the IMF also included an estimate of the so-called balance-sheet effect for the private sector, including private enterprises and households (International Monetary Fund 2009, p. 26). The IMF scenario was thus carefully considered, taking into account widespread private-sector borrowing in euro prior to the crisis. But in the end the decision was to keep the exchange rate fixed.

Not everyone was impressed with this decision. Torbjörn Becker at the Stockholm Institute of Transition Economics commented as follows:

> For some reason the exchange rate is almost sacred in Latvia, but the exchange rate is a tool, not a goal in itself. The real goals are welfare, economic prosperity and stability for as many Latvians as possible, not only the minority with loans in foreign currency. What is stability when the only thing stable is the exchange rate?
>
> (Becker n.d.)[12]

And Reinert and Kattel (2014) observed as follows on the fixed exchange-rate policy of the Baltics:

> When the 2008 crisis hit, the decisions not to devalue the three Baltic currencies saved real-estate speculators and penalized local production. Consistently, individuals-as-producers have been sacrificed in order to incentivize individuals-as-consumers. Since we all play both roles in the economy, this systematic neglect of the production side of the economy is at the very core of the present imbalances and crises.
>
> (Reinert and Kattel 2014. p. 72)

The question remains whether the government of Latvia or the EU ever considered what the nation's will was on this issue. The author of this book has not found any decisive evidence, but in a country characterized by about the most unequal income distribution, social exclusion and poverty to be found anywhere in Europe (see Chapter 10), one could speculate that the wealthier segment of the Latvian population was more likely to have borrowed larger amounts of euro than the poorer segment. The richer élite would perhaps be more likely to support an EU fixed exchange-rate policy that was also supported by the Scandinavian/Swedish bank owners.

EU economic policies are not formulated using democratic processes. The European Central Bank (ECB) is independent and, as Arestis and Sawyer (2006) point out, monetary policy is not to be operated by politicians but by experts (Arestis and Sawyer 2006, p. 9). Who would use national elections for decision-making in such a system? It has been noted that 'a growing body of evidence suggests that variables like democracy are important for real exchange rate determination' (Eichengreen 2008, p. 16). Democracy is still fragile in the Baltic States. It is likely that the government was influenced by representatives of the foreign banks that would seek to influence, and perhaps pressure, government officials to take action favourable to them. The EU would lend support to protect contagion within the EU and the euro area.

In addition to Latvia, the other Baltic States also implemented fixed exchange-rate policies with serious social consequences for their people, including massive outward migration of the young and educated. This last phenomenon was especially marked in the cases of Latvia and Lithuania, where the fixed exchange-rate policies were accompanied by austerity programmes that served to compound the trend. As Arestis and Sawyer (2006) have stated, no fiscal policy is exercised at the EU level and the fiscal policy of national governments is subject to conformity with the Stability and Growth Pact (Arestis and Sawyer 2006, p. 7). Fiscal policy has thus been severely downgraded within the EU. Keynesian fiscal stimulus has mostly been ruled out as a possible policy response.

Are fixed exchange rate regimes feasible?

In a 2010 report, Torbjörn Becker et al. discuss different exchange rate regimes in Central and Eastern Europe (which includes the Baltic States), and the path to euro adoption. According to their report, which was entitled *Whither Growth in Central and Eastern Europe? Policy Lessons for an Integrated Europe*: 'Exchange rate policies [...] greatly affected how countries [...] fared in both the boom and bust phases of the current crisis. In particular, fixed exchange rates seem on average to have amplified the excesses and imbalances in the boom, and contributed to more severe declines in the bust' (Becker et al. 2010, p. 46). According to the report, '[t]he crisis clearly demonstrated the important role of cross-border financial flows in creating booms and the associated vulnerabilities in the bust' (Becker et al. 2010, p. 46). This finding is relevant to the Baltic States, which were flooded with cross-border finance in the years prior to the 2008/09 crisis—finance that dried up when the crisis occurred, followed by some of the worst GDP declines seen anywhere in the world. The fixed exchange rate regimes escalated this development as:

> [...]these persistent inflows were also encouraged by fixed exchange-rate strategies that led private actors to **underprice risk**. Private capital funded a too-rapid credit expansion, which led in several cases to booming real estate prices and excessive wage inflation, ultimately contributing to declining competitiveness, massive current-account deficits, and the substantial build-up of foreign debt.
>
> (Becker et al. 2010, p. 47)

The Baltic States certainly experienced this kind of boom, incurring large current account deficits (see Figure 5.1). Becker et al. (2010) divide the Central and Eastern European countries into groups, which they refer to as BB5 (Baltic and Balkan EU members), WB6 (Western Balkan EU candidate countries) and CE5 (Central European EU members). According to their analysis: .

> [...] capital flows to the BB5 [Bulgaria, **Estonia, Latvia, Lithuania** and Romania—emphasis added] and WB6 [Albania, Bosnia and Herzegovina, Croatia, the former Yugoslav republic of Macedonia, Montenegro and Serbia] countries **were heavily biased towards the financial and real-estate sectors** [emphasis added]. Although some of this was in the form of FDI [foreign direct investment], much was in loans that contributed to a rapid and significant build-up of foreign debt.
>
> Capital flows to the CE5 countries [Czech Republic, Hungary, Poland, Slovakia and Slovenia] on the other hand **were more in the form of FDI [foreign direct investment] to the manufacturing sector. This prevented the build-up of balance-sheet vulnerabilities and instead contributed to the strengthening of the competitiveness of the tradable sector. Fixed exchange rates contributed significantly to making foreign loans (rather than FDI) the dominant form of inflowing capital, especially for the banking and real-estate sectors** [emphasis added].
>
> **Fixed currencies were associated with significantly negative real interest rates for domestic borrowers, coupled with the impression that exchange rates would not adjust to deal with this imbalance** [emphasis added]. This became a self-reinforcing cycle with the monetary expansion leading to even higher domestic inflation and more negative real interest rates from the perspective of local borrowers. **Since credit was supplied by foreign banks—which did not have to rely on raising funds on local markets—supply was more or less unlimited as long as nominal interest rates were attractive** [emphasis added].
>
> (Becker et. al. 2010, pp. 49–50)

> With negative real interest rates associated with foreign borrowing, it should be no surprise that lending to the private sector increased rapidly in most fixed exchange rate countries [...] such as **Bulgaria, Estonia and Latvia** [emphasis added].
>
> (Becker et al. 2010, p. 50)

Negative real interest rates can be viewed as the equivalent to a subsidy for borrowers, who in effect were paid for taking loans as long as the exchange rate remained fixed:

> Cross-border financial flows resulted in the build-up of vulnerabilities that greatly influenced the cost of the crisis in countries with all kinds of

> exchange-rate regimes. But these flows and associated imbalances were more pronounced in countries with fixed exchange rates. Fixed exchange-rate countries tended to experience higher current-account imbalances and external debt, the share of loans was larger and the share of FDI was lower in total capital inflows, the composition of FDI inflows was biased in favour of finance and real estate-related activities, credit growth was faster, inflation was higher, unit labour costs rose faster, and real interest rates were lower than in floating exchange rate countries, on average. These characteristics and vulnerabilities contributed to sharper contractions in real growth and a larger rise in unemployment during the crisis in fixed exchange-rate countries than in countries with flexible exchange-rate regimes.
>
> (Becker et al. 2010, p. 75)

> **Looking forward, national exchange-rate strategies should take into account the problems with fixing the exchange rate too early in the catch-up phase and being stuck with an overvalued exchange rate and large stock of private debt** [emphasis added].
>
> (Becker et al. 2010, p. 75)

The Baltic 'bubble' versus Polish exceptionalism

When considering the crisis in the Baltic States it is also worth reviewing the experience of other neighbouring emerging economies in Europe, including Poland. With almost 40 million people, Poland is a much larger country than any of the Baltics. Like the Baltic States, Poland had strong trade links with Russia (Allington and McCombie 2016). Polish banks had been acquired by foreign financial institutions during the privatization process. According to Allington and McCombie (2016), foreign owners held major shareholdings in 37 commercial banks, accounting for 68.1% of the total assets in the banking sector. By 2009, Italy controlled 13.3% of banking sector assets, followed by Germany with 10.4%, the Netherlands with 8.6% and France with 5.8%. This proved to be a sufficiently diversified ownership structure to reduce the degree of exposure to economic events in a single country, but not, of course, a euro area-wide crisis (Allington and McCombie 2016, p. 213). This is a very different development from that seen in the Baltic States, where banking ownership was primarily in the hands of a single country, Sweden, which made both the Baltics and Sweden vulnerable during the crisis.

Banking supervision was also stricter in Poland than in the Baltic States. As Allington and McCombie (2016) note, recommendations on 'Good Practices Regarding Mortgage-Secured Credit Exposure' were introduced by the Polish Commission for Banking Supervision in June 2006. This consisted, *inter alia*, of two elements: (i) a higher creditworthiness valuation was required when customers applied for a residential loan in a foreign currency; and (ii) the recommendations set high standards for disclosing foreign exchange-related risks. Banks were advised to offer a Polish złoty loan first, but when customers insisted on a foreign- currency loan, the banks were required to disclose the risks associated with foreign currency borrowing and provide a simulation of repayments given specified levels of złoty depreciation and increases in interest rates (Allington and McCombie 2016, p. 223). Foreign borrowing was restricted for low-income customers, using stress-testing analysis (cases where debt repayment would exceed 50 % of monthly income) (Allington and McCombie 2016, p. 223).

These measures are notable, especially as, in the Baltic situation, the exposure of private creditors who had borrowed in euros was among the main arguments to stick with a fixed exchange-rate policy throughout the financial crisis, until the euro was eventually adopted in all three Baltic States.

As regards the crisis experience of Eastern European economies (EEE), those with floating exchange rates received FDI inflows, mainly in the manufacturing sector, while those with fixed rates had a higher concentration in the financial and housing sector (Allington and McCombie 2016, p. 213). Countries with floating exchange rates, with the notable exception of Romania, did better, with Poland, Slovakia and the Czech Republic recording falling labour costs in manufacturing: a similar internal devaluation had occurred in Germany in the late 1990s. Those EEE with pegged rates also had expanding non-tradable sectors with a competitiveness gap (Allington and McCombie 2016, p. 214).

Allington and McCombie refer to research by Lane (2008) showing that accession to the EU in 2004 fostered greater capital inflows, and progressive financial integration led to an increase in foreign ownership in the banking sector that boosted credit growth and [fuelled] a pre-crisis boom (Lane 2008). By 2008 foreign banks owned 80% of EEE banking assets, with major shareholdings in the hands of Austrian, German, Italian and French banks, as well as Scandinavian banks—in particular, in the Baltic States (Gardó and Martin 2010).

As noted above, the banks were to a large extent in foreign ownership in Poland as they were in the Baltics, but diversification in Poland with investments from many countries meant that no single country would have a strong bargaining situation *vis-à-vis* the government in a crisis situation. Such diversification would perhaps have been difficult in the Baltics, as their economies are much smaller than the Polish economy. But one could ask why measures that were taken in Poland to temper capital inflows and restrict borrowing in foreign currency were not taken in the Baltics. One could view this as the shared responsibility of the Baltic governments and the foreign banks' home governments, because excessive private-sector debt could translate into a nationwide crisis, as indeed turned out in this case. The Swedish Government, with the oldest central bank in the world, is no novice to financial sector supervision and management and had experienced a crisis in the early 1990s that bore a striking resemblance to the Baltic crisis in 2008/09. Nevertheless, as will be discussed below, it appears not to have taken preventive measures to a similar degree as did Poland.

The crisis in Finland and Sweden in the early 1990s versus the Baltics in 2008/09

Two of the Nordic countries—Sweden and Finland—experienced a severe financial crisis in the early 1990s, when the Baltic States were still part of the Soviet Union. It is interesting to review the experience of those two Nordic countries leading up to the crisis in the 1990s, as well as their response to the crisis itself, and compare this with their reaction to the crisis in the Baltic States in 2008/09, about a quarter of a century later, when the economies of the Baltic States were hit exceptionally hard.

The focus of the analysis is especially on Sweden, as for a long time it has had strong Baltic ties, especially in Estonia and Latvia, but to a lesser extent Lithuania (which, historically, has stronger ties with Poland). In fact, the Swedish empire had territorial control of much of the Baltic region during the 17th and early 18th centuries and it was perhaps not surprising that Sweden sought to re-establish strong Baltic relations during the vacuum left by the collapse of the Soviet Union. This was accomplished via trade and cross-border migration of Nordic and Baltic people, but also via extensive financial flows to the Baltic States. Naturally this could create tensions with Russia and the Russian minority[13] in the Baltic States, which is especially large in Estonia and Latvia. Finland's connections were more concentrated in Estonia because of geographic proximity, a similar language and cultural ties. In fact, the Nordic countries could be viewed as playing a mentoring role with regard to the post-Soviet Baltic States by assisting them to reintegrate into Europe. There is no reason to believe that this increased interest in, and interaction with, the Baltics was ill-intended, but it could obviously have side effects and be influenced by global developments, including in the EU, Russia and the USA, as well as by the 2008/09 global economic crisis itself. Moreover, conflicts of interest could arise between the Nordics and the Baltics, both within the region and between and among the different countries.

The Nordic countries, most notably Sweden, influenced developments in the Baltic States before, during and after the 2008/09 crisis, especially due to financial interlinkages with the Baltic States. This came in addition to important trade flows and mobility of people across Baltic-Nordic borders, but by the late 2000s Swedish banks had come to dominate the banking sector in all three Baltic States. Prior to the crisis, cheap money had been flowing into the Baltics; as the global crisis, with its roots in the US housing market, developed, the inflows were brought to a sudden halt.

Consider the case of Latvia, the country which was to be hardest hit among the Baltic States. As a result of large capital inflows, the local currency (the lat) became overvalued, resulting in a loss of competitiveness. At some point investors began to question the sustainability of the system, causing capital flows to turn around and ultimately bringing about a dramatic fall in GDP, a rise in unemployment and an increase in social hardship.

It is perhaps fair to assume that Sweden should have been able to draw some lessons from its earlier crisis in the 1990s and avoid playing such a large role in fuelling a real-estate bubble in the Baltics in 2008/09, resulting in a banking crisis that threatened not only Sweden's own economy and financial sector but also caused concern within the EU and the euro area, and had devastating and long-lasting effects on the economic development of the Baltic States. But as Reinhart and Rogoff (2009) state in their book *This Time is Different: Six Centuries of Financial Folly*, '[t]he fading memories of borrowers and lenders, policy makers and academics, and the public at large do not seem to improve over time, so the policy lessons on how to 'avoid' the next blow-up are at best limited' (Reinhart and Rogoff 2009, p. 287).

In the introduction to his 1991 work *The Risk of Economic Crisis*, Harvard professor Martin Feldstein (1991) notes that the depression of 1930 was the last time that the industrial world had experienced a financial crisis followed by an economic collapse. Consequently, economists devoted relatively little work to the analysis of crisis in recent decades, being more concerned to understand the economy during normal times than during times of crisis (Feldstein, 1991, p. 1)[14]. In the 1990s, many economists had forgotten the great depression of 1930, and by 2008/09 the recession of the 1990s had been forgotten. This also raises questions about institutional memory within organizations such as the Swedish Riksbank, the oldest central bank in the world, although one can hardly blame a single institution for a failure which resulted from a chain of events happening in several countries simultaneously. Arguably, the European Commission, the ECB and the IMF should also have played a more active role in helping to avoid this catastrophe, by providing not only analysis, but also action. They knew about the Nordic-Baltic banking interlinkages but did little about it. The Baltic crisis was not only a local disaster. It was also a man-made inter-regional crisis that was affected by a global crisis.

The image of Sweden today is that of a prosperous country, a Nordic welfare state and a mature democracy. As discussed in an earlier chapter of this book, Sweden's experience during the 2008/09 crisis was more akin to that of a rich country entering a recession than it was to the descent into serious crisis experienced by the Baltic States during the same period. However, in the early 1990s Sweden had experienced such a crisis, with a sharp drop in GDP, banks collapsing and soaring public debt. Prior to the onset of the Swedish crisis, a credit boom (fuelled by a rapid deregulation of credit in the early 1980s[15]) had prompted a surge in asset prices affecting both residential and commercial property. This asset price bubble was fuelled by negative real interest rates, both due to high inflation, but also because interest on loans was deductible from income tax, in turn creating strong incentives to borrow and invest. People were subsidized—in fact, paid—to invest. The financial deregulation of 1985 fundamentally affected the behaviour of borrowers and lenders. It gave strong incentives for companies and households to increase their borrowing at prevailing interest rates. And, as Jonung et al. (2008)[16]

note, financial deregulation '… also changed the environment for banks, now they were facing more open and aggressive competition for market shares. They adjusted to the new situation by expanding credit as borrowers stood in line to increase their debt'. (Jonung et al. 2008, p. 18).

After the fall of the Berlin Wall in 1989[17], a clear slowdown occurred in the international economy. The German Bundesbank tightened its monetary policy and other European central banks, including the Swedish Riksbank, raised interest rates. In 1991, in contrast to the stance it had maintained during the past two decades, the Riksbank made serious attempts to defend its peg with the European Currency Unit (ECU)[18]. Rising nominal interest rates in Sweden, along with falling inflation and reduced tax deductions on loan interest, resulted in a sharp increase in real interest rates from about -2 % to +4 % (Chabert and Clavel 2012, p. 2). The property bubble burst, and a deterioration of bank asset portfolios resulted in a banking crisis. The property and banking crisis then resulted in a sharp contraction in GDP.

In November 1992, the Swedish krona was allowed to float and depreciated by around 23% against the ECU. A long recovery was facilitated by this sharp depreciation and a rapid fall in short- and long-term interest rates (Jonung et al. 2008, p. 38). Sweden did not have to comply with rules on fiscal discipline monitored by a third party, such as the EU, and allowed automatic stabilizers[19] to play their role in full. Besides, not being a member of a currency union, Sweden was not constrained in devaluing its currency. This is a very different situation to that which the Baltic States faced in 2008. As EU member states since 2004, they had to comply with EU requirements, including the 'Maastricht criteria[20]' on fiscal discipline, and had to keep their exchange rate fixed in order to be eligible to enter the euro area after the crisis was resolved.

Like Sweden, Finland was also forced to devalue its currency in 1992, but Finnish politicians, who also wished to prepare the national economy for future membership in the EU and future participation in the monetary union, believed that abandoning the currency peg would harm that goal. The Finnish position in 1992 was more similar to that of the Baltic States in 2008: however, at that time Finland ultimately had no other choice than to devalue. Finland went on to join the European Exchange Rate Mechanism (ERM) in 1996 and fully to embrace the Economic and Monetary Union (EMU) in January 1999, by becoming a member of the euro area when it was founded (Jonung et al. 2008, p. 47). As discussed in Chapter 4, economic considerations were not the only factor leading to Finland's decision. Security from a potentially unstable Russia was a key component in Finland's calculations.

In a welfare state such as Sweden, automatic stabilizers are more powerful than in transition countries such as the Baltic States that not only have much lower per capita income but that also, due to their neoliberal political traditions, allocate a much lower portion of their income to support their welfare systems. The welfare systems are also better protected in welfare states like Sweden, as Jonung et al. (2008) note: '[t]he tightening of fiscal policy was […]

hampered in the late 1980s by constitutional obstacles to austerity measures, notably the fact that a simple parliamentarian majority was sufficient to increase spending while a two-thirds majority was needed for reductions in entitlement programs' (Jonung et al. 2008, pp. 15–16). While Sweden did reform its welfare systems in the aftermath of the crisis in the 1990s, it did not implement austerity programmes to anywhere near the extent that the Baltics did in 2008/09. As Jonung et al. (2008) state,

> The welfare state—that is the large public sector—in both Finland and Sweden remained basically unchanged during the 1990s although the replacement ratios of many benefits decreased. The recovery did not bring about any major scaling back of public services.
>
> (Jonung et al. 2008, p. 39)

After the crisis in the 1990s, Sweden did not reinstate its exchange rate peg to the ECU, but instead adopted a floating exchange rate, combined with a policy targeting an inflation rate of around 2%. The final government decision to devalue was perhaps helped because powerful trade unions in Sweden understood that an 'internal devaluation' was not the best alternative for the export industry (Jonung et al. 2008, p. 25–26). The floating of the krona boosted exports, allowing Sweden to return to strong GDP growth. This recovery was largely powered by the contribution of exports. Loosening of monetary policy, including currency depreciations, helped not only Sweden but also Finland to recover. As Jonung et al. (2008) state:

> [t]he effect of the depreciation turned out to be surprisingly long-lasting. According to the standard view of macroeconomic textbooks, a nominal change in the exchange rate has only a temporary effect on production. In the long run, prices, not volumes, are affected. This pattern is not supported by the Finnish post-crisis experience: the effects of depreciation in the beginning of the 1990s were maintained well into the first years of the 21st century.
>
> (Jonung et al. 2008, p. 32)

Sweden's central bank, the Riksbank, had its share of problems with implementing monetary policy in Sweden for decades leading up to the crisis in the 1990s. The Riksbank drew its lessons from this, and it is notable that it did not return to a fixed exchange rate post-crisis. However, it did not recommend this course of action to the Baltic States when they were similarly affected in 2008/09.

Of course, the policies implemented by Sweden in the 1990s cannot be reproduced for euro area countries grappling with a sovereign debt crisis and operating within a monetary union, as was the case for the Southern European economies (Greece, Italy, Portugal and Spain). The Baltic States, however, had not yet adopted the euro in 2008/09 and their levels of public debt were low—much lower in than in the Southern European countries, and much lower than the EU or euro area averages. There would thus have been more room for stimulus policy—if, that is, the EU had not insisted on austerity.

The course of action Sweden recommended to the Baltic States during the 2008/09 crisis was very different from the policies Sweden itself implemented in the early 1990s. For Sweden, where any implementation of austerity programmes on the scale later seen in the Baltics was likely to have produced serious public and political unrest, the outcome of currency devaluation was a success. Automatic stabilizers were allowed to run their course. Some years later, in September 2003, Sweden—by now an EU member state—rejected membership of the euro area in a democratic referendum to keep its krona floating and not fixed.

Summing up: Sweden versus the Baltics

Given the lessons learned during its own economic crisis in the 1990s, it is interesting to sum up how the Swedish Government reacted to the 2008/09 crisis in the Baltic States. Post-crisis in the 1990s, Sweden would not return to a pegged exchange rate for its currency but it insisted on the adoption of a fixed exchange-rate policy in the Baltics in 2008/09, thus protecting its banks' portfolios. Once Sweden entered the EU, its population rejected the euro, but the Swedish government encouraged the Baltics to adopt the euro after the 2008/09 crisis, but without a national referendum such as had been held in Sweden. This was clearly a case of 'Do as we say and not as we do'.

While Sweden experienced the problems associated with a price-wage spiral with frequent devaluations in the 1970s and 1980s, it learned its lessons in terms of the domestic economy, and exchange-rate flexibility has served the country well since then. However, there is evidence to show that, in its cross-border economic relations with the Baltics, some of the old mistakes were repeated: this time, it was the Baltic peoples who would bear the costs of the mistakes.

Jonung et al. (2008) attempt to draw some lessons from the crisis[21], and it is worth quoting those lessons at some length:

> The financial crisis of the 1990s demonstrated, however, that the policy of the hard *markka* [then the currency of Finland] and the hard *krona* [currency of Sweden] actually amplified the boom and deepened the economic downturn. When an economy has ended up in a debt deflation process with an overvalued currency, loss of competitiveness, rising current account deficit and mounting financial imbalances due to rising real rates of interest and falling asset prices, the policy-makers can and—as a normative proposition—should arrest the process by a change in the foreign value of the domestic currency. This was a major policy lesson that Finland and Sweden were forced to learn in the early 1990s. In short,

> devaluation (depreciation) was deemed a better alternative than deflation by policy-makers.
>
> (Jonung et al. 2008, p. 10)

> The depreciation of the *krona* in November 1992 marked the culmination of the crisis and the beginning of the recovery in Sweden. As the *krona* was floating, interest rates were gradually lowered. The turnaround and the recovery started in 1993. Economic growth turned positive in 1993 and remained strong throughout the rest of the 1990s, with the exception of a short downturn in 1996–97 [...]. Almost all indicators of economic activity showed positive numbers after 1993–94.
>
> (Jonung et al. 2008, p. 36)

These are the lessons drawn from the crisis in Finland and Sweden, both of which devalued their currency in 1992. Finland later decided to adopt the euro, but Sweden continued with its own national currency, floating exchange rate and an inflation target. Sweden did not apply the learned lessons in the Baltics, where austerity programmes were introduced and the exchange rate was kept fixed. The policy followed by Sweden resembles more closely the Keynesian approach, which protects the welfare state for the relatively rich country, but the approach utilized in the Baltics is more monetarist in character, imposing austerity on poorer countries.

The consequences of negative real interest rates

Negative real interest rates create perverse incentives for investors, be they households or businesses. Iceland, a Nordic country, experienced periods of negative real interest rates in the 1980s. In effect, those who had access to credit from banks at negative real interest rates received a subsidy. It is possible to run a non-viable enterprise forever with such a subsidy, as long as real interest rates remain negative and the lending bank is willing to supply additional funds. If one borrows at negative real interest rates, one can invest in housing, for example, and allow inflation to reduce the real debt over time. Decisions that were rational for those with access to loans at negative real interest rates can become irrational when real rates become positive again. This can be devastating for investors if interest rate movements are sudden and dramatic, as occurred in Sweden in the early1990s and in the Baltics in 2008/09, making it difficult for debtors to service their loans and eventually resulting in their defaulting on those loans. Defaults reduce the value of bank portfolios and can result in a banking crisis.

Decisions made during periods of negative real interest rates can be rational and profitable from the standpoint of the individual who happens to have access to loans, but do not necessarily make sense for society collectively. For example, a sudden increase in real interest rates because of external events, such as a regional or global financial crisis, will at some point reveal bad decisions. An investment that made sense for an individual or a firm during a period of negative interest rates can suddenly become non-viable when interest rates become positive—and if the individual who overinvested cannot repay their debt. In the new environment of positive real interest rates, this becomes a problem not only for that individual, but also for society as a whole. Investors often respond to a rise in real interest rates by rushing to sell their assets to reduce their debt burden. They may face dramatically reduced asset prices. Bank lending portfolios decline in value, weakening the banks' balance sheets. A sudden increase in real interest rates can undermine a country's financial system and create a financial crisis. Eventually, the costs may be passed to taxpayers via a government bailout, as was seen, for example, during the 2008/09 crisis in Europe.

Negative real interest rates encouraged individuals to make poor decisions in Iceland in the 1980s that later damaged the country's whole economy. Negative real interest rates contributed to the housing bubble in Sweden and Finland in the 1990s by creating incentives to invest so that—as in Iceland—negative real interest rates became a subsidy. People were paid to take risks and invest in housing. A rapid increase in real interest rates resulted in a banking crisis in both Sweden and Finland in the 1990s. The significant rise in the real rate of interest constituted a central feature of boom-bust cycle imbalances within both the financial system (a banking crisis) and the foreign exchange market (a currency crisis).

A similar story played out in the Baltic States before the 2008/09 crisis hit, fuelled primarily by Swedish banks wishing to establish themselves in new and emerging markets and compete for market share, as they had previously done in their home market. In fact, the negative real interest rate cycle looks remarkably similar in Sweden between 1989 and 1994 as it did in the Baltics from 2007–12 (See Jonung et al. 2008, p. 65, Figure 7 and Bukevičiūtė and Kosicki 2012, p. 6, Chart 7). Prior to 2008 in the Baltics, Sweden repeated the same mistakes it had made at home in the early 1990s, but now—as this was a matter of cross-border lending—it could, with EU support, ensure that the Baltics would pay for the damage created by its banks. The EU is not supposed to be a 'transfer union' but this time funds were transferred to rescue damaged bank portfolios via Baltic austerity programmes. This crisis was worsened by the fact that the loans were to a large extent in foreign currencies, most notably euro, to Baltic borrowers receiving salaries in local currencies.

The 2008/09 crisis in Latvia, one of the three Baltic States, was in many ways a standard balance-of-payments crisis. It was preceded by vulnerabilities typical in these circumstances, including large capital inflows from abroad; negative real interest rates; a bubble in housing; a sharp increase in imports; the domination of imports by consumer goods, rather than investment; rapid growth in private credit; large and unhedged borrowing in foreign currency; a large current account deficit; and foreign capital inflows predominately in the form of 'hot' money instead of FDI (See Frankel and Saravelos 2012).

As has been pointed out by Bukevičiūtė and Kosicki[22], long-term interest rates on mortgages during the overheating years were strongly negative and significantly below the euro-area average in all three Baltic States. This created a strong incentive to take out a mortgage (Bukevičiūtė and Kosicki 2012, p. 6)[23]. The foreign banks provided low interest-rate loans in foreign currencies, most notably in euros, during a period of high inflation in the Baltics. This resulted in negative real interest rates, and a situation where households and firms were effectively paid to borrow in euro. As Bukevičiūtė and Kosicki (2012) point out:

> [t]he predominance of adjustable-rate mortgages in the Baltic States makes households more vulnerable to interest rate shifts, as the pass-through from interest rate increases to debt servicing can be sizable. Interest rate changes and potential future house price declines are the main risks facing indebted households. It should be noted that, in the Baltic States, the impact of increasing debt-servicing costs could be particularly strong for many highly-indebted low-income households.
>
> (Bukevičiūtė and Kosicki 2012, p. 5)

The increase in real interest rates in the Baltics in 2009 was dramatic. Real rates went from about -6% in 2008 to (on average) about + 4 % in 2009, a movement of 10 % in one year. During the same period, inflation in all the Baltic States fell dramatically: see Figure 5.4 below.

In 2010, real interest rates rose to about 6% in Lithuania and about 7% in Latvia, before falling in 2011. As Blanchard et al. (2013a and 2013b) point out, credit standards were being tightened in Latvia by early 2007. This drive was led by subsidiaries of Swedish banks. According to Blanchard et al. (2013a), lending rates for mortgages denominated in lats increased from 2007 onwards, reaching about 14% by the end of 2007. This increase reflected a

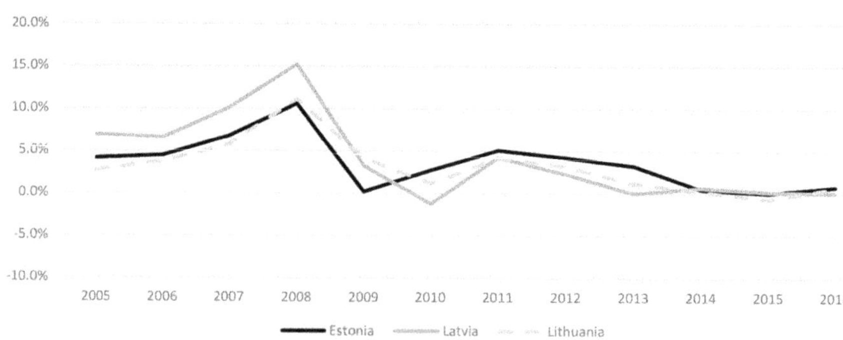

Figure 5.4 Baltic States: Inflation, average consumer prices 2005–16 (% change)
Source: International Monetary Fund (2017).

growing perceived risk in the exchange rate. Real mortgage rates in euros were increasingly negative. Using wage or house price inflation, they find that real interest rates were even more negative (Blanchard et al. (2013a and 2013b). During the adjustment period in 2009–10, when real interest rates became positive again, they exceeded those in the euro area by a significant margin, due to negative inflation (Bukevičiūtė and Kosicki 2012, p. 6).

The consequences of low or negative real interest rates in the Baltic States should not have been much of a surprise to Sweden, since the Swedish economy had suffered from comparable shifts in the early 1990s. In fact, as Jonung et al. (2008) remind us, referring to the Swedish experience of the 1990s, '[t]he low and often negative real interest rates made it tempting to raise loans—both within Sweden and from abroad—for investments and consumption. The final result was the creation of a financial bubble in the Swedish economy, built on excessive indebtedness within the private sector, and a corresponding over-lending within the financial system' (Jonung et al. 2008, p. 18). During this time, similar developments occurred in Finland, resulting in a contraction, as Jonung et al. (2008) point out: 'High real interest rates together with shrinking asset values depressed domestic demand' (Jonung et al. 2008, p. 23). And further: 'High real interest rates in combination with weaker expectations led to falling investment, first in the construction sector, soon in all sectors' (Jonung et al. 2008, p. 24).

As post-crisis empirical evidence shows, the policy of fixed exchange rates demanded by the EU and Swedish bank owners only made a bad situation worse in the Baltic States. Becker et al. (2010) note that:

> [...]imbalances were more pronounced in countries with fixed exchange rates. Fixed exchange-rate countries tended to experience higher current account imbalances and external debt, the share of loans was larger and the share of foreign direct investment was lower in total capital inflows, the composition of FDI inflows was biased in favour of finance and real estate-related activities, credit growth was faster, inflation was higher, unit labour costs rose faster, and real interest rates were lower than in floating exchange rate countries, on average.
>
> (Beckeret al. 2010, pp. 74–75)

In contrast, as Bakker and Klingen (2012) note:

> [c]ountries with *flexible exchange rates* [...] can dampen booms by letting the nominal exchange rate appreciate. Such an appreciation helps prevent overheating of the economy and further lowers inflation by reducing import prices, which keeps real interest rates higher. Many of the countries that avoided a credit boom (the Czech Republic, Poland, the Slovak Republic) had flexible exchange rate regimes and saw a substantial appreciation of their nominal exchange rates during the boom years.
>
> (Bakker and Klingen 2012, p. 282)

When asking the IMF about the Baltic situation, the author of this book received the following email from the IMF[24].

> Regarding the role of real interest rates in the boom-bust cycle in the Baltics (and Central and Eastern Europe more generally), we would agree with you that the fixed exchange rate regimes exacerbated the cycle for the peggers. To our mind, the main mechanism was the inability for the exchange rate to appreciate, which would have helped cool the upswing.

This fixed exchange rate demanded by foreign bank owners and the EU as a condition for euro area membership made a devastating crisis even worse in the Baltics. Thus a high premium was paid for 'stability' and security in the Baltics—a cost that Sweden did not itself have to bear.

Notes

1 A peg means that a currency is anchored to another currency or basket of currencies.

2 The SDR (Special Drawing Right) is an international reserve asset, created by the IMF in 1969 to supplement its member countries' official reserves, see further www.imf.org/en/About/Factsheets/Sheets/2016/08/01/14/51/Special-Drawing-Right-SDR.

3 See further www.imf.org/external/pubs/ft/dp/2016/eur1603.pdf.

4 Exchange regimes in emerging Europe vary as follows:
Fixed
Euro area membership: Estonia, Latvia, Lithuania, Slovakia, Slovenia
Unilateral use of the euro: Kosovo, Montenegro
Currency boards: Bosnia and Herzegovina, Bulgaria
Flexible
Managed arrangements: Croatia, former Yugoslav republic of Macedonia
Inflation targeting and floating: Albania, Czech Republic (Czechia), Hungary, Poland, Romania, Serbia
See further Bakker (2017): www.imf.org/external/region/BAL/rr/2017/033017.pdf.

5 PIIGS is an acronym used to refer to the five euro area nations that were considered weaker economically following the 2008/09 financial crisis: Portugal, Italy, Ireland, Greece and Spain.

6 See further www.baltic-course.com/eng/baltic_states/?doc=52471 and www.baltictimes.com/news/articles/30545/. In spite of Swedish urging for the Baltics to join the euro area, Sweden itself did not join.

7 The real exchange rate and economic growth, see the full report online: http://documents.worldbank.org/curated/en/868701468152077108/The-real-exchange-rate-and-economic-growth.

8 Latvia was the only Baltic State to receive financial assistance from the IMF during the crisis.

9 According to the empirical evidence: 'There is now substantial literature [...] linking the level of the real exchange rate to output and employment growth. Galindo, Izquierdo and Montero (2006) show that real overvaluation slows the growth of industrial employment for a sample of 9 Latin American countries. Marquez and Pages (1998) find the same thing for 18 countries in Latin America and the Caribbean in an earlier period. Hausmann, Pritchett and Rodrik (2004) examine

episodes when growth accelerates by at least two percentage points and that acceleration lasts for at least eight years. Considering 80 some episodes, they find that real depreciation is among the factors that are significantly associated with their incidence. Aghion et al. (2006) find that countries suffering from real overvaluation experience slower productivity growth. This effect shrinks in magnitude, as noted above, as countries become financially more developed'. (Eichengreen 2008, p. 16). 'Rodrik (2006) finds that rapidly growing developing countries tend to have unusually large manufacturing sectors and that growth accelerations are associated with structural shifts in the direction of manufacturing'. (Eichengreen 2008, p. 17).

10 Hence the IMF suggested a 15% devaluation in Latvia in 2008. See also IMF Country Report No. 09/3 January 2009. Republic of Latvia: Request for Stand-By Arrangement—Staff Report; Staff Supplement; Press Release on the Executive Board Discussion; and Statement by the Executive Director for the Republic of Latvia.

'Latvia faces intense liquidity pressures and needs to take steps to address concerns over external debt sustainability. These strains were triggered by the impact of global financial turmoil on the banking sector, which is highly dependent on foreign funding. However, the underlying cause of these problems is the build-up of vulnerabilities during the post EU accession boom, which left banks and the private sector highly indebted and unprepared to cope with a sudden stop of capital inflows. These problems are exacerbated by the high level of external debt and an **overvalued currency**' [emphasis added], see further www.imf.org/en/Publications/CR/Issues/2016/12/31/Republic-of-Latvia-Request-for-Stand-By-Arrangement-Staff-Report-Staff-Supplement-Press-22586.

11 See www.imf.org/external/pubs/cat/longres.aspx?sk=25765.0

12 Torbjörn Becker is the Director of the Stockholm Institute of Transition Economics (SITE) at the Stockholm School of Economics, see further www.hhs.se/en/Research/Institutes/site/people/person/?personId=15841033.

13 For more details, see endnote discussion in Preface.

14 Urban Beckström, then governor of the Swedish Riksbank, referred to Feldstein's observation in a speech he made in the USA in August 1997.

15 The cap on interest rates on lending was removed in March 1985, the cap on loans in November 1985, and the limitations on currency risk were abolished at the end of 1986 (See Chabert and Clavel 2012, p. 2). In fact, deregulation in the financial markets started earlier in Sweden. According to Jonung, et al. (2008) 'World War II unleashed a process of far-reaching regulation of the Swedish economy. At the start of the war, capital account controls (*valutaregleringen*) were introduced. They were complemented in the 1950s with a series of instruments that made it possible for the Riksbank to set the interest rate and steer credit flows according to political priorities. The objective of the regulations of the financial system was to facilitate a policy of low interest rates (*lågräntedoktrinen*), which aimed at keeping interest rates below the levels that would have prevailed in the absence of the regulatory system' (Jonung et al. 2008, p. 17).

16 See further: http://ec.europa.eu/economy_finance/publications/pages/publication_summary13549_en.htm.

17 The reunification of Germany— which can also be considered a consequence of the political weakening of the Soviet Union—boosted Germany's budget deficit and fuelled inflation. Due to the anti-inflation policy of the Bundesbank, European interest rates climbed in the European Exchange Rate Mechanism (ERM), within which Finland was committed to keeping its exchange rate pegged (Jonung et al. 2008, p. 26).

18 The ECU was, replaced by the euro in 1999 as the official unit of currency used in the EU.

19 Automatic stabilizers are economic policies and programmes designed to offset fluctuations in a nation's cyclical economic activity, and are automatically triggered, without explicit intervention by the government or policymakers. The best-known automatic stabilizers are corporate and personal taxes, and transfer systems such as unemployment insurance and welfare.

20 Agreed in Maastricht in 1991 by the EU member states as part of the preparations for introduction of the euro: also known as convergence criteria.

21 Lars Jonung served as chief economic advisor to conservative Swedish Prime Minister Carl Bildt during the crisis, i.e. between 1992 and 1994. See also www.jonung.se/books/.

22 Lina Bukevičiūtė, European Central Bank, Directorate General Economics and Daniel Kosicki, European Commission, Directorate Financial Stability and Monetary Affairs.

23 See Bukevičiūtė and Kosicki 2012, Chart 7: Real interest rates on lending for house purchases, original maturity over 10 years.

24 Email received from the IMF on 1 November 2016.

References

Aghion, P. Philippe, Bacchetta, P., Ranciere, R. and Rogoff, K. (2006), '*Exchange Rate Volatility and Productivity Growth: The Role of Financial Development*,' NBER Working Paper No. 12117 (March), National Bureau of Economic Research.

Allington, N. F. and McCombie, J. S. (2016). 'An Eastern European Perspective on the Recent Financial Crisis and an Examination of Poland's Exceptionalism'. In P. Arestis and M. Sawyer (eds) *Emerging Economies During and After the Great Recession*, Houndmills, Basingstoke: Palgrave Macmillan, pp. 195–231.

Arestis, P. and Sawyer, M. (2006). 'Macroeconomic Policy and the European Constitution'. In P. Arestis and M. Sawyer (eds) *Alternative Perspectives on Economic Policies in the European Union*, Houndmills, Basingstoke: Palgrave Macmillan.

Austers, A. (2014). 'How great is Latvia's success story?' *Intereconomics, 49*(4), pp. 228–238. Available at: http://archive.intereconomics.eu/year/2014/4/how-great-is-latvias-success-story/search/+(The+Impact+of+the+Crisis+on+EU+Competitiveness+in+International+Trade)/20/ (Accessed on 11 August 2017).

Bakker, B. B. (2017). *Exchange Rate Regimes in Emerging Europe. 5th Regional Meeting of Governors Umag*, 30–31 March 2017. Available at: www.imf.org/external/region/BAL/rr/2017/033017.pdf (Accessed on 11 December 2017).

Bakker, B. B. and Klingen, C. A. (eds) (2012). *How Emerging Europe Came Through the 2008/09 Crisis: An Account by the Staff of the IMF's European Department.* Washington, DC: International Monetary Fund.

Becker, T. (n.d.). *Latvia's Options—Internal versus External Devaluation.* Available at: www.hhs.se/contentassets/558fa19998a247258a3cc96b82a239bf/latvias_options_internal_vs_external_devaluation.pdf (Accessed on 1 August 2017).

Becker, T., Daianu, D., Darvas, Z., Gligorov, V., Landesmann, M., Petrovic, P., Pisani-Ferry, J., Rosati, D., Sapir, A. and Weder di Mauro, B. (2010). *Whither Growth in Central and Eastern Europe? Policy Lessons for an Integrated Europe.* Bruegel Blueprint No. 11 (Brussels: Bruegel). Available at: http://bruegel.org/wp-content/uploads/imported/publications/101124_bp_zd_whither_growth.pdf (Accessed on 15 December 2017).

Belhocine, N., Crivelli, E., Geng, N., Scutaru, T., Wiegand, J. and Zhan, Z. (2016). *Taking Stock of Monetary and Exchange Rate Regimes in Emerging Europe.*

Washington, DC: International Monetary Fund. Available at: www.imf.org/external/pubs/ft/dp/2016/eur1603.pdf (Accessed on 11 January 2018).

Blanchard, O. J., Griffiths, M. and Gruss, B. (2013a). '*Boom, Bust, Recovery: Forensics of the Latvia Crisis*'. Final Conference Draft to be presented at the Fall 2013 Brookings Panel on Economic Activity, 19–20 September 2013. Available at: www.scribd.com/document/205371312/Boom-Bust-Recovery-Forensics-of-the-Latvia-Crisis (Accessed on 11 August 2017).

Blanchard, O. J., Griffiths, M. and Gruss, B. (2013b). 'Boom, bust, recovery: forensics of the Latvia crisis'. *Brookings Papers on Economic Activity*, 2013(2), p. 325–388.

Bukevičiūtė, L. and Kosicki, D. (2012). 'Real estate price dynamics, housing finance and related macro-prudential tools in the Baltics'. *ECFIN Country Focus, 9*(2), pp. 1–8. Available at: http://ec.europa.eu/economy_finance/publications/country_focus/2012/2012/cf_vol9_issue2_2012.pdf (Accessed on 1 August 2017).

Chabert, G. and Clavel, L. (2012). *Lessons for today from Sweden's crisis in the 1990s.* Directorate General of the Treasury (DG Trésor). Available at: www.tresor.economie.gouv.fr/Ressources/File/377309 (Accessed on 21 August 2017).

Eichengreen, B. (2008). 'The real exchange rate and economic growth'. *Commission on Growth and Development Working Paper*; no. 4. Washington, DC: World Bank. Available at: http://documents.worldbank.org/curated/en/868701468152077108/The-real-exchange-rate-and-economic-growth (Accessed on 2 December 2017).

Feldstein, M. (1991). 'The Risk of Economic Crisis'. *National Bureau of Economic Research Conference Report*. Chicago, IL: University of Chicago Press.

Frankel, J. and Saravelos, G. (2012). 'Can Leading Indicators Assess Country Vulnerability? Evidence from the 2008–2009 Global Financial Crisis'. *Journal of International Economics* 87(2, July).

Galindo, A., Izquierdo, A. and Montero, J. M. (2006). *Real Exchange Rates, Dollarization, and Industrial Employment in Latin America: , Working Paper No. 575*, Washington, DC: Inter-American Development Bank (November).

Gardó, S. and Martin, R. (2010). 'The Impact of Economic and Financial Crisis On Central, Eastern and South-Eastern Europe: A Stock Taking Exercise', *ECB Occasional Paper Series*, no. 114, Frankfurt: European Central Bank.

Griffiths, M. (2012). 'Latvia: The Domino That Did Not Fall'. In B. B. Bakker and C. A. Klingen (eds) *How Emerging Europe Came Through the 2008/09 Crisis: An Account by the Staff of the IMF's European Department*. Washington, DC: International Monetary Fund.

Grönn, M. A. and Fredholm, M. M. W. (2013). *Baltic and Icelandic experiences of capital flows and capital flow measures* (IMF Working Paper WP/13/242). Washington, DC: International Monetary Fund.

Hausmann, R., Pritchett, L. and Rodrik, D. (2004), '*Growth Accelerations'*, NBER Working Paper No. 10566 (June) , National Bureau of Economic Research.

International Monetary Fund (2009). *Republic of Latvia: Request for Stand-By Arrangement—Staff Report; Staff Supplement; Press Release on the Executive Board Discussion; and Statement by the Executive Director for the Republic of Latvia*. IMF Country Report No. 09/3. Available at: www.imf.org/external/pubs/ft/scr/2009/cr0903.pdf (Accessed on 1 January 2017).

International Monetary Fund (2017). *World Economic Outlook Database*. Available at: www.imf.org/external/pubs/ft/weo/2017/02/weodata/index.aspx.

Jonung, L., Kiander, J. and Vartia, P. (2008). *The great financial crisis in Finland and Sweden—The dynamics of boom, bust and recovery, 1985–2000* (No. 350).

Directorate General Economic and Financial Affairs (DG ECFIN), European Commission. Available at: http://ec.europa.eu/economy_finance/publications/pages/publication13551_en.pdf (Accessed on 1 August 2017).

Lane, P. R. (2008). '*The Macroeconomics of Financial Integration: A European Perspective*'. Discussion Paper no. 265, Institute for International Integration Studies, Trinity College, Dublin.

Marquez, G. A. and Pages, C. (1998), *Trade and Employment: Evidence from Latin America and the Caribbean: Working Paper No. 336*, Washington, DC: Inter-American Development Bank.

Obstfeld, M. (2013). 'Crises and the international system'. *International Economic Journal, 27*(2), pp. 143–155.

Reinert, E. S., and Kattel, R. (2014). 'Failed and Asymmetrical Integration: The Baltics and the Non-financial Origins of the European Crisis'. In Sommers, J. and Woolfson, C. (eds) *The Contradictions of Austerity: The Socio-Economic Costs of the Neoliberal Baltic Model*. Abingdon and New York: Routledge, pp. 64–86.

Reinhart, C. M. and Rogoff, K. S. (2009). *This Time is Different: Six Centuries of Financial Folly*. Princeton, NJ and Oxford: Princeton University Press.

Rodrik, D. (2006), '*Industrial Development: Stylized Facts and Policies*', unpublished manuscript, Kennedy School of Government (August).

World Bank (2017). *Doing Business 2018. Reforming to Create Jobs*. Available at: www.doingbusiness.org/reports/global-reports/doing-business-2018 (Accessed on 7 December 2017).

6 The challenges of euro area membership: Economic benefits versus security concerns, and the euro area versus NATO

When the Bretton Woods system of pegged, but adjustable, exchange rates broke down, European governments created the European Monetary System (EMS), which was instituted in 1979. The EMS had two components. These were the Exchange Rate Mechanism (ERM) and the European Currency Unit (ECU). The ECU was a basket of currencies of the countries that were members of the EMS. The ERM used an adjustable peg, as the Bretton Woods agreement had done previously. The European Union (EU) Single Market, with removal of capital controls, created pressure for the establishment of a common currency in Europe—the euro—and the formation of the euro area. In 1999 the ECU was transformed into the euro and the ECU ceased to exist. Euro coins and banknotes were then put into circulation in 2002.

After becoming members of the EU in 2004, all three Baltic State governments sought to join the euro area and adopt the euro as a common currency. Prior to euro adoption, they had pegged their local currencies to other currencies or to a currency basket, as discussed in the previous chapter, and by doing so forming an 'incomplete' monetary union. It is unclear whether there was popular support for the adoption of the euro, as no referendums were held in the Baltic States, as had occurred, for example, in the Scandinavian countries of Denmark and Sweden. This is perhaps one indication of how immature and fragile democracy in the Baltics was at this time (and, to some extent, still is). There tends to be a difference between what Baltic governments do and what their citizens want, or is in their best interests, as there is between the wishes of the Baltic 'élite' and those of ordinary Baltic citizens. Indeed, it can be argued that a similar situation exists in the EU, where economic policy—especially monetary policy—is to be determined by technocrats sitting in an independent European Central Bank (ECB), and there is little fiscal policy other than an emphasis on a balanced budget.

Estonia was the first of the Baltic States to join the euro area in 2011; Latvia subsequently joined in 2014 and Lithuania in 2015. The only Nordic country to adopt the euro was Finland. Sweden and Denmark rejected euro area membership in referendums[1]. Denmark then formed an incomplete monetary union by pegging its krone to the euro. Sweden has kept its krona with a floating exchange rate and inflation target. As non-EU members, Iceland and Norway were not eligible to adopt the euro even if their governments and populations desired to do so; both, however, remain in good standing *vis-à-vis* the EU (See Hilmarsson 2016). It is true that Kosovo and Montenegro both adopted the euro unilaterally, but their case is different, as both countries used the Deutsche Mark prior to euro adoption. The EU leadership has also clearly communicated to Iceland and Norway that unilateral adoption of the euro would be considered an unwelcome action. Currently there is little appetite in those countries to join the EU, let alone adopt its common currency.

The euro has had a bumpy road so far and the euro area has been suffering a long period of stagnation. In many euro area countries, gross domestic product (GDP) in 2016 was barely higher than in 2007. Unemployment remains high, especially among young people. The most talented and educated people tend to move from poor and poorly-performing countries, such as the Baltic States, to richer, better-performing countries, both within and outside the euro area, including the United Kingdom, Germany and the Scandinavian countries. Inequality in the Baltics remains intolerable. While it is already clear that the Baltics are facing a lost decade in terms of economic growth, they are at risk of a lost quarter of a century. Slow growth and lost human capital is likely to leave long-lasting scars on the Baltics. Finland has also been experiencing stagnation.

The euro area crisis has a familiar aspect but it has been made more intractable by several idiosyncratic features of EMU—see, for example, Obstfeld (2013):

- The absence of a currency devaluation option other than depreciation of the shared currency, the euro. This is because each member country in a monetary union is faced with a fixed exchange rate *vis-à-vis* other member countries.
- The existence of a currency union without fiscal union. This is very different from the federal situation in the USA, where fiscal transfers from one state to another are more acceptable to the electorate than transfers across countries within the euro area. The euro area does not constitute a 'family' to the same extent as the USA.
- No fiscal policy is exercised at the EU level, while at the national level there is an upper limit of 3% of GDP on the fiscal budget (Arestis and Sawyer 2006, p. 7).
- Excessive austerity is a condition for loans, a result of ideology and diverse national politics. The richer countries in the euro area want, as far as possible, to eliminate or at least minimize transfers to the weaker/poorer member states. According to them, the EU is not a 'transfer' union.
- Treaty and political constraints exist regarding both the ECB's role and fiscal bailouts.

- Banks receive excessive exposure to local sovereign debt.
- The absence of a full banking union (with supervisory, resolution, and deposit insurance capacities) and the threat to national solvency from the sheer size of bank balance sheets—completing the 'doom loop' linking banks and sovereigns (see for example Obstfeld 2013, p. 149).

In a famous article, Robert Mundell (1961) made it clear that the countries of the euro area were too diverse to easily share a common currency. He was rather sceptical about the chances of a successful monetary union in Europe (Mundell, 1961). In a later paper, he appeared to be more optimistic about the benefits of a monetary union (see Mundell 1973 for more discussion; see also De Grauwe 2016 and Stiglitz 2016). Mundell, a professor of economics working in the USA, has been hailed as one of the fathers of European monetary union and received the Nobel Prize in Economics in 1999.

It is likely that those who originally conceived of the idea of the euro as a common currency for Europe were inspired by the success of the US dollar as the common currency for all fifty states of the USA. Why, after all, could Europe not also unite under a shared currency? While perhaps some of the complications emerging after the introduction of the euro were unexpected and unpredictable, its founders must have been aware of at least some of the problems that could materialize as a consequence of adopting a single currency. Europe has many top economists and some of the architects of the euro were experienced policymakers. But the euro has never been solely an economic object. It has been suggested that Helmut Kohl, who was Chancellor of Germany during the period in question, agreed to the euro's creation in return for French President François Mitterrand's acceptance of the reunification of Germany (Stiglitz 2016, p. 6). Thus, in addition to the economic theory behind the euro, it was also a political project where European security considerations played a significant role. Once the euro was adopted and in circulation, member states would have little choice other than to rally together and defend it. A common currency creates ties between member states, and if those are severed by the exit of one member state, the consequences seem unpredictable and the risks appear to be high. This has become increasingly evident when the possible exit of Greece from the euro area has been discussed. In fact, the Maastricht Treaty has no provisions for an exit from the euro area.

Barry Eichengreen (2015) stated that 'Germany wants Greece to choose between economic collapse and leaving the eurozone[2]. Both options would mean economic disaster; the first, if not both, would be politically disastrous as well.[3]' Joseph Stiglitz, who is highly sceptical about the future of the euro, holds a different view, recently commenting that 'those in the eurozone, as well as many economic pundits, have been successful in convincing the crisis countries that the departure from the euro would be extraordinarily costly' (Stiglitz 2016, p. 54). Recent EU efforts to keep Greece within the euro area, together with the sacrifices made by its government and people, suggest that all parties want to avoid exit and consider it a high-risk scenario. If the Baltics wanted to make a link with Europe that would be irreversible, then joining the euro area perhaps made sense. But at what cost for economic and human development?

While the Baltic States have shown some recovery in the post-crisis period, the review of their recent economic performance earlier in this book shows that their growth rate has slowed and has been low, especially for transition countries seeking to catch up with rich European countries, such as the Nordics, in the foreseeable future. Their growth performance also cannot be considered impressive when considering how much ground they lost when the crisis hit. Their social fabric has been damaged, and this will slow long-term growth. The pre-2008/09 crisis 'tiger' growth was driven by capital flowing from Scandinavian countries, most notably Sweden. Free capital movements across borders were thus at best a mixed blessing for the Baltics. According to the International Monetary Fund (IMF) (2014), the Baltics experienced creditless recoveries in the first years following the crisis[4]. This was hardly surprising, given banks' concern that private individuals and companies in the Baltics would have difficulty paying back their debt post-crisis, and foreign banks were concerned about the quality of their overall portfolio in the Baltic States. Tensions with Russia did not improve the risk profile of the Baltic States, and this has undoubtedly contributed to the reluctance of foreign banks to enlarge their lending portfolio.

Labour mobility facilitated by EU and Schengen membership (see Chapter 4) has taken its toll in the Baltics, with young people migrating in large numbers to countries such as the UK and Ireland, but in spite of that unemployment remains high, especially among the young. It will take the Baltics a long time to catch up with high-income Nordic countries at their current growth rate. The exit of young people will not help restore long-term growth, either. In fact, the Baltics may fall further behind their rich neighbours to the north instead of catching them up. There is a risk of 'divergence' rather than the initially intended 'convergence'. The aspect of GDP growth known as 'convergence' is the tendency for levels of per capita income and productivity to converge towards those prevailing in Western Europe. The cost of adopting the euro was a fixed exchange rate and internal devaluations that almost never work. History shows that those neoliberal policies often lead to large contractions in GDP along with massive unemployment and human suffering. Debt crises typically do not occur in countries that have borrowed in their own currency, because their central bank can print the money needed. A common currency, however, increases the risk of a sovereign debt crisis. The Baltic States do not control the euro printing press in Frankfurt. A fixed exchange rate followed by euro adoption increased the default risk for those countries and they avoided default only through extreme austerity. Euro area membership has weakened their national sovereignty. A high price has been paid for close and 'irreversible' ties with Europe.

The absence of a currency devaluation option

A single currency such as the euro entails a fixed exchange rate among the member countries and a single interest rate within the monetary union. The devaluation option is not available as long as a country remains a member of the currency union—other than, of course, the depreciation of the shared currency. The question regarding the effectiveness of the euro area raises questions such as whether or not economic cycles in the area are broadly synchronized, about the degree of intra-union trade[5], financial and labour mobility, and wage flexibility. Different growth rates in countries within the currency union can also exert pressure, because countries within the euro area cannot use independent monetary and exchange rate tools to help them readjust. A policy that may suit the majority of countries may not suit them all. The economies within the euro area are diverse, as can be expected in a group of 19 countries of different sizes, structure and geographical locations. A common currency can thus become a straitjacket. Once in a common currency area, the Baltic States and Finland were locked into a system of fixed exchange rates, unable to exercise independent monetary and exchange rate policy to achieve readjustment. Given the small size of their economies, the Baltics and Finland have only token influence at the ECB. They have little say in any efforts aimed at depreciating the shared currency or determining the single interest rate, as their economies only account for a tiny share of the euro area economy. The local currencies of the Baltics were overvalued when the 2008/09 crisis erupted, and if they entered the euro area with an overvalued exchange rate—in spite of internal devaluation and programmes of extreme austerity—this could have long-lasting effects on their economic growth and unemployment rate. Among the Nordics, Iceland, Norway and Sweden have chosen a floating exchange rate, which affords them more flexibility. The Danish krone is pegged to the euro, but in theory Denmark could devalue if it decides to break ties with the euro area. Thus the richer Nordic countries have mostly chosen flexible exchange rates outside the monetary union and fiscal policies that tend to be more Keynesian than neoliberal. The Nordic welfare model, with progressive tax and safety nets, has strong automatic stabilizers. However, some of the rich Nordics, especially those with banking interests in the Baltics, advocated euro area membership and austerity programmes for the poorer Baltic States.

Currency union without fiscal union

The euro area is a currency union without a fiscal union. The EU has made efforts, however, to enforce fiscal discipline: these have included the Stability and Growth Pact (SGP)[6] and the Fiscal Compact[7]. There is no fiscal policy at EU level and the common EU budget is small, at about 1% of GDP (Arestis and Sawyer 2006). Under the Fiscal Compact, budget deficits at national level among the EU member states (i.e., not only within the euro area) are intended to remain below the equivalent of 3% of GDP, and general government debt below 60% of GDP. These criteria—the so-called convergence criteria—have not proved binding so far, especially as regards larger nations such as Germany and France, as will be discussed later in this book. It seems to have been assumed that a strict limit to deficits and debt would be the key to the viability of the common currency. Somehow the architects of the euro seemed to believe that, in the absence of excessive fiscal deficits and government debt, trade imbalances would not be a problem. Before the 2008/09 crisis, the fiscal budgets of the Baltic States were in surplus or near balance, and public debt was low, while their current accounts had huge deficits (see overview earlier in this book) and private sector debt grew. Iceland had a fiscal surplus, but a huge current account deficit. So the economic rationale behind the convergence criteria is somewhat hard to understand. But the key problem to be discussed here is the absence of fiscal union within the EU and the euro area.

The fundamental problem here is the lack of solidarity within a diverse group of nations that do not seem to have any common purpose or vision. If a state in the USA faces a disaster it can rely on the federal government for assistance. At the time of writing in late 2017, Hurricane Irma had just struck the US state of Florida, just days after Hurricane Harvey had hit the state of Texas. In both cases, the US federal government provided massive assistance and relief. In the aftermath of such events, the US President sends a clear message to the US Congress emphasizing that the USA is all one family and insists on urgent action to the aid of those devastated states. Objections are not heard. Would the EU provide similar assistance to Greece in the event of a comparable disaster? The answer is no. It has been repeatedly stated, most often by Germany, that the euro area is not a 'transfer union'. Europe is not a federal state, nor is it 'one family', as the USA claims to be, and it has only a minuscule common budget, amounting to just 1% of its GDP, which is largely used to fund agricultural subsidies. In contrast, federal spending in the USA is equivalent to some 20% of national GDP. The USA operates national welfare programmes and the US federal government contributes to unemployment insurance. The EU and the euro area do not have comparable institutions. The founders of the euro did not foresee or want a substantially larger communal budget—a Union-wide system of fiscal federalism, nor was it planned to make any other significant transfers of fiscal funds from one national government to another.

Excessive austerity

The Baltic States exercised fiscal discipline before the 2008/09 crisis hit and were relatively quick to restore discipline following the crisis (see Table 2.4). This is in line with the neoliberal policies favoured by their governments, ministries of finance and central banks, among others, and also complies with the emphasis placed by the EU on the goal of a balanced budget, and the absence of an EU fiscal policy. In the post-Soviet Union period there has seemed to be an unwavering faith in free markets in the Baltics that is also apparent within the European Commission. In contrast, the government of Iceland—which resembles more closely the Nordic welfare model—was much more Keynesian in its response to the economic crisis. Iceland had fairly large fiscal surpluses before the crisis and then ran large and long-lasting fiscal deficits, allowing more room for automatic stabilizers to be activated and run their course (see Table 2.4). The merits of the austerity required for IMF and EU loans during the 2008/09 crisis are highly questionable, especially when implemented in countries such as Latvia with weak social safety net systems. Estonia and Lithuania did not request an IMF loan; however, the EU required them to keep a fixed exchange rate as a condition for subsequent euro adoption, which meant aggressive application of the austerity 'medicine'. The dominant powers within the euro area believed that low deficits and debt levels would protect the Baltics from the worst effects of the crisis; this did not transpire. The euro area powers also believed that the best way to restore the health of a country in recession was a large dose of austerity (Stiglitz 2016, p. 18). Sweden also advocated fixed exchange rates in the Baltics and supported the introduction of austerity programmes to help rescue its banks. Because of free flows of capital within the EU, Swedish banks had flooded the Baltics in the run-up to the economic crisis with loans, mostly denominated in euros, which created real estate bubbles.

Austerity meant cutbacks in public expenditure, including in public programmes such as health, education and other basic services, to lower fiscal deficits. History shows that severe austerity programmes have a negative effect on GDP growth, with the imposition of austerity measures in the midst of a recession (as was the case in the Baltic States in 2008/09) also being associated with sharper contractions in GDP, greater increases in unemployment and a more adverse impact on populations.

Western Europe has historically favoured a 'social capitalist' model, incorporating systems of social protection. Automatic stabilizers, included in government budgets to counteract economic shocks arising from recession, are an important social achievement that took years to develop in most rich countries throughout the world. With the adoption of the euro, many European countries have moved towards neoliberalism and monetarism. In an unfavourable equilibrium during a crisis, governments may find it difficult to use automatic stabilizers, given that they are restricted by the Fiscal Compact from running a budget deficit exceeding 3% of GDP, as per the Maastricht criteria. As De Grauwe (2016) has stated, if monetary union implies destroying automatic stabilizers, it is unclear if the social and political basis for such a union can be maintained (De Grauwe, 2016, p. 118).

Rich countries in the euro area, such as Germany, did not feel much pressure from rising government bond spreads and did not apply any significant austerity measures during the 2008/09 crisis. Poorer euro area member states, such as Greece and Portugal, saw their spreads surge, as did Ireland.

Vulnerable euro area candidate countries, such as the Baltic States, also experienced a surging of government bond spreads and were forced, because of their status, to implement severe austerity measures and effectively fund the bailout of foreign banks, resulting both in sharp contractions in GDP and increasing government debt-to-GDP ratios.

We can conjecture that the Baltic States' governments might have received the message that if they did not accept the conditions, the foreign banks would pull out of their economies, which would then be devastated, preventing the countries from adopting the euro. This would have represented a serious threat to countries that wanted irreversible ties with Europe, perhaps more for security than for economic reasons. Countries such as Norway—which remains outside the EU and the euro area—and Sweden, an EU member state, but with its own currency and flexible exchange rates (like Norway)—only experienced what could be described as a rich-country recession, not a crisis.

Among the problems with austerity is that it leads to economic slowdown when a stimulus is needed. It lowers revenues and increases social expenditures, including employment benefits. In the Baltics, social safety nets are weak and even those measures could not be activated; instead, they were cut severely. Austerity resulted in massive and long-lasting unemployment, along with large-scale migration from the Baltics that will reduce future GDP growth potential in the long term. Overall austerity policies weakened the EU even further as the euro convergence criteria discussed above practically eliminated the use of fiscal policy to stimulate economies.

Keynesian economics, on the other hand, would call for increasing expenditure and cutting taxes during a recession, to increase economic activity and reduce both unemployment (with its associated misery and waste of resources) and the long-term costs of lower GDP growth. In the euro area, this has been turned upside down. Thus expenditure has been cut back in times of recession, and taxes raised; controlling inflation has been more important than controlling unemployment; and exchange rate stability has been prioritized over the welfare of the population. As all too often in their history, the Baltic governments have made poor choices, under pressure from outside forces.

The absence of a full banking union

The absence of a full banking union is a key concern within the euro area, and the fight over this union is tangible evidence of the difficulty of decision-making within the enlarged EU, with its 28 member states. Indeed, few issues have been more contentious since the euro was created. With a common currency, European banks have become more interconnected, with banks engaging in cross-border activities. However, their national regulators have failed to take into account how this could affect neighbouring banks and countries, leading *inter alia* to the conclusion that the prevailing system of national regulators in each of the EU-28 member states is insufficient to monitor cross-border banking activities. The solution would be a banking union where three elements were needed: single supervisory, single resolution and single deposit insurance mechanisms (Eichengreen 2015, p. 12, De Grauwe 2016, p. 178). The EU has been taking steps to address those issues[8].

The ECB, which is responsible for the prudent supervision of credit institutions located in the euro area, is expected to contribute to the safety and soundness of the banking system and the stability of the financial system within the EU and each participating member state[9]. However, the situation within the Nordic-Baltic region is awkward because the Nordic—mainly Swedish—owners of the Baltic banking system exist outside the currency union, while the Baltic States exist within the union. It is thus unclear how the ECB can effectively perform its role, although it can certainly make efforts to co-operate with the Scandinavian central banks, especially the Swedish Riksbank. Sweden does not intend to join the EU banking union in the foreseeable future. Prior to the 2008/09 crisis, Iceland aggressively expanded its overseas banking operations, as permitted under the system, and then had serious disputes with the UK, the Netherlands and the EU, which tried to attribute blame to Iceland alone.

A common resolution framework for banks in the euro area is still lacking, although progress has been made. A system is needed that makes it possible to resolve a crisis at the euro area level. Currently, national governments are responsible for resolving a crisis, taking over troubled banks and restructuring them. This can result in very large budget deficits and increases in debt, causing a solvency crisis for national governments. (Ireland is an example of this.) Some progress has been made in setting up a common resolution mechanism in the euro area through a resolution fund, although its size may be insufficient to deal with a future banking crisis (see for example De Grauwe 2016, p. 178). The European Stability Mechanism, a new EU institution established in 2012 and funded by bond sales and capital from euro area countries, lends to countries in trouble and helped recapitalize Spain's banks (Stiglitz, 2016, p. 23), but more needs to be done.

The final element—and the one which is most obviously lacking—is deposit insurance. In the euro area every government has its own deposit insurance mechanism with national contributions. Each national government has been responsible for its own banks. In the event of a large-scale crisis this commitment could become a problem for the sovereign. The USA has a federal agency (the Federal Deposit Insurance Corporation) that bails out banks in the USA. This is not done at a federal level within the EU, but by individual states. With some countries strong, such as Germany, and other countries weaker and still in crisis, such as Greece, capital naturally flows from weaker countries to stronger countries. In effect, it is less safe to deposit one's money in Athens than in Frankfurt, because the government of Greece is in a weaker position to come to the rescue of its banks than the government of more robust Germany.

A free flow of capital within the EU has certain advantages, but there are side effects, too. The Baltic States were vulnerable when the 2008/09 crisis struck, with funds flowing back to richer Nordic countries. The Baltics were suddenly perceived as more risky, resulting in reverse capital flows. Naturally, with a mostly foreign banking system, credit growth was slow in the post-crisis period. Within the euro area, the Baltics remain rather weak compared to larger, richer European Economic Area (EEA) member states. There is a need for a common insurance scheme within the euro area. This would mean that during a crisis funds would need to be transferred from member countries to another.

As Obstfeld (2013) has pointed out, a threat to national solvency exists in some euro area countries from the sheer size of bank balance sheets—completing the 'doom loop'[10] linking banks and sovereigns (see for example Obstfeld 2013, p. 149). A bank that holds many government bonds on its balance sheet becomes dependent on its government's credit rating. Any deterioration of that credit rating can thus create a solvency problem for the bank. Conversely, a deterioration in the financial health of a country's banks can affect the state budget because the government may end up having to bail out a bank, and a subsequent economic downturn can reduce government tax revenue. This situation has affected a number of southern European countries, notably Greece (which has faced the greatest challenges), Italy, Portugal and Spain.

The euro area and its member states are at risk because of large bank balance sheets within the area, but also because of interlinkages with countries outside the euro area, including, for example, EU member states that have not adopted the euro, as well as countries in the EEA that are not EU member states. In 2008, just before the financial crisis struck, the assets of Iceland's banks had a total value equivalent to almost 10 times the country's GDP. When 85% of the Icelandic banking system collapsed in October 2008, its cross-border banking activities embroiled the country's government in disputes with the UK, which was not a member of the euro area, and the Netherlands, which was. As Buiter and Sibert (2008) pointed out, Iceland's situation was extreme, but according to them other countries are suffering from milder versions of what they label as a fundamental vulnerable 'quartet' of circumstances, i.e.: (1) A small country with (2) a large, internationally exposed banking sector, (3) its own currency and (4) limited fiscal spare capacity relative to the possible size of the banking sector solvency gap. The countries that they name as examples are Switzerland, Denmark and Sweden and even to some extent the UK, although it is significantly larger than the others and has a minor-league legacy reserve currency (Buiter and Sibert, 2008).

The Danish and Swedish banking systems are not as large in terms of the countries' economies—as measured by GDP—as was the case in Iceland, but they still present a risk both to the countries themselves and to the euro area as a whole. In Denmark, bank assets in December 2012 were more than three times the value of GDP, and in Sweden, they were four times as large as

GDP. Both Denmark and Sweden are outside the euro area, but they have outward exposure via their banking systems beyond their domestic market into the euro area; most notably, Sweden has exposure in the Baltic States. Conversely, the Baltic States have inward exposure from Sweden because of banking claims from Sweden on the Baltics. When the 2008/09 crisis erupted, the Baltics were outside the euro area, but they had all committed to euro adoption, which became a reality after the crisis. Thus these interlinkages continue to pose challenges in the post-crisis period, for the Baltics and for the entire euro area. As Hüttl and Schoenmaker (2016) report, at the end of 2014 three Nordic banks: Nordea (Sweden), SEB Group (Sweden), and Danske Bank (Denmark) held assets amounting to 18%, 14% and 12%, respectively, of total assets in the euro area, with a particularly strong presence in Finland and the Baltic States (Hüttl and Schoenmaker 2016, p. 6). Neither Denmark nor Sweden is a euro area member state. The government of Sweden has declared that it does not intend to take part in the banking union that is being created by the EU[11]. This is notable and could be a source of concern for the euro area. As Hüttl and Schoenmaker (2016) also argue, membership of Denmark and Sweden in the banking union would increase the effectiveness and efficiency of supervision of the larger European cross-border banks, allowing supervision and resolution at the consolidated level (Hüttl and Schoenmaker, 2016, p. 9).

The European Central Bank

The ECB and the national central banks together constitute the Eurosystem, the central monetary authority of the euro area. The main objective of the Eurosystem is to maintain price stability: safeguarding the value of the euro[12]. Stabilizing output and keeping high levels of employment are among the objectives of the ECB, but these are only secondary to the main objective of price stability. The ECB may be the strongest institution within the EU, but it lacks democratic accountability. In fact, we can say that the EU has built a fortress around the ECB to protect it from political interference—indeed, a much stronger fortress than that built by the US Federal Reserve. As De Grauwe (2016) has pointed out, when the chairman of the Federal Reserve testifies to the US Congress, he is speaking to an institution that can change its status by a simple majority. In contrast, when the president of the ECB appears before the European Parliament, he knows that it has no power to change the ECB statutes. Changing the ECB Treaty requires unanimity among EU member states, including those member states that do not participate in European monetary union (De Grauwe 2016, p. 167). This gives the ECB enormous power, and should it make serious mistakes, it is not clear what sanctions could be applied. It has often been argued that the ECB was modelled after the German Bundesbank, but in fact, as the Bundesbank statutes can be altered by a simple majority vote in the German parliament, the ECB is the more powerful.

In the post-crisis period, the ECB's ability to preserve the euro has been questioned and it has sought to reassure the world about its commitment. For example, in a 2012 speech, ECB President Mario Draghi stated: 'Within our mandate, the ECB is ready to do whatever it takes to preserve the euro. And believe me, it will be enough'[13]. But as noted above, the ECB's primary mandate is to focus on inflation in a continent with a serious problem of high long-term unemployment and slow GDP growth. (In particular, youth unemployment has become a critical issue.) This narrow focus on inflation traces its roots back to the Maastricht Treaty of 1992.

In contrast, the US Federal Reserve reformed after the 2008/09 global crisis. It now focuses on inflation, but also on unemployment, GDP growth and stability. With limited fiscal policy options within the euro area, given both fiscal deficit and debt-to-GDP constraints as well as the inability to transfer fiscal funds across national borders (in the absence of a transfer union), a special burden is placed on monetary policy within the euro area. As stated above, monetary policy is also ineffective because of the very narrow mandate on inflation targeting. The ECB should be charged with setting interest rates in a manner that encourages economic growth and full employment, rather than merely inflation (see, for example, Arestis and Sawyer 2006, p. 23).

However, the ECB, along with the European Commission, often supported by the IMF and member states with vested interests (such as Sweden, in the case of the Baltics) appear very willing to come to the rescue of private banks. The cost of rescuing foreign banks in Latvia led to an increase in Latvia's debt-to-GDP ratio from 7% in 2007 to 37% in 2016, in Lithuania from 16% in 2007 to 40% in 2016 and in Estonia from 4% in 2007 to 9% in 2016 (See Figure 6.1)[14].

The Baltic States were not the only victims. According to Stiglitz (2016), Jean-Claude Trichet demanded that Ireland assume the liabilities of its

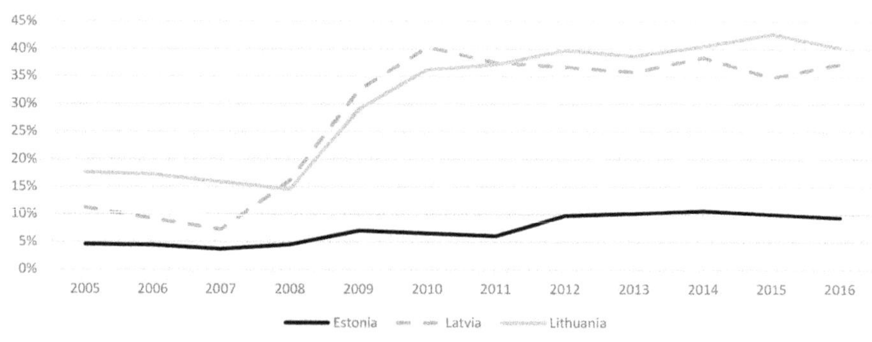

Figure 6.1 Baltic States: General government gross debt 2005–16 (% of GDP)
Source: International Monetary Fund (2017).

bankrupt banks, and the cost of restructuring those banks led to an increase in Ireland's debt-to-GDP ratio from 24% in 2007 to an estimated 95% in 2015 (Stiglitz 2016, p. 156).

This debt increase was not because of ordinary spending, but because of bank bailouts. In Iceland the three largest banks, representing 85% of the banking system, went bankrupt. Since Iceland is not an EU or euro area member state, the European Commission or the ECB could not insist that ordinary taxpayers bear the costs, as was done in the Baltics and in Ireland and other euro area countries.

Arguably, the current German model employed by the ECB was more suitable for the most prosperous members of the euro area who, like Germany, favour price stability, rather than the poorest members, which need growth to catch up. Scandinavian history shows that Keynesian fiscal policies along with floating exchange rates sometimes resulted in high inflation, but in spite of instability from time from time there was strong economic growth over long periods: indeed, that is what made those countries rich. Social justice provided by the welfare state contributed to stability and growth in those countries.

Under the euro area straitjacket, the Baltics can perhaps not be considered dead economies. However, they have certainly been facing stagnation in the years since the crisis. Why is it that the ECB became so conservative, so neoliberal? Why did the EU choose the German model and reject the Anglo-French model during the Maastricht negotiations? De Grauwe (2016) offers two explanations: first, the intellectual development favouring monetarism and second, the strategic position of Germany, giving high priority to price stability (De Grauwe, 2016). Since the 2008/09 crisis, Keynesianism has revived at the cost of still-prevailing monetarism, but it remains to be seen for how long.

The euro area and national security

Arguably, Europe proceeded too quickly with full monetary union. However, security considerations were involved, as well as purely economic issues. EU membership, followed by euro area membership, firmly integrated the Baltic States into a union with Western European nations. The Baltics all share borders with Russia. They are not the only countries that would consider euro area membership as important for their security. Greece, which borders Turkey, may also view euro area membership as improving its security profile, integrating that country further into Europe.

The Russian revolutionary Lenin (Vladimir Ulyanov) has been quoted as saying: 'The surest way to destroy a nation is to debauch its currency'[15]. During the first and second World Wars one could, for example, expect that Germany would try to undermine the pound sterling and the French franc, and the UK and France the German mark, and so on. However, once Germany and France shared a common currency, they were bound by a mutual interest in preserving that currency for the sake of their economies and the well-being of their own peoples. In fact, as Eichengreen (2008) points out, the institutions of European integration were designed to lock Germany into Europe to ensure that the continent's largest producer would apply its industrial might to peaceful purposes (Eichengreen, 2008, p. 10, see also Eichengreen 2007).

A peaceful Germany was an important motive for European integration and the pressure only grew after the unification of West and East Germany, which resulted in a country with a larger land mass, population and economic capacity. Some will go so far as to give the EU credit for the absence of war in Europe for 70 years. The single market, which entailed the removal of capital controls, created pressure for establishing a common currency, the euro. The euro greatly decreased the incentive of these old rivals to become embroiled in major wars like those characterizing the first half of the last century. It might thus have made good sense for those two countries to adopt the euro even if they had known and understood the possible economic complications and financial risks involved—some foreseeable, others not. It is perhaps more questionable whether the euro should have been adopted by countries in southern and northern Europe. Developments in southern Europe have been especially challenging, involving Greece, Italy, Portugal and Spain, while other countries have also had problems, most notably Ireland and to some extent Finland. It may also be naïve to assume that the establishment of the EU and of the euro are the only reasons we now have a peaceful Europe. Nuclear deterrence is another factor that discourages nations from going to war.

In retrospect it seems obvious that the Baltic States and Finland adopted the euro not only for possible economic gains, but also because further European integration could provide them with added security, most notably against any potential threat from Russia. Finland, Estonia and Latvia all have eastern borders with Russia, while Lithuania borders on the Kaliningrad Oblast, an exclave of the Russian Federation in which Russia maintains a strong military presence. Meanwhile, the Russian minority[16] in the Baltic States accounts for about 25% in Estonia and 27% in Latvia. In Lithuania this proportion is lower, at about 6%. Having borders with Russia and the presence of a Russian minority has created tensions in the Baltic States and can be a source of instability and insecurity. A higher risk profile discourages cross-border engagement from foreign investors, especially as regards long-term investment.

It should be noted that many ethnic Russians were born in the Baltics and consider them to be their home country. Tensions in the Baltics concern not only the Baltic governments themselves, but also the Russian authorities. In June 2006 Russian President Vladimir Putin announced proposals to introduce a national policy aiming at encouraging ethnic Russian immigration to Russia[17].

The Baltic States, NATO and reliance on the USA

The Baltics are all North Atlantic Treaty Organization (NATO) member states as indeed are Denmark, Iceland and Norway, while Finland and Sweden remain outside NATO. In the event of a conflict with Russia involving the Baltic States the pressure would be on a response from NATO and especially the USA, which remains the backbone of NATO. Article 5 of the NATO Treaty on Collective Defence commits NATO member states to protect each other and sets a spirit of solidarity within the NATO Alliance[18]. As discussed in Chapter 4, the USA has progressively reduced its military presence in Europe since the fall of the Berlin Wall and the collapse of the Soviet Union, and US commitment to NATO has been called into question, most recently with the election of Donald Trump as US president, who has labelled NATO as 'obsolete'[19]. There are also growing tensions and distrust between the EU and US leadership.

With the adoption of the euro by the Baltic States, we can perhaps argue that the pressure on NATO to provide defence has been reduced and that euro member states—including the major powers of Germany and France—now have added responsibility, especially within the 19 member-state euro area but also for all 28 EU member states. However, the preparedness of the larger euro area member states and the EU in general to protect the smaller member states during a military conflict is open to doubt, though a conflict in the Baltics would be of serious concern to all EU— and especially euro area—member states.

As also stated in Chapter 4, the ability of the USA to serve as a guarantor of peace and stability in Europe and in other regions of the world has been reduced. In 1944, at the time of the Bretton Woods conference towards the end of the Second World War, the US economy represented about 50% of global GDP. While the economies of continental Europe and Japan were devastated by the war, North American territory had remained largely undamaged. In 1950 the USA represented about 40% of world GDP, reducing to about 30% in the 1960s and falling to around 20–25% of global GDP by the 1990s[20].

Thus, while the US economy is growing in absolute terms, in relative terms it continues to become ever smaller. While the USA remains the greatest superpower in the world, new powers have arisen, including the BRICS grouping of large emerging economies—comprising Brazil, Russia, India, the People's Republic of China and South Africa. Their economies have grown and they demand a greater say in world affairs. It follows that pressure will increase on the EU member states and euro area member states to take the lead in their own defence, especially powers such as Germany and France.

Thus the EU may increasingly need to take over US leadership in NATO. An additional complication in Europe will result from the decision of the UK, a key player in Europe strategically and militarily, to exit the EU. The UK's role in Northern Europe is especially important for global security, and it will still remain a NATO member state.

Some politicians in the USA have made absurd statements about the Baltic States. Newt Gingrich, a former Speaker of the US House of Representatives, is quoted as having told CBS News that 'Estonia is in the suburbs of St Petersburg [...] 40% of Estonia is Russian...I'm not sure I would risk nuclear war over some place that is the suburb of St Petersburg'[21]. Statements such as this, from an influential US politician, must be especially shocking, not only for Estonians and all inhabitants of the Baltics, but also for all EU member states as well as for European NATO member states. During the election year of 2016, then-presidential candidate Donald Trump was quoted as saying 'Pulling back from Europe would save this country millions of dollars annually. The cost of stationing NATO troops in Europe is enormous. And these are clearly funds that can be put to better use'[22]. Non-NATO member states such as Sweden and Finland are also deeply concerned. Sweden has a big stake in the Baltics, especially in the financial sector. Sweden's defence minister has been quoted as saying that his country was worried by the presence of warships in the Baltic Sea, complaining the move was likely to keep tension in the region high and affects all the countries around the Baltic Sea[23]. For Sweden, the risk profile for the Baltics is higher than it was before Russia invaded and then annexed the Crimean peninsula from Ukraine. Ironically, the decline in Finnish-Russian trade has not only impeded recovery of the Finnish economy, which is facing its fourth year of low-to-negative GDP growth, but has also weakened its ability to invest more in its military[24].

In August 2016 the three Baltic States—Estonia, Latvia and Lithuania—celebrated the 25th Anniversary of the restoration of their independence, while 2018 sees the centenary of their original independence. The Baltic States still see themselves as on the frontline of a potential conflict with Russia under Vladimir Putin's administration. Russia is seen as an unpredictable neighbour and tensions with Russia have heightened.

During the 25th anniversary the then US Republican presidential candidate Donald Trump suggested that he might abandon NATO's pledge to defend all alliance members automatically if elected. The NATO alliance was formed by Western nations in 1949 in response to perceived threats posed by the Soviet Union and communist expansion in Europe. During the anniversary, Joe Biden, then US vice-president, met with Baltic leaders from Estonia, Latvia and Lithuania and criticized the then Republican presidential nominee, saying his comments on NATO were 'nothing that should be taken seriously', adding, 'I don't think he even understands what Article 5 is'[25]. In fact, Article 5 has to do with collective defence and, according to NATO: 'The principle of collective defence is at the very heart of NATO's founding treaty. It remains a unique and enduring principle that binds its members together, committing them to protect each other and setting a spirit of solidarity within the Alliance'—NATO 2018).

It is clear that the USA is not as committed to NATO obligations as in the past. In 1994 US President Bill Clinton gave a speech at the Monument of Freedom in Riga, Latvia. There he said: '[W]e will stand with you. We will help you....We will be partners so that your nation can be forever free' (Clinton 1994). The USA may no longer have the will or the resources to carry the burden of defence for Europe. Furthermore, it has an increasing tendency (as do certain other nations) to act on its own interests first and foremost. For example, the USA withdrew in 2006 from its commitment to maintain a defence force in Iceland, regardless of the Icelandic Government's views at that time.

The governments of the Baltic States joined the euro area without consulting their citizens via referendums. The fixed exchange rate policy has arguably slowed their economic recovery in the aftermath of the economic crisis, but security concerns and the wish to create irreversible links with Western Europe presumably also weighted high in the minds of their governments.

Notes

1 A referendum held in Sweden in September 2003 saw 55.9% of eligible voters electing against membership of the euro area. As a consequence, Sweden decided in 2003 not to adopt the euro for the time being. If they had voted in favour, Sweden would have adopted the euro on 1 January 2006: see www.riksbank.se/en/Press-and-published/Speeches/2003/Heikensten-The-Riksbank-and-the-euro1/. A referendum held in Denmark in September 2000 rejected membership of the euro area; the turnout was 87.6% of eligible voters, with 46.8% voting yes and 53.2% voting no: see www.eu.dk/.
2 The euro area as described in this book is synonymous with what is elsewhere termed the eurozone.
3 See further: www.project-syndicate.org/commentary/greece-debt-agreement-risks-by-barry-eichengreen-2015-07.
4 There were some variations among them. In Estonia, real credit is no longer contracting. In Latvia and Lithuania, where credit expansion is yet to resume, measures aimed at reducing private sector debt overhang—such as improvements in insolvency regimes—could spur credit demand, while reducing credit risk, thus encouraging supply. According to the IMF, the Baltic economies could, over the medium term, explore initiatives to deepen capital markets and reduce dependence on bank credit. See further: www.imf.org/external/pubs/ft/scr/2014/cr14116.pdf.
5 See further: http://ec.europa.eu/eurostat/statistics-explained/index.php/Intra-EU_trade_in_goods_-_recent_trends.
6 See further: https://ec.europa.eu/info/node/4287/.
7 See further: www.ecb.europa.eu/pub/pdf/other/mb201203_focus12.en.pdf.
8 See further: https://ec.europa.eu/info/business-economy-euro/banking-and-finance/banking-union_en.
9 See further: www.ecb.europa.eu/ecb/orga/escb/ecb-mission/html/index.en.html.
10 See, for example, www.bloomberg.com/view/articles/2017-12-15/europe-s-sovereign-bank-doom-loop-can-t-be-broken.
11 See further: www.government.se/sweden-in-the-eu/eu-policy-areas/economic-and-financial-affairs/.
12 See further: www.ecb.europa.eu/ecb/orga/escb/ecb-mission/html/index.en.html.
13 See further: www.ecb.europa.eu/press/key/date/2012/html/sp120726.en.html.
14 See further: International Monetary Fund 2017.
15 See further: http://quotes.liberty-tree.ca/quotes_by/vladimir+ilyich+lenin.
16 For more details, see endnote discussion in Preface.
17 See further: www.rferl.org/a/1070573.html.

18 See further: www.nato.int/cps/en/natohq/topics_110496.htm.
19 See further: www.independent.co.uk/news/world/europe/europe-atonshished-donald-trump-nato-comments-obsolete-eu-military-organisation-russia-agression-a7529776.html.
20 See 1987 interview with Paul Samuelson at: https://vimeo.com/151661109.
21 See further: www.cbsnews.com/news/newt-gingrich-trump-would-reconsider-his-obligation-to-nato/.
22 See further: www.washingtonpost.com/opinions/global-opinions/under-president-trump-america-may-no-longer-lead-the-free-world/2016/11/09/921bbbbe-a67b-11e6-ba59-a7d93165c6d4_story.html?utm_term=.64ead8a1ff4d.
23 See further: www.reuters.com/article/us-russia-defence-baltic-sweden-idUSKCN12Q1HB.
24 See further: www.defensenews.com/story/defense/policy-budget/2015/06/27/finland-sweden-russia-nato-baltics-tensions-budgets-gdp/29289941/.
25 See further: www.cnn.com/2016/08/23/politics/joe-biden-trump-nato-comments/ For further information also see www.reuters.com/article/us-latvia-usa-biden-idUSKCN10Y0ZT and http://abcnews.go.com/Politics/joe-biden-tells-baltic-leaders-donald-trump-understand/story?id=41593419.

References

Arestis, P. and Sawyer, M. (2006). 'Macroeconomic Policy and the European Constitution'. In P. Arestis and M. Sawyer (eds), *Alternative Perspectives on Economic Policies in the European Union*, Houndmills, Basingstoke: Palgrave Macmillan.

Buiter, W., and Sibert, A. (2008). '*The collapse of Iceland's banks: the predictable end of a non-viable business model*'. Available at: https://voxeu.org/article/iceland-s-banking-collapse-predicable-end-and-lessons-other-vulnerable-nations (Accessed on 28 September 2017).

Clinton, W. (1994). *Remarks to Citizens in Riga: July 6, 1994*. Available at: www.presidency.ucsb.edu/ws/?pid=50448 (Accessed on 22 August 2017).

De Grauwe, P. (2016). *Economics of monetary union*. Oxford: Oxford University Press.

Eichengreen, B. (2007). '*The European economy since 1945: coordinated capitalism and beyond*'. Heritage Lectures, No. 1012. Available at: www.heritage.org/europe/report/the-european-economy-1945-coordinated-capitalism-and-beyond (Accessed on 22 August 2017).

Eichengreen, B. (2008). *The European economy since 1945: coordinated capitalism and beyond.* Princeton, NJ: Princeton University Press.

Eichengreen, B. (2015). *Hall of Mirrors: The Great Depression, the Great Recession, and the Uses—and Misuses—of History.* New York: Oxford University Press.

Hilmarsson, H. Þ. (2016). 'Iceland and the Challenge of European Integration: Is European Union Membership Feasible?' In Lino Briguglio (ed.) *Small States and the European Union. Europa Economic Perspectives.* London: Routledge.

Hüttl, P. and Schoenmaker, D. (2016). '*Should the 'outs' join the European banking union?' Policy Contribution 2016/03*, Bruegel. Available at: http://bruegel.org/wp-content/uploads/2016/02/pc_2016_03.pdf (Accessed on 29 September, 2017).

International Monetary Fund (2014). *Baltic Cluster Report. IMF Country Report No. 14/116.* Available at: www.imf.org/external/pubs/ft/scr/2014/cr14116.pdf (Accessed on 21 November 2017).

International Monetary Fund (2017). *World Economic Outlook Database.* Available at: www.imf.org/external/pubs/ft/weo/2017/02/weodata/index.aspx.

Mundell, R. (1961). 'A Theory of Optimal Currency Areas', *American Economic Review*, 51(4): pp. 657–665.

Mundell, R. (1973). 'Uncommon Arguments for Common Currencies', in H. G. Johnson and A. K. Swoboda (eds), *The Economics of Common Currencies*, London: Allen and Unwin, pp. 114–132.

NATO (2018). '*Collective Defence—Article 5*'. Available at: www.nato.int/cps/en/natohq/topics_110496.htm (Accessed on 29 September 2017).

Obstfeld, M. (2013). 'Crises and the international system'. *International Economic Journal*, *27*(2), pp. 143–155.

Stiglitz, J. E. (2016). *The Euro—How a Common Currency Threatens the Future of Europe*. New York and London: W. W. Norton & Company.

7 Nordic–Baltic banking interconnectedness and its consequences

With the single European market came not only free movement of goods, services and labour, but also free capital flows across national borders. As discussed in Chapter 6, this becomes a problem when the European Union (EU) banking union remains incomplete. The advantages of a common market with goods and services are obvious, as are the merits of free flows of labour, although more sensitive and at much lower levels in the EU than in the USA. The merits of free capital flows cross-border in the EU, including the Nordic-Baltic region, are more frequently disputed. In the Nordic-Baltic region, only the Baltics and Finland are within the euro area, but the continental Nordics–whose banks are also the main operators within Baltic financial systems—remain outside, and are not direct participants in, efforts to build an EU banking union. But if free capital flows were to be restricted then we need to think about an alternative to free capital flows across borders.

In 2006, two years before the global economic and financial crisis struck, large parts of the banking sectors of Denmark, Finland, Norway and Sweden were under Nordic control, i.e. there were extensive interlinkages via cross-border liabilities. According to data from the Bank for International Settlements (BIS)[1], liabilities as a percentage of total foreign liabilities were especially high in Finland, but also in Denmark and Norway—in all cases, due to the influence of Sweden. A clear exception to this rule was the Icelandic banking sector, which was predominantly in domestic ownership and did not have strong cross-border interlinkages with the continental Nordics. The Swedish financial groups had a large presence in the other Nordic-Baltic countries, but the presence of other Nordic groups in Sweden was less significant. Swedish, and to a lesser degree Finnish, financial institutions, occupied a leading position in the Baltic banking sectors. According to the International Monetary Fund (IMF), liabilities to Sweden were particularly high in Estonia, but slightly less pronounced in Latvia and Lithuania (see Table 7.1) (International Monetary Fund 2007).

In 2007 the IMF issued a report entitled 'Financial integration in the Nordic-Baltic region: challenges for financial policies' (International Monetary Fund 2007). As the report noted, Nordic-Baltic cross-border financial sector linkages were reflected in the BIS-reported foreign claims in the region.

The foreign claims of Nordic banks showed increasing exposure to other Nordic countries. This trend was driven by the cross-border integration of the Nordic financial sectors. BIS data indicated that the Nordic-Baltic cross-border cluster had become more pronounced in recent years (International Monetary Fund 2007).

Nordic claims on the Baltic States grew rapidly until the economic and financial crisis hit in 2008. The Nordic banks' exposure to the Baltics was small relative to their Nordic exposure, but significant in comparison with the Baltic States' other foreign liabilities. In 2006, liabilities to the Nordic countries represented approximately 82% of the total foreign liabilities of the Baltic banks. Strikingly, 71% of the foreign liabilities of the Baltic banks were to Sweden and 11% to Finland (see Table 7.1 below). The strategic refocusing of the Nordic countries towards their core Nordic market and the Baltic States was accompanied by reduced exposure to some of the major financial centres. According to the IMF, the Nordic countries cut back exposure to the USA and the United Kingdom, but increased exposure to Germany (International Monetary Fund 2007). Liabilities to all the Nordics as a percentage of total foreign liabilities increased significantly in Germany and also increased in the UK from 1999 to 2006, but remained the same for the USA (see International Monetary Fund 2007, Table 2.8, p. 26).

Table 7.1 Liabilities of the Nordic and Baltic Banking Systems to the Nordic Countries 1999–2006 (% of total foreign liabilities)

	Liabilities to Denmark		*Liabilities to Finland*		*Liabilities to Norway*		*Liabilities to Sweden*		*Liabilities to all Nordics*	
	Q4 1999	*Q3 2006*	*Q4 1999*	*Q3 2006*	*Q4 1999*	*Q1 2004*	*Q4 1999*	*Q3 2006*	*Q4 1999*	*Q3 2006*
Nordic Countries	**3.9**	**7.9**	**3.7**	**5.2**	**0.1**	**0.5**	**10.8**	**27.9**	**18.5**	**41.4**
Denmark	-	-	1.2	6.4	0.0	0.5	9.9	33.5	11.1	40.5
Finland	3.3	1.8	-	-	-	0.1	23.3	60.2	26.6	62.1
Iceland	1.5	-	0.8	0.1	3.0	0.4	3.5	0.8	8.8	1.3
Norway	4.2	10.4	2.0	4.1	-	-	23.6	31.9	29.8	46.3
Sweden	7.0	19.3	8.3	8.9	-	1.1	-	-	15.3	29.3
Baltic States	**0.0**	**0.0**	**8.7**	**11.1**	**0.0**	**0.0**	**42.6**	**70.9**	**51.3**	**82.1**
Estonia	-	-	10.9	13.2	-	-	59.8	78.8	70.6	92.0
Latvia	-	-	9.6	8.8	-	-	45.0	67.9	54.5	76.7
Lithuania	-	-	4.2	11.3	-	-	10.3	65.5	14.5	76.7

Source: Bank for International Settlements Consolidated Banking Statistics and International Monetary Fund (2007).

Notes: Liabilities on immediate borrowers basis; data for liabilities to Norway not publicly available after March 2004.

As the numbers in Table 7.1 show, Swedish financial groups played an important role in the process of regional financial sector integration. The direction of foreign claims and liabilities in the region underscores the importance of Swedish groups in the Nordic-Baltic financial sectors. It is Sweden that has the largest share of claims on other Nordic countries in total banking system assets and that has emerged as the most common lender in the region. The same trend is evident in the Baltics, where more than 70% of foreign borrowing is due to Sweden. Swedish financial groups hold dominant market shares in the Baltic financial sectors.

Financial sector developments in the Nordic-Baltic countries over the decade prior to the 2008 crisis indicated increased regional integration of institutions and markets. Institutional integration took the form of closer ownership linkages between the Nordic financial institutions and their expansion in the Baltics. Foreign financial sector presence in the region is predominantly from other Nordic countries (International Monetary Fund 2007).

Financial conglomeration and cross-border expansion of large Nordic financial groups in the Nordic-Baltic region created financial institutions that became of systemic importance in different countries and sectors. Financial conglomeration has increased concentration in the financial sectors as a whole. The large Nordic financial institutions increased their reliance on market-based funding, and capital market operations represented an important part of their overall activity. The institutional complexity and the expanded international reach of the large Nordic financial groups underscore the importance of a unified approach to their supervision as well as the need for co-operation and co-ordination among supervisors both at the sectoral and at the regional level (International Monetary Fund 2007).

The question remains: what action did the IMF take when seeing the potentially dangerous interlinkages between the Nordic and Baltic banking systems in 2006? The report issued by the IMF in 2007 was useful, and the data it references from the BIS ought to have alarmed the authorities in the continental Nordic-Baltic region. The comment from the IMF regarding the importance of co-operation and co-ordination among supervisors was also consequential.

At this time, it was well known that the different levels of European integration sought by the Nordic countries and the Baltic States could make this co-operation complicated. All the Baltic States sought to join the euro area, while the Nordic countries, with the exception of Finland, did not. Thus the main players within the Baltic banking sector would be outside an EU banking union, while the Baltics remained within. It was also known that bank assets were very high in relation to GDP in Sweden and Denmark. At the end of 2012, total Swedish bank assets were equivalent to 400% of the country's GDP, and the corresponding figure for Denmark was more than 300%. This represented a danger for the whole region. The vulnerabilities were that these were small countries, possessing a large banking sector, their own currency and limited fiscal capacity to assist their banking sector during a crisis. This is what made Iceland's banking model non-viable. The same situation applied, and still applies, to the Danish and Swedish banking sectors, although the situation that led to the fall of the Icelandic banking system was more extreme.

In 2013 Grönn and Fredholm wrote a paper, published as an IMF working paper, entitled *Baltic and Icelandic experiences of capital flows and capital flow measures*, in which they noted the significant size of the Swedish and Danish banking sectors *vis-à-vis* their domestic economies, linked partly to large-scale activity by the Nordic banks in other Nordic countries. They noted further—in the context of growing interlinkages between financial systems in the Nordic-Baltic region, and the overall dominance of the Nordic banks in the Baltic States—the danger of risks in one country spreading to others in the chain. (Grönn and Fredholm 2013, p. 6).

As already noted, Iceland does not have large interlinkages with Scandinavian banks and has none with Baltic banks. According to BIS data, the interlinkages between continental Nordic and Baltic banking systems mainly relate to the Swedish banking sector. This was a problem before the 2008 crisis struck: it continued to pose a problem about five years later when Grönn and Fredholm wrote their paper, and is still a problem in 2018. The Swedish authorities seem helpless to deal with this issue, although they are aware of it, express concern, and try to take action.

In November 2016, the following statement appeared on the website of the Riksbank, Sweden's central bank and an authority under the Riksdag, the Swedish parliament:

> Banks and households need to increase their resilience. The Swedish banking system is vulnerable due to its size, concentration and interconnectedness [...] As the major Swedish banks have extensive cross-border operations, primarily through their presence in the Nordic Region, the Baltic States and the United Kingdom, they are also exposed towards short-term liquidity risks in other currencies. [...] The major Swedish banks are also taking significant structural liquidity risks. These arise as a result of the banks having a large proportion of mortgages with long maturities on the asset side, while having a comparatively high proportion of short-term wholesale funding on the liability side. The banks must therefore renew their funding several times during the mortgage's maturity period. The banks should therefore continue to reduce their structural liquidity risks, for example by extending the maturity of their funding.[2]
>
> (Riksbank 2016)

In its statement, the Swedish Riksbank notes that its actions are supported by the European Commission and the IMF.

It remains to be seen what action will be taken. But warnings from the Swedish Riksbank have not always had their intended effect. As Grönn and

Fredholm state: 'although Sveriges Riksbank already in 2005 started to regularly publish assessments of the looming risks in the Baltic countries in the Financial Stability Report, the Swedish banks continued to fuel the credit growth in the Baltic countries' (Grönn and Fredholm 2013, p. 17–18). This behaviour had serious consequences in the Baltic States, especially in Latvia, which was the hardest-hit country and which was also threatened by continental Nordic banking systems because of the extensive interlinkages discussed above.

The incumbent Latvian Prime Minister, Valdis Dombrovskis (2009–14), was not impressed with the actions of the Swedish authorities before the onset of the 2008/09 global economic and financial crisis. In their 2011 book, entitled *How Latvia Came through the Financial Crisis*, he and his co-author Anders Åslund state: '[t]he Swedish Riksbank and the Financial Supervisory Authority [...] should also have paid attention to excessive exposure of the Swedish commercial banks to the Baltic economies, but they did nothing' (Åslund and Dombrovskis 2011, p. 29). According to Åslund and Dombrovskis, the Swedish authorities thus failed in their supervisory role in the Baltic States.

The IMF working paper by Grönn and Fredholm (2013) documented the risks and the still obvious vulnerabilities caused by the interconnected continental Nordic and Baltic banks in the aftermath of the crisis (Grönn and Fredholm 2013, p. 6). A common pre-crisis problem in both Iceland and Latvia was that the housing bubble had to a large extent been funded by loans in euro (or other foreign currencies) taken by people with income in local currency. As Grönn and Fredholm state, 'Another characteristic is that many of these banks were exposed to a large share of unhedged borrowers, with income in domestic currency and loans in foreign currency' (Grönn and Fredholm 2013, p. 6).

This is one key reason why some people in Latvia, perhaps those belonging to the élite , had a common interest with foreign banks. They, like the foreign banks, feared the balance sheet effects of devaluation. As Grönn and Fredholm state:

> ... there is no risk as long as the fixed exchange rate is maintained, but can potentially imply large credit losses if the currencies were to depreciate. Since investors had underestimated the potential risks in the Baltic countries, the Nordic parent banks were allowed continued access to cheap funding at a price corresponding to the risk of the banking groups. The consequence of the Nordic parent banks not assessing their own risk properly in turn led to the interest rate offered to the Baltic borrowers being too low. This inadequate risk management contributed to large capital flows to these countries as the Nordic banks underestimated the risks of the exposure in the Baltic countries.
>
> (Grönn and Fredholm 2013, p. 7)

When commenting on Iceland, Grönn and Feldhom (2013) state that:

> Before the crisis, Iceland's private sector had accumulated a relatively large share of FX-denominated debt as the tightening of monetary policy led to much higher interest rates on loans in Krona than in foreign currency. In addition to the macrofinancial risks posed by the FX-denominated debt, a large part of Icelandic household debt was also indexed to inflation. This exposed the financial sector to similar risks as the household balance sheets could be seriously impaired because of the rapid pass-through to the exchange rate.
>
> (Grönn and Fredholm 2013, p. 7)

In Iceland the government could not defend the local currency in the third quarter of 2008, although its intention was to do so, and thus sharp depreciation materialized. All three major banks fell, and many households and businesses faced financial hardship. Some loans were partly cancelled, and some were declared to be on illegal terms; the government implemented a plan to assist the most vulnerable households.

The key difference between Iceland and Latvia (and the other Baltic States) was that the Icelandic banking system was local, and did not have extensive interlinkages with the Scandinavian/Swedish financial sector or other foreign banking systems. This is why neither the continental Nordics, nor the EU, the USA or indeed any other country showed much interest in rescuing the Icelandic banks. In contrast, continental Nordic/Swedish banking interlinkages with the Baltic States ensured their full attention to problems in the Baltics. The case of Latvia was extreme: here, the EU and Sweden practically took over and ran the country through the worst crisis period with a fixed exchange rate and extreme austerity. The Riksbank also became, in effect, the Baltic central bank.

In Latvia, external forces kept the lat at par with the euro. There was no way that Latvia could have kept the peg on its own account, as had Iceland on its króna in 2008, or Sweden on its krona and Finland on its markka in the 1990s. The lat was defended with a concerted EU/Nordic/IMF bailout package, with conditions for harsh austerity measures being imposed in one of the poorest EU member states. Latvia was, and remains, a country with weak or, perhaps more accurately, almost non-existent welfare systems, and the most unequal income distribution in the EU. Grönn and Fredholm (2013) comment as follows: 'However, it was not until after the crisis had materialized that broader austerity measures were implemented and approved by the Latvian government in the general government budget for 2009. The fiscal tightening was a prior action set by the IMF, EU and bilateral lenders' (Grönn and Fredholm 2013, p. 7).

Dombrovskis, now European Commission Vice-President for the Euro and Social Dialogue, and his co-author state that 'Latvia also learned from the Swedish and Finnish banking and devaluation crisis in the early 1990s that banking collapses and devaluation should be avoided if possible' (Åslund and Dombrovskis 2011, p. 117). This is perhaps a strange comment, given that both Finland and Sweden which (unlike Latvia) have strong welfare systems, both eventually allowed their currency to depreciate sharply during the 1990s crisis, which in both countries was followed by a period of strong export-led growth. In addition to devaluation, these countries did not implement austerity programmes to anything like the extent of those implemented in the Baltic States. In Sweden, automatic stabilizers were allowed to run their course.

A report published by the EU in 2008, and authored by Jonung and colleagues, reviews the recovery of Finland and Sweden from 1993 to 2000. When commenting on Finland, the authors state that 'the biggest macroeconomic change contributing to the recovery was the loosening of monetary policy, including the currency depreciation in the aftermath of the 1992 EMS [European Monetary System] crisis' (Jonung et al. 2008, p. 31). The cumulative depreciation of the markka was more than 30%, and according to the report, exports were the first component of GDP to recover. The effects of depreciation turned out to be long-lasting. Unemployment in Finland fell from 17% in 1994 to 10% in 2000 and to 6% in 2008. When commenting on Sweden, Jonung et al. state that: '[t]he depreciation of the krona in November 1992 marked the culmination of the crisis and the beginning of the recovery in Sweden' (Jonung et al. 2008, p. 36). A large depreciation increased Swedish competitiveness. Economic growth turned positive in 1993 and exports were the major driving force behind the Swedish recovery.

It is hard to see what lessons Latvia was able to learn in 2008/09 from the crisis in Finland and Sweden in the 1990s, since both the latter countries depreciated their currency sharply followed by export-led growth. This was also the experience in Iceland, whose currency depreciated during the 2008/09 crisis. Had austerity programmes been implemented in Finland and Sweden, they would not have had such severe effects as they did when implemented in Latvia, since both the Nordic countries have strong welfare systems in place and strong safety nets for the most vulnerable.

The key factor driving crisis response in the Baltic States was interconnectedness with continental Nordic banking systems. As Dombrovskis and his co-author commented: 'Devaluation would have broken the Latvian banking system and caused mass bankruptcies because of currency mismatches. Disorderly devaluation would presumably have spread to Lithuania and Estonia, as well as caused a Swedish banking crisis' (Åslund and Dombrovskis 2011, p. 116). This could have threatened the whole interconnected Scandinavian banking system and then destabilized the euro area, which was extremely vulnerable in late 2008. And the IMF's chief economist later commented in a report on Latvia: 'If your financial sector is largely composed of foreign subsidiaries, it is a good idea to be friends with the parent banks' (Blanchard et al. 2013, p. 33).

Debt, public and private, pre- and post-crisis

Before the onset of the 2008/09 economic crisis, the Baltic States did not run large fiscal deficits. In fact, government budgets were either in surplus or close to balance. In retrospect, arguably the Baltics should have had sizeable surpluses during the boom years 2005 to 2007. Government debt as a percentage of GDP in 2007 was remarkably low, much lower than either in the euro area or the EU, and lower than in the Nordic countries (see Figures 7.1 and 7.2 below). However, during the 2008/09 crisis, that debt rose sharply and has remained so to date (see Figure 7.1). Government debt as a percentage of GDP nevertheless remains very low in Estonia; however, in Latvia and Lithuania it reaches levels similar to general government debt in Denmark, Norway and Sweden (see Figure 7.2). Rising debt levels in the Baltics are at least directly and indirectly related to the foreign bank bailout during the 2008/09 crisis. In 'good' years, banks take profits with high salaries, bonuses, dividends to shareholders and are willing to take high risks. During 'bad' years, the arch-enemy of the free market—the state—comes to the rescue, government debt rises and taxpayers foot the bill. With a Baltic tax system of a flat tax on income, taxes are disproportionately borne by the poorest segment of the population.

Private sector debt in the Baltic States grew rapidly after the accession of the Baltics to the EU in 2004 (see Figure 7.3). This is no surprise, as the Baltics were viewed as more stable as EU member states. At the same time, their risk profile was seen as almost equivalent to the Nordic countries, which was questionable. But the weaknesses in the system were disregarded by the foreign banks, which fuelled expansion with low-interest foreign currency loans. Arguably, the regulators and bankers were not sufficiently experienced to respond to overheating in a timely way. This, however, is not an entirely satisfactory explanation given that the Baltic banks were branches and subsidiaries of Nordic banks, which should have been able to draw on painful memories from the crisis in the Nordics in the 1990, as already discussed.

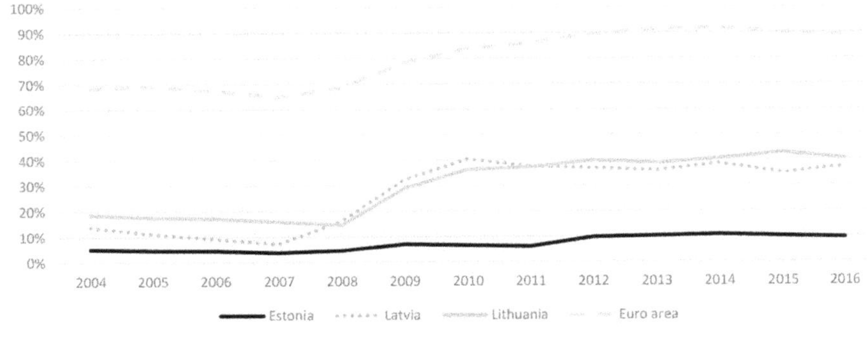

Figure 7.1 Baltic States: General government gross debt 2004–16 (% of GDP)
Source: International Monetary Fund (2017).

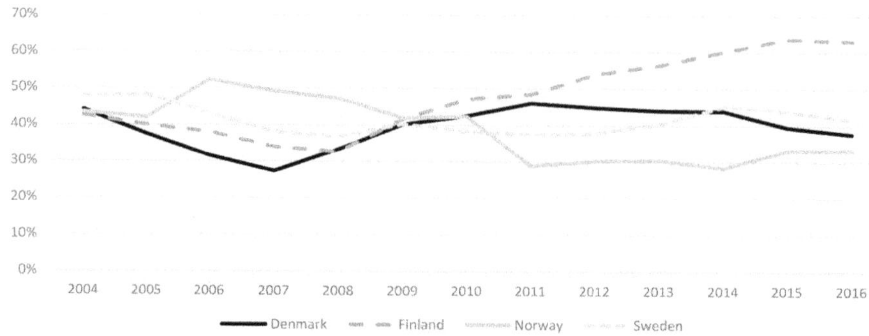

Figure 7.2 Continental Nordic countries: General government gross debt 2004–16 (% of GDP)
Source: International Monetary Fund (2017).

Private sector debt reached a peak as a percentage of GDP in the Baltics in 2009/10, by which date it had doubled from its 2004 level (see Figure 7.3 below). The Baltics were thus flooded with credit that subsequently declined as a percentage of GDP as the crisis abated. From a situation termed by many a 'lending mania', lenders swung to the other extreme, namely risk aversion, contributing to an economic collapse.

Private debt as a percentage of GDP in Denmark, Finland and Sweden was higher than in the Baltics both before and after the 2008/09 crisis. No wonder that the oldest central bank in the world, the Swedish Riksbank, was, and remains, so concerned by it. These debts continue to present a threat to the financial sector in the three countries, and especially in Denmark and Sweden, although debt levels have reduced from their 2009 peak (see Figure 7.4 below).

Moreover, those debts threaten not only Denmark and Sweden but the whole Nordic-Baltic region and can adversely impact the whole EU and euro area. The fact that the principal players in the Baltic banking system are

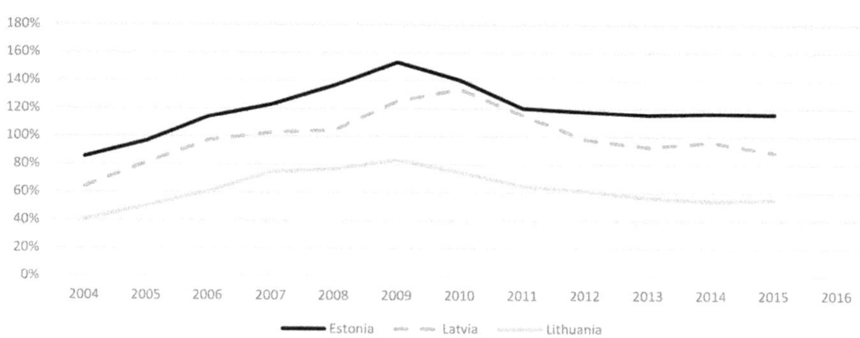

Figure 7.3 Baltic States: Private sector debt consolidated 2004–16 (% of GDP)
Source: Eurostat (2017).

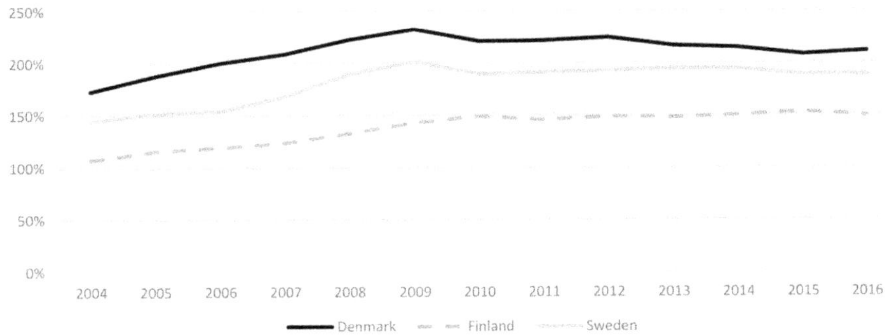

Figure 7.4 Continental Nordic countries: Private sector debt consolidated 2004–16 (% of GDP)
Source: Eurostat (2017).

outside the euro area and the creditors are within exacerbates the situation; moreover, Sweden has no plans for joining the EU banking union, making supervision and monitoring more complex.

Notes

1 See www.bis.org/.
2 The following statement was posted on the website of the Swedish Riksbank on 23 November 2016 entitled: *Banks and households need to increase their resilience.* See http://archive.riksbank.se/en/Web-archive/Published/Press-Releases/2016/Banks-and-households-need-to-increase-their-resilience-/.

'The Swedish banking system is vulnerable due to its size, concentration and interconnectedness. The banks are also exposed to liquidity risks. It is therefore important to ensure that the major banks have adequate capital and liquidity. It is also necessary to manage the risks of the continued high and rising housing prices and increasing household indebtedness. There are short-term liquidity risks in the banking system that, in the long run, can pose risks to financial stability. .... As the major Swedish banks have extensive cross-border operations, primarily through their presence in the Nordic Region, the Baltic States and the United Kingdom, they are also exposed towards short-term liquidity risks in other currencies...The major Swedish banks are also taking significant structural liquidity risks. These arise as a result of the banks having a large proportion of mortgages with long maturities on the asset side, while having a comparatively high proportion of short-term wholesale funding on the liability side. The banks must therefore renew their funding several times during the mortgage's maturity period. The banks should therefore continue to reduce their structural liquidity risks, for example by extending the maturity of their funding.' For more on the following, please refer to the website. 'Leverage ratio requirement to safeguard the banks' resilience' and 'High housing prices and high indebtedness are a risk' (Riksbank 2016).

References

Åslund, A. and Dombrovskis, V. (2011). *How Latvia Came Through the Financial Crisis.* Washington, DC: Peterson Institute for International Economics.

Blanchard, O. J., Griffiths, M. and Gruss, B. (2013). '*Boom, Bust, Recovery: Forensics of the Latvia Crisis*'. Final Conference Draft to be presented at the Fall 2013 Brookings Panel on Economic Activity, 19–20 September 2013. Available at: www.brookings.edu/wp-content/uploads/2016/07/2013b_blanchard_latvia_crisis.pdf (Accessed on 11 August 2017).

Eurostat (2017). *Database*. Available at: http://ec.europa.eu/eurostat/data/database.

Grönn, A. and Fredholm, M. W. (2013). *Baltic and Icelandic experiences of capital flows and capital flow measures.* (IMF Working Paper WP/13/242). Available at: www.imf.org/external/pubs/cat/longres.aspx?sk=41130.0 (Accessed on 7 February 2017).

International Monetary Fund (2007). *Financial integration in the Nordic-Baltic region: challenges for financial policies.* Available at: www.imf.org/external/pubs/cat/longres.aspx?sk=21421.0 (Accessed on 31 October 2017).

International Monetary Fund (2017). *World Economic Outlook Database.* Available at: www.imf.org/external/pubs/ft/weo/2017/02/weodata/index.aspx.

Jonung, L., Kiander, J. and Varita, P. (2008). *The great financial crisis in Finland and Sweden—The dynamics of boom, bust and recovery, 1985–2000* (No. 350). Directorate General Economic and Financial Affairs (DG ECFIN), European Commission. Available at: http://ec.europa.eu/economy_finance/publications/publication13551_en.pdf (Accessed on 1 August 2017).

Riksbank (2016). *Banks and households need to increase their resilience.* Available at: http://archive.riksbank.se/en/Web-archive/Published/Press-Releases/2016/Banks-and-households-need-to-increase-their-resilience-/ (Accessed on 24 November 2017).

8 International organizations as economic policy advisers for small states: the Baltics as victims?

The Nordic countries and the Baltic States are all small states exposed to international organizations. Small states tend to a varying degree to form alliances either with larger states or international organizations, or both. Success in building these alliances can be critical for their prosperity and even for their survival. There appears to be an increasing trend for small states to seek shelter within multilateral institutions, some of which have a global membership while others are regional. Small countries also sometimes form alliances as a group within international bodies, as indeed the Nordic countries and the Baltic States have done via NB8 co-operation in organizations such as the European Union (EU)[1], the North Atlantic Treaty Organization, the European Bank for Reconstruction and Development (EBRD), the Council of Europe, the Organization for Security and Co-operation in Europe, the United Nations, and others (For more detail about NB8 co-operation see Birkavs and Gade 2010). At the Bretton Woods institutions—the World Bank and the International Monetary Fund (IMF)—the NB8 share offices. The Baltics are now members of the Nordic Investment Bank. Co-operation among the NB8 is an important umbrella which can shield and strengthen them when they act as a group instead of making individual moves. But this requires consensus among those countries—a consensus that does not always exist.

The Nordic countries and the Baltic States all participate in European integration and are, to a varying degree, dependent on EU institutions, either as EU member states or as European Free Trade Association member states, and all are participants in the European Economic Area, as well as Schengen. They all have access to the EU single market, which is critical for their prosperity. They are all members of the World Bank and the IMF. Only the continental Nordics are participants in non-European regional institutions such as the African Development Bank, the Asian Development Bank and the Inter-American Development Bank.

As with all member states, the IMF regularly monitors and reports progress in the Nordic and Baltic economies. During the 2008/09 crisis the EU and the IMF provided financial assistance to Latvia, in an effort to prevent a financial sector collapse, and to Iceland, following the collapse of 85% of its banking system. The Nordic countries contributed to both loan packages.

The Baltic States all received assistance from the World Bank Group after reclaiming independence from the Soviet Union in 1991. This took two separate forms: firstly, loans to fund specific projects in many different sectors of the economy; and secondly, policy-based loans accompanied by technical assistance grants. World Bank Group assistance began to be phased out in the Baltics once they became EU member states in 2004, thus qualifying for assistance from various EU funds both prior to and following EU accession, as well as loans from the European Investment Bank and the EBRD. The Nordic Investment Bank also supported the Baltics. (The World Bank would normally phase out its lending to countries classified as high-income economies, as indeed the Baltics had become, since it primarily assists developing or middle-income emerging countries.) World Bank assistance re-emerged in 2008 when the World Bank Group contributed to a loan package for Latvia. The Nordic countries have not received assistance from the World Bank Group in recent history but they are important contributors of funding and ideas to shape the World Bank's five institutions, and in fact they co-operated closely with the World Bank when it was active in the Baltics. The Nordic countries and the Baltic States also participate in regional institutions such as the EBRD, which has also been active in reconstruction in the Baltic States and provided assistance to Latvia during the 2008/09 crisis.

The Bretton Woods and EU institutions as advisors to EU member states

If we consider, for example, the Bretton Woods and EU institutions, those organizations engage in research and publish their analytical work. The question thus arises: how technically good is this work, and can the advice given by such institutions to their member states ever be anything close to neutral? (This is an important question, because those organizations not only fund projects whose return can be estimated, but also engage in policy dialogue with governments, provide them with advice and set policy conditions.) Furthermore, given their policy agenda, can the IMF or the World Bank Group conduct research without bias? Are they influenced by other countries, such as the USA, in whose capital the headquarters of those institutions are based? At the Bretton Woods conference towards the end of the Second World War, the British economist John Maynard Keynes expressed strong objections to the headquartering of these institutions in Washington, DC, in close proximity to the US Congress, the White House and the US Treasury. According to some observers, this gives the USA enormous leverage at the World Bank, far beyond its shareholding (See Wolfensohn 2010).

The question also arises whether the institutions within the EU can conduct research and give advice without bearing in mind the interests of individual EU member states, especially the larger and more powerful member states.

For example, the European Central Bank (ECB), which is based in Frankfurt, is intended to be independent; it has an Executive Board and a Governing Council—which is its main decision-making body—as well as a General Council[2]. The Governing Council and the General Council include both representatives of the participating member states and representatives of the EU as a whole. This is perhaps intended to balance national and EU interests. However, according to some observers the policies of the ECB have on occasion resembled those that would be pursued by the German Bundesbank in similar circumstances (See for example Eichengreen 2008, p. 370).

Doubtless, the staff recruited by the EU, the ECB, the IMF, the World Bank Group, and so on can be expected to be technically competent professionals. The question is more whether they can ever be truly neutral and base their views on a professional assessment. As Cornell professor Ravi Kanbur (2003) points out: 'the central issue is that frameworks for understanding and interpreting information and knowledge in the development process are contested' (Kanbur 2003, p. 259). Furthermore, as Kanbur goes on to discuss, this is more likely to be a problem in social sciences than natural sciences, where 'there is no uniform, underlying framework in which research and its findings can be assessed'[3]. Kanbur, who also had a long and distinguished career at the World Bank, concludes that the World Bank as a whole cannot possibly be viewed as an independent arbiter of social science research. There is a widespread perception that its research is in the service of a particular line or policy stance to the exclusion of others. World Bank staff, while generally good professionals, do face constraints, which is entirely to be expected in an operational organization (Kanbur 2003).

In fact, there are cases where employees of international organizations have been apparently dismissed for publicly expressing opinions based on their research. An example of this is that of William Easterly, a former economist at the World Bank, who lost his job following the publication of his book *The Elusive Quest for Growth* (Easterly 2001), which was critical of the development policies followed by the Bank. Despite his subsequent appointment to a professorship at New York University's Department of Economics, Easterly's case shows that it is risky to express views publicly that are not supported by the top management of the institution and its largest, most powerful member states.

The Bretton Woods institutions—the World Bank and the IMF—often emphasize the need for what they label as 'government ownership' of country-specific programmes. Governments are to choose their own policies and defend their own policy decisions. However, the World Bank and IMF conduct their own analysis in order to come up with policy recommendations and conditions. It is questionable whether they can be viewed as neutral researchers, observers or advisors, and some observers claim that their policy agenda mainly comes from richer or larger countries—in effect the largest shareholders of the Washington-based Bretton Woods institutions—and that this agenda needs to be defended. This can clearly be seen in the dispute which arose following the collapse of Icesave in 2008, between Iceland on the one side and the UK and the Netherlands on the other (See Chapter 3), during which the IMF clearly favoured the stance adopted by the two EU nations against Iceland.

Potentially, politicians may put pressure on Bretton Woods institutions: both the World Bank and the IMF have representatives of member governments sitting on their executive boards. In addition, both have a staff of professionals, selected on the basis of their merits. The issue of ensuring neutrality and professionalism is equally relevant to the institutions of the EU, which include political appointees from member states in addition to their professional staff. The Commissioners who make up the European Commission are allocated between member states: however, their task is not to defend the interests of their own country or indeed any other country, but to act in the interests of the EU.

Critics of EU economic policy have claimed that the interests of specific nations—especially the larger and more powerful—can do prevail; it has been suggested that, during the 2008/09 crisis in the Baltic States, Nordic—mainly Swedish—interests had to be defended at whatever cost, no matter how high the resultant human cost in the Baltic States. Hence the European Commission insisted on a fixed exchange-rate policy by reference to the Maastricht criteria (which have also been the subject of criticism, with opponents claiming they were somewhat arbitrarily determined) and the fact that the Baltic States were seeking euro area membership.

It is interesting to note that when Germany, France and Italy ran into conflict with the EU's fiscal regulations—then known as the Stability and Growth Pact—by running budget deficits in excess of 3% of GDP, they incurred no penalties or fines. Germany and France received warnings from the European Commission in 2003–04, but were granted exemptions, and the pact was subsequently amended (in 2005) to allow more flexibility. For small countries (such as Portugal, see Eichengreen 2008, pp. 372–373) the pact would be applied more strictly (in 2001). This was widely viewed as ironic, given that German negotiators insisted in the early 1990s that the Maastricht Treaty should include an Excessive Deficit Procedure.

The agreed policy stance within international organizations can also be a straitjacket for some member states. At national level, the EU limits fiscal deficits to the equivalent of 3% of GDP under the Maastricht criteria. This may be insufficient to allow for the activation of automatic stabilizers in countries with strong welfare systems and safety nets, such as the Nordic countries. Such a policy also provides little room for the investment which is needed in transition countries such as the Baltics. It can reduce growth within the whole union during normal periods and be an impediment to recovery during times of crisis. The 3% fiscal deficit limit is based on questionable analytical grounds, with roots more neoliberal than Keynesian.

Furthermore, the EU may choose not to produce analytical justification for its stance. It can simply take action that is favoured by larger, stronger nations against smaller, weaker nations. As De Grauwe (2013) argues: 'What is surprising is that the European Commission has assumed the role as agent of the creditor nations in the eurozone[4], pushing austerity as the instrument to safeguard the creditor nations' (De Grauwe 2013, p. 13).

The central issue is that frameworks for understanding and interpreting information and knowledge to formulate economic policy response are contested: there is no 'correct' policy. The ECB's emphasis on inflation-targeting differs from the stance adopted by the Federal Reserve in the USA after the 2008/09 crisis. In addition to the importance that the ECB attaches to inflation, the Federal Reserve also places emphasis on GDP growth, unemployment and stability (Stiglitz 2016, p. 8). This narrow focus on inflation within the EU is likely to be favoured by richer, stronger EU member states, most notably Germany, since it reflects Bundesbank policy.

In spite of the arguments above, this does not imply that there should not be research departments within organizations such as the Bretton Woods institutions, the EU, the ECB, and others. Clearly, these institutions will need to carry out research to interact with outside analysts and engage in policy dialogue. But it is important that international organizations welcome criticism and are willing to make adjustments based on research by outside institutions and individual researchers. One should not underestimate the damage that austerity has done to the social fabric of the Baltic States or, for that matter, Greece.

The question remains whether institutions such as the Bretton Woods institutions and the EU, including the European Commission and the ECB, can be viewed as independent arbiters of social science research. As noted above, they are primarily owned and run by the world's richest countries, and they have their own specific operational policies that need to be defended. Their critics contend that their research is in the service of a particular line or policy stance to the exclusion of others, with social sciences research being considered to be much more of a contested terrain than natural science in this regard. With an 'independent' central bank—the ECB—and limited room for fiscal policy, the EU has attempted to divorce economic policy from politics. But it is widely contended that economic policy should also be decided democratically, with the involvement of elected politicians informed with help from experts. Fixed exchange rates, an independent central bank and limited fiscal policy operate to reduce the role of democratically-determined economic policy. However, it would be naïve to assume that the larger countries in the EU cannot set the tone. Stability, with fewer risks of free-riding and slow growth, may be music to the ears of the more economically robust member states, like Germany. However, stagnation is no paradise for countries in transition, which seek support and the opportunity to 'catch up' economically.

Notes

1 Six of the NB8 countries are EU member states, but all are part of the European Economic Area.

2 The Executive Board of the ECB consists of: (i) the President, (ii) the Vice-President and (iii) four other members. All members are appointed by the European Council, acting by a qualified majority. The Governing Council consists of (i) the six members of the Executive Board, plus (ii) the governors of the national central banks of the 19 euro area countries. The General Council comprises (i) the President of the ECB, (ii) the Vice-President of the ECB and the governors of the national central banks (NCBs) of the 28 EU Member States (European Central Bank 2018), see further. www.ecb.europa.eu/ecb/orga/decisions/govc/html/index.en.html.

3 See relevant extracts from Kanbur's argument, quoted below: 'Leaving to one side complex technical and institutional issues of managing knowledge flow, **the central issue is that frameworks for understanding and interpreting information and knowledge in the development process are contested** [emphasis added].[…] **The central question is whether research in institutions like the [World] Bank, which have to take stances and views on policy in their operations, can ever command wide enough trust to be an [international public goods]. This is in no way to impugn the motives of the many fine individuals who do research in these institutions. But they do face constraints, which is entirely to be expected in an operational organization** [emphasis added]. The point is not whether there should or should not be a research organization in an operational institution, as any such institution will need a group dedicated to specific analysis and to interacting with outside analyses. **The point is rather whether [international financial institution] research can claim the mantle of an [international public good], and thence the aura and the resources that flow from it in the current climate favoring [international public goods]. Our conclusion on this is a skeptical one, at least when there is a widespread perception that the research is in service of a particular line or policy stance to the exclusion of others. This is perhaps more likely in social science research where, unlike research in the natural sciences, much of the terrain is contested and there is no uniform, unifying framework in which research and its findings can be assessed**' (Kanbur 2003, p. 259–260, emphasis added).

Furthermore 'Social science is not like natural science. It is contested terrain to a much greater extent. Moreover, **the [World] Bank as a whole cannot possibly be viewed as an independent arbiter of social science research** [emphasis added]. It is owned by the rich countries and it has operational policies that need to be defended. These features mean that social science research done by the [World] Bank itself cannot fully lay claim to the mantle of an [international public good]. […]The fifth and final implication of the reasoning in this chapter is that more of the research at the [World] Bank should be farmed out to universities and transparently independent institutions, where at least perceived independence will enhance its value as an [international public good]' (Kanbur 2003, p. 263).

4 The term 'eurozone' is synonymous with 'euro area'.

References

Birkavs, V. and Gade, S. (2010). *NB8 Wise Men Report*. Available at: www.stjornarradid.is/media/utanrikisraduneyti-media/media/Skyrslur/NB8-Wise-roMen-Report.pdf (Accessed on 20 April 2017).

De Grauwe, P. (2013). 'The creditor nations rule in the eurozone'. In P. De Grauwe, G. Magnus, T. Mayer and H. Schmieding, *The future of Europe's economy: Disaster or deliverance?*London: Centre for European Reform. Available at: www.lse.ac.uk/europeanInstitute/pdfs/CER-report-18.9.13.pdf (Accessed on 10 June 2017).

Easterly, W. (2001). *The elusive quest for growth: economists' adventures and misadventures in the tropics.* Cambridge, MA: MIT Press.

Eichengreen, B. (2008). *The European economy since 1945: coordinated capitalism and beyond.* Princeton, NJ: Princeton University Press.

European Central Bank (2018). *Governing Council.* Available at: www.ecb.europa.eu/ecb/orga/decisions/govc/html/index.en.html (Accessed on 2 April 2017).

Herbertsson, T. þ. and Mishkin, F. S. (2006). *Financial stability in Iceland.* Reykjavík: Iceland Chamber of Commerce, available at: www.vi.is/files/555877819Financial%20Stability%20in%20Iceland%20Screen%20Version.pdf (Accessed on 10 May 2017).

Kanbur, R. (2003). 'International financial institutions and international public goods: operational implications for the World Bank'. In A. Buira (ed.) *Challenges to the World Bank and IMF: developing country perspectives,* London and New York: Anthem Press, pp. 251–266.

Portes, R., Baldursson, F. M. and Ólafsson, F. (2007). *The Internationalisation of Iceland's Financial Sector. Iceland Chamber of Commerce.* Available at: www.vi.is/files/15921776Vid4WEB.pdf (Accessed on 20 April 2017).

Stiglitz, J. E. (2016). *The Euro—How a Common Currency Threatens the Future of Europe.* New York and London: W. W. Norton & Company.

Wolfensohn, J. D. (2010). *A Global Life: My Journey among Rich and Poor, from Sydney to Wall Street to the World Bank.* New York: Public Affairs.

9 The Nordic welfare model and the Baltic States' Anglo-Saxon bias

The Nordic countries and the Baltic States now form a well-integrated region in terms of trade, labour mobility and investment. The Baltics and the continental Nordics are also integrated in terms of their financial sector cross-border interlinkages, with risks of regional contagion. As citizens of European Economic Area (EEA)[1] and Schengen member states, Nordic and Baltic citizens can travel freely across each other's borders. The Nordic countries and the Baltic States also co-operate closely within various international organizations where their representatives share offices, such as the Bretton Woods institutions in the shape of the International Monetary Fund (IMF) and the World Bank Group.

The Nordic and Baltic peoples are in many ways like-minded and despite interruptions—most recently, the period of Soviet rule in the Baltics—have been in contact for centuries. During the 17th and 18th centuries, large parts of Estonia and Latvia formed part of the Swedish empire. Nevertheless, today, a little more than a quarter of a century after their separation from the Soviet Union, the economic policies, welfare and tax systems of the Baltic States are as far away from the Nordic welfare model as one could possibly get. Post-independence, the Baltics went from one extreme to another: from communist central planning to neoliberal free market economies. (In Estonia, economic policy was influenced by Milton Friedman and the Chicago school of economics, as will be discussed below.) Post-Soviet Union wealth and income became concentrated in the coffers of a relatively small élite. It is highly questionable whether this system is sustainable.

The famous British economist John Maynard Keynes once commented that 'Capitalism is the astounding belief that the most wickedest [sic] of men will do the most wickedest of things for the greatest good of everyone'. (Keynes, n.d.) When discussing the 2008/09 financial crisis in his book *The Price of Inequality*, Stiglitz (2013) states that: 'The wealth given to the élites and the bankers seemed to arise out of their ability and willingness to take advantage of others' (Stiglitz, 2013, p. xliv). This comment seems to fit the Baltic situation.

But capitalism is a useful system—if governments can successfully and democratically intervene for the common good. While the welfare systems of

Nordic countries are undergoing constant review and reform, these systems remain one of the key characteristics of Nordic societies and the Nordic welfare model (see Hannibalsson 2017). According to Christine Ingebritsen, a leading scholar in Scandinavian studies, 'Scandinavians remain committed to the provision of universal benefits and to playing a role in international society consistent with the golden age of welfare capitalism' (Ingebritsen 2006, p. 12). For the Baltic States the question arises whether or not they are likely to become members of this group of like-minded northern European social welfare states or whether they will remain as neoliberal societies with high income inequality and weak welfare systems.

While the Nordic countries allow market forces to play a significant role in their societies, governments intervene to correct what they perceive as market failures, redistributing income through progressive income tax, taxing property owners and maintaining social 'safety nets' to help the most vulnerable. This is what they term welfare capitalism. In contrast, Baltic capitalism—with its flat income taxes and low taxes on wealthy property owners—to some observers seems much more 'wicked' in Keynes' terms, in that it reflects a less equitable sharing of the tax burden. The Nordics have placed economic and social justice high on the policy agenda—the importance of doing so being something other major countries, such as the United Kingdom and, even more so, the USA, are now learning the hard way, as the effects of uneven income distribution are reflected in internal tensions and divisions.

As pointed out in a comprehensive report by Torben M. Andersen and colleagues (2007) entitled *The Nordic Model—Embracing globalization and sharing risks*, the Nordic model is widely regarded as a benchmark for other countries (Andersen et al. 2007). As the authors state, the Nordics are often seen to have succeeded better than other countries in combining economic efficiency and growth with a relatively peaceful labour market, a fairly even distribution of income, and social cohesion (Andersen et al. 2007).

In a meeting between the author of this book and the IMF in July 2016, during which economic and social progress in the Baltic States was discussed and compared with the Nordic countries, one IMF official commented that 'it is hard to look good if you are compared with the Nordics'. This is a commonly expressed view. As Ingebritsen notes: 'Scandinavia provides examples of how power and wealth can be distributed more equitably; how gender and class differences can be minimized; and how state authority can be used in a positive way to temper markets and social injustice' (Ingebritsen 2006, p. 2). Scandinavians have not hesitated to intervene with market forces and have used government institutions and systems to produce results that are seen as more equitable than neoliberal, hands-off policies would achieve. Andersen et al. argue that, in order to correct the 'wickedness' in capitalism of which Keynes spoke, the Nordics have embraced both globalization and the welfare state, and that the security offered by collective mechanisms for sharing risks has been instrumental in enhancing a favourable attitude to globalization and competition (See Andersen et al 2007).

Collective risk-sharing can thus continue to offer a safety net that helps workers and their families cope with risks and adapt to new requirements during times of crisis, transition and change. At the same time, the Nordic welfare model is widely seen as consistent with a good business and investment climate with a vibrant private sector and foreign investment, research and innovation. This is, for example, reflected in the World Bank's 'Doing Business' reports, which constantly rank the Nordic countries among the top performers worldwide for creating a favourable investment and business climate (World Bank 2017).

Furthermore, as Anderson et al. point out: 'Professional economists have often been puzzled by the relatively good economic performance of the Nordic model, given its high taxes and its generous social protection systems as well as the role of strong labour unions and wage coordination' (See Andersen, et al. 2007, p. 16)[2]. Clearly, some losses of economic efficiency must be caused by some of the characteristics of the Nordic welfare model, and numerous studies have been devoted to analysing the economic costs of a large welfare state.

However, it is equally clear that numerous factors appear to have made up for those disadvantages. Arguably, the Nordic model has become a mechanism for generating political support for growth-enhancing technical change, free trade and open markets by creating systems through which the winners from structural transformation compensate the losers, at least to some extent (See Andersen et al. 2007, p. 18). In the future, the pressure will be on European countries to deliver their preferred mix of public and private goods more efficiently. As Eichengreen (2007) points out, the Scandinavian countries are widely cited as examples of societies that have already begun moving in this direction by successfully maintaining essential social protection while enhancing the efficiency of their provision (Eichengreen 2007, p. 421–422). A reasonable degree of social and political cohesion would also seem to be of fundamental importance in the Baltic States, in order to maintain political stability and growth sustainability. It could reduce ethnic strife and political tensions, while improving the region's security profile.

Although the Baltic States have sought international co-operation with the Nordic countries in international organizations, also engaging with them in trade, investment and financial sector cooperation, they have followed them to a lesser degree in terms of economic policy. Moreover, they do not follow the Nordic welfare model at all as regards the design of their tax and welfare systems. Since their resumption of independence in 1991, the Baltic States have followed a very different political, economic, and social path from their richer Nordic neighbours. Adopting the Nordic welfare model in its entirety would be out of reach and unsustainable at their current income level. Nor is there reason for them to copy the Nordics on every account. Nevertheless, the Baltic States could attempt to implement a watered-down Nordic model, if that was their wish, and thus attain something closer to the welfare systems of some of the other richer European countries, perhaps with European Union

(EU) support. This could also help them keep a greater proportion of their young people within their borders. Currently the Baltics are closer to the free-market neoliberal Anglo-Saxon model (see different categories for country groups in Table 9.2 below).

Mart Laar served as prime minister of Estonia in 1992–94 and again in 1999–2002. In an interview with the *Brussels Journal* during the Baltic boom in 2005 and before the crash in 2008 he commented: 'It is very fortunate that I was not an economist'. He went on:

> I had read only one book on economics—Milton Friedman's *Free to Choose.* I was so ignorant at the time that I thought that what Friedman wrote about the benefits of privatisation, the flat tax and the abolition of all customs rights, was the result of economic reforms that had been put into practice in the West. It seemed common sense to me and, as I thought it had already been done everywhere, I simply introduced it in Estonia, despite warnings from Estonian economists that it could not be done. They said it was as impossible as walking on water. We did it: we just walked on the water because we did not know that it was impossible.
>
> (Laar 2005)

Mart Laar thus decided to implement neoliberal policies in Estonia in a more orthodox way than any other country in the world had ever done, assuming, according to himself, that this was common practice 'in the West'.

The neoliberal era started in the 1980s as a revolt against the welfare state and was based on a belief in market infallibility. Markets self-corrected, ran the theory, and the government should get out of the way. Arguably, the results of this policy became clear in 2008 on a global scale, including in the Baltics.

We should bear in mind that Estonia had been a republic within the Soviet Union, and that Estonians were not well-informed about economic and welfare policies in other countries when Laar took office—not even about those operating in Scandinavia, in spite of the region's close geographic proximity to Estonia. This shows how isolated the country had been and how ill-prepared it was during its early days of independence. Nevertheless, Estonia is often perceived as the Baltic State that is most likely to lead in initiating reforms.

From the re-establishment of independence in the region in 1991, Baltic reforms were characterized by the creation of an ultra-liberal business-friendly environment that was to help attract foreign investment. A balanced fiscal budget and strict monetary policy with fixed exchange rates was to give the Baltics a strong reputation as reliable borrowers. A fully open trade regime led to a rapid reorientation of foreign trade towards the West, especially towards the EU common market. The social welfare system, on the other hand, was intended to inspire 'people to assume responsibility for their own future' (Laar 2007, p. 9, see also Bohle and Greskovits 2012). Neither a high degree of social inclusion nor safety nets for the most vulnerable were on the agenda. It was the survival of the fittest, and the fittest had accumulated wealth that in some cases was based on privatization of government property in a corrupt environment. The World Bank diplomatically referred to 'state capture'.

Free markets, fiscal discipline, fixed exchange rates and economic integration were among key priorities, but income inequality persisted (see Table 9.1): Social justice was not on the agenda. The Baltic States' reforms were not to be soft with a human face. It should not come as a surprise that, in terms of indicators such as the at-risk-of-poverty rate, the Gini index or the income quintile share ratio[3], the Baltics have among the worst records of poverty and uneven income distribution in the EU and the euro area, as well as the EEA.

The Gini index is a standard measure of inequality. If income were shared exactly in proportion to population, for example, with both the bottom and top 10% getting 10% of the income, then the Gini index would be zero. If on the other hand all the income went to the richest person, the Gini index would be 100. So the lower the Gini index, the greater the income equality. More equal societies—such as the Nordics and the Central European countries, with the exception of Poland (see Table 9.1)—have a Gini index of 30 or below. In more unequal societies such as the Baltics and the South-Eastern European countries of Bulgaria and Romania, the Gini index is above 30 and sometimes closer to 40.

Compared to the Nordic welfare states the Baltics have a very uneven income distribution, weak safety nets and weak welfare systems, which in combination made their citizens extraordinarily vulnerable during the 2008/09 crisis. Poverty, social exclusion and income inequality remain serious problems, even if they are compared to countries at similar income levels, such as the Czech Republic, Slovakia and Slovenia. Income distribution in the Baltics is also more uneven than in Ireland and the UK (the Anglo-Saxon countries of Europe—see Table 9.1). Unemployment has remained high since the crisis and outward migration—especially among the youngest segment of their populations—is likely to have a negative effect on long-term growth in the Baltic States.

Public spending in the Baltics is low and government operations are on a small scale, particularly with respect to transfer payments. Public expenditure is generally lower than in the 'CE 4' country group (see Table 9.2 below) or the Nordic countries, and the share of GDP devoted to social benefits is substantially lower. According to the IMF, the Baltic States are closer to the Anglo-Saxons than the Nordics as regards the structure of their private sectors (International Monetary Fund 2014, p. 4). In fact, in terms of poverty, social exclusion and income inequality the Baltic States are close to Bulgaria and Romania, countries that have less advanced economies and much lower income levels (see Table 9.1).

The Baltic States have relatively high rates of labour taxation and low rates of profit taxation. In contrast to their weak performance on social indicators,

Table 9.1 Gross domestic product (GDP) per capita (current prices, US $ at purchasing-power parity) and selected social indicators 2015

	GDP per capita (US $)	*Proportion of population at risk of poverty or social exclusion*	*At-risk-of-poverty rate (%)*	*Gini coefficient/ index*	*Income quintile share ratio*
Baltics					
Estonia	28,685	24.2	21.6	34.8	6.2
Latvia	24,678	30.9	22.5	35.4	6.5
Lithuania	28,591	29.3	22.2	37.9	7.5
Nordics					
Denmark	47,229	17.7	12.2	27.4	4.1
Finland	41,055	16.8	12.4	25.2	3.6
Iceland	45,746	13.0	9.6	23.6	3.4
Norway	68,410	15.0	11.9	23.9	3.5
Sweden	48,315	18.6	16.3	26.7	4.1
Anglo-Saxon					
Ireland	65,679	26.0	16.3	29.8	4.5
UK	41,482	23.5	16.6	32.4	5.2
Central Europe					
Czech Republic	32,317	14.0	9.7	25.0	3.5
Hungary	26,539	28.2	14.9	28.2	4.3
Poland	26,612	23.4	17.6	30.6	4.9
Slovakia	28,591	18.4	12.3	23.7	3.5
Slovenia	29,879	19.2	14.3	24.5	3.6
South-Eastern Europe					
Bulgaria	19,288	41.3	22.0	37.0	7.1
Romania	20,936	37.4	25.4	37.4	8.3
EU-28		***23.8***	***17.3***	***31.0***	**5.2**
EUR-19		***23.1***	***17.2***	***30.8***	**5.2**

Source: International Monetary Fund (2017) and Eurostat (2017).

Note: EUR-19: the 19 countries of the euro area.

Table 9.2 Baltic Comparator Country Groups

Baltic States	*Nordic countries*	*Anglo-Saxon countries*	*Central Europe 4 (CE 4)*	*South Eastern Europe 2 (SEE 2)*
Estonia Latvia Lithuania	Denmark Finland Iceland Norway Sweden	Australia Canada Ireland New Zealand UK USA	Czech Republic (Czechia) Hungary Poland Slovakia	Bulgaria Romania

Source: International Monetary Fund (2014), author's construction.

they rank relatively highly on business indicators, according to the World Bank's 'Doing Business' Report (World Bank 2017). As stated above, the introduction of low corporate taxes and a liberal economic regime in all three states in the 1990s following the restoration of independence was primarily aimed at attracting foreign investment and promoting investment growth and thus GDP growth. The question arises whether European integration has led to convergence towards European levels of productivity and welfare, or whether, conversely, this has led to the increasing divergence and long-term unsustainability of the Baltic economies.

It can be argued that EU overemphasis on fiscal discipline exacerbated the impact of the 2008/09 crisis on the Baltic States. Extreme austerity was implemented, with cuts in expenditure on healthcare and education. Internal devaluation was enforced, since depreciation of the local currencies would have resulted in the exclusion of the Baltics from the euro area, membership of which was a priority at the time for these countries, perhaps more for reasons of security than for reasons of economics.

Had the Baltics wanted to implement policies closer to the Nordic model, they could, for example, have introduced a system of progressive income taxation[4], instead of a flat-rate tax, and either a higher tax on property or some form of capital gains tax, in order to pass some of the burden to the more wealthy members of society[5]. Some of this revenue could then have been used to support the most vulnerable, including young people, who as a consequence might have remained in their home countries to seek work, instead of migrating abroad. The Baltics had very low levels of public debt when the 2008/09 crisis struck. Government debt subsequently increased, not as a result of the creation of a social safety net, but rather to enable foreign bank recovery after the financial crisis—in other words, the state intervened in order to save a system of unregulated capitalism.

Notes

1 Among the Nordic countries, Denmark, Finland and Sweden are EU members. Iceland and Norway have access to the common market as members of the European Economic Area. The Baltic States are all EU member states.

2 Anderson et al. also discuss further an important aspect of the Nordic model, in that it makes access to such basic welfare services independent of income and employment status. But it is also a problematic feature, which may in the long run lead to an impasse in public finances. This is so for two reasons: (1) Wagner's Law of increasing state spending, and (2) Baumol's Law, which explains why services such as health care and education continue to become more expensive. The two phenomena taken together imply a tendency for total spending on welfare services to rise faster than GDP over time (See Andersen et al. 2007, p. 19).

3 The ratio of total income received by the 20% of the population with the highest income (top quintile) to that received by the 20% of the population with the lowest income (lowest quintile). Income must be understood as equivalized disposable income.

4 At the time of writing Latvia seems to be taking some modest steps to introduce a progressive income tax.

5 As Stiglitz has pointed out, countries with less progressive taxation have more inequality (Stiglitz 2013).

References

Andersen, T. M., Holmström, B., Honkapohja, S., Korkman, S., Söderström, H. T. and Vartiainen, J. (2007). *The Nordic Model—Embracing globalization and sharing risks*, Helsinki: The Research Institute of the Finnish Economy (ETLA). Available at: http://economics.mit.edu/files/5726 (Accessed on 23 August, 2017).

Bohle, D. and Greskovits, B. (2012). *Capitalist Diversity on Europe's Periphery.* Cornell Studies in Political Economy. Ithaca, NY: Cornell University Press.

Eichengreen, B. (2007). *The European economy since 1945: coordinated capitalism and beyond.* Princeton, NJ: Princeton University Press.

Eurostat (2017). *Database.* Available at: http://ec.europa.eu/eurostat/data/database.

Hannibalsson, J. B. (2017). *What Can We Learn From The Nordic Model?*, Social Europe. Available at: www.socialeurope.eu/what-can-we-learn-from-the-nordic-model (Accessed on 23 August, 2017).

Ingebritsen, C. (2006). *Scandinavia in World Politics.* Lanham, MD and Oxford; Rowman & Littlefield.

International Monetary Fund (2014). *Baltic Cluster Report. IMF Country Report No. 14/117.* Available at: www.imf.org/en/Publications/CR/Issues/2016/12/31/Baltic-Cluster-Report-Selected-Issues-41541 (Accessed on 30 August 2017).

International Monetary Fund (2017). *World Economic Outlook Database.* Available at: www.imf.org/external/pubs/ft/weo/2017/02/weodata/index.aspx.

Keynes, J. M. (n.d.). *John Maynard Keynes Quotes.* Available at: www.brainyquote.com/quotes/john_maynard_keynes_137774 (Accessed on 23 August 2017).

Laar, M. (2005). 'Walking on Water: How to Do It'. *The Brussels Journal.* Available at: www.brusselsjournal.com/node/202 (Accessed on 23 October 2017).

Laar, M. (2007). *The Estonian Economic Miracle*, No. 2060, 7 August 2007. Washington, DC: The Heritage Foundation. Available at: www.heritage.org/report/the-estonian-economic-miracle (Accessed on 7 January 2018).

Stiglitz, J. E. (2013). *The Price of Inequality——How Today's Divided Society Endangers Our Future.* New York and London: W. W. Norton & Company.

World Bank (2017). *Doing Business 2018. Reforming to Create Jobs.* Available at: www.doingbusiness.org/reports/global-reports/doing-business-2018 (Accessed on 7 December 2017).

10 Fragile Baltic democracy and the challenges posed by outbound migration

Currently all the Nordic countries and the Baltic States are democracies. This has not always been the case—not even in recent history. The Baltics were part of a totalitarian regime from the Second World War until 1991, when the Soviet Union fell apart. All the countries in the Nordic-Baltic group are involved in European integration, with six out of eight countries being full European Union (EU) member states: only Iceland and Norway are not, and they have other mechanisms of co-operation with the EU, as discussed earlier in this book. The EU is a supranational institution, and within it views are divided on the most feasible level of integration, and whether full political union should be the aim. There are also disputes on how democratic the EU is today. EU law and regulations are promulgated by the European Commission, the executive arm of the EU, which is not directly elected by European voters. The head of the European Commission is also not elected. The Baltic States have generally been more interested in close European integration than the Nordics. Both regional and global integration have been high on their agenda since the re-establishment of their independence in 1991.

The populations of the Baltic States have generally appeared to be more submissive, silent and 'loyal' than those of the Nordic countries when faced with controversial government decisions, even if those decisions carry significant consequences for the economic welfare of the populace. This could clearly be seen during the 2008/09 crisis, when the austerity measures introduced by Baltic States governments resulted in, *inter alia*, widespread salary reductions; large increases in unemployment in countries with relatively weak welfare systems by European standards; a highly unequal income distribution; and persistent high levels of corruption. In contrast, a high degree of public outrage followed the collapse of the majority of the Icelandic banking system during the crisis. Iceland's government—including the entire cabinet and central bank management—were forced to resign: early parliamentary elections had to be called, and bank managers received prison sentences.

Unlike in the Soviet Union, when their borders were closed, exit or outward migration has become a serious challenge in the post-crisis Baltic States (see Table 10.1 below). This trend has been widely attributed to the enforcement of austerity (labelled by the EU as 'fiscal discipline') and the fixing of the exchange rate as a condition for euro area membership. A circular flow of people moving in and out across the Baltic borders could be feasible. Movements of people seeking new experiences and education can be valuable. But massive one-way outward migration out of the Baltics results in a process of 'brain drain', and negatively affects long-term economic growth. Outward migration—mostly by skilled and highly-skilled young people—appears permanent, according to a recent International Monetary Fund (IMF) staff discussion note (Atoyan et al. 2016).

Morten Hansen, an economist at the Stockholm School of Economics in Riga, was reported by the German broadcaster Deutsche Welle to have stated in an interview: '...that Latvians, Estonians and Lithuanians see themselves as Europeans and they would do almost anything to remain in the European family' (Hansen 2015). However, he reportedly wondered 'whether deep down the Greek people really have that same feeling of belonging to Europe, [which] makes him question whether they are really committed to staying within the [euro area] when push comes to shove' (Hansen 2015). The Baltic States' clear commitment to achieving closer European integration, including euro area membership, has encouraged speculation that their situation was, to some extent, exploited by European (and particularly Nordic) interests in order to rescue their foreign banks at the expense of poorer nations. Not everyone has been impressed with the results of the Baltic success story. Paul Krugman (2011) wrote: 'I find myself quoting Tacitus: "They make a desert and call it peace"—or, in this case, adjustment'. Then he added: '[s]till, this is one way the euro zone[1] could survive intact' (Krugman 2011).

'Exit, Voice and Loyalty'

Why might the Baltic people be willing to accept the economic difficulties imposed on them during the 2008/09 crisis, in order to remain in the EU 'club' and adopt the euro? Albert O. Hirschman's 1970 classic *Exit, Voice and Loyalty* may provide a framework to explain the behaviour of the Baltic peoples in the post-Soviet period, and, specifically, following the global economic crisis.

The basic concept discussed by Hirschman is as follows in the case of nation states: Citizens of nations, in this case the Baltic States, have essentially two possible responses when they perceive that the state is demonstrating a decrease in quality of life for its citizens. They can *exit*, that is, leave the country; or, they can *voice* their concern, i.e. attempt to repair or improve the state of affairs in the country through communicating complaint or proposing change. The citizens of a country may thus respond to increasing political repression in two ways: emigrate or protest, i.e. exit or voice.

One could argue that the greater the availability of exit, the less likely it is that voice—or protest—will be used. So, according to Hirschman's theory of exit, voice and loyalty, 'exit' translates into leaving one country and migrating to another country, while 'voice' describes the option of articulating discontent, which as Hirschman noted, 'can be graduated, all the way from faint grumbling to violent protest' (Hirschman 1970, p. 16). Hirschman modelled these options as mutually exclusive.

The easier the availability of an exit option, the lower the likelihood of voice. For rulers, emigration serves as a safety valve by which the discontented renounce their possibility to articulate protest. 'Latin American powerholders have long encouraged their political enemies and potential critics to remove themselves from the scene through voluntary exile. The right of asylum, so generously practiced by all Latin American republics, could almost be considered as a "conspiracy in restraint of voice."' (Hirschman 1970, p. 60–61).

However, not always did 'exit subvert voice', as Hirschman himself acknowledged in a 1993 article (Hirschman 1993). In East Germany in 1989, it was the escalating dynamic of out-migration that led those who wanted to stay to take to the streets to demand change. Exit triggered voice, and both worked in tandem. This has not yet happened in any of the Baltic States.

Exit need not be physical, but can be mental or emotional. For example, under totalitarian states, such as the Soviet Union or Nazi Germany, many people could not physically exit the country, so outward migration was almost impossible. But they did not want to participate in the system either. In these cases, citizens could be said to exit from civic or political participation, as they were neither loyal to the government nor were they willing to voice their dissatisfaction because doing so could lead to imprisonment, exile, or even death. Many thus mentally and emotionally exited their countries for the duration of a repressive regime they did not agree with but felt they could not fight or topple.

During the Soviet era, exit was practically impossible for citizens of the Baltic States as the borders with the West were closed and guarded. Their country had become a de facto province of the Soviet Union and was under the strict control of Soviet officials in Moscow. Voicing opposition openly against the Soviet regime could be dangerous. There was no freedom of speech. Moreover, under this severe oppression the Baltic peoples were hardly able to use their own language, but were expected to communicate in Russian. It was possible to be passive, which would translate into mental or emotional exit while living in a totalitarian union. Exit was thus not physical, but emotional. Emotional exit would be the only viable option left for the masses, who would silently bide their time until the eventual end of the regime.

With the fall of the Berlin Wall in 1989, East Germans were able to flee to West Germany. The impact of this change would become dramatic for Europe and the EU. The Soviet Union collapsed in 1991 and Baltic accession negotiations with the EU could be initiated. Part of the Russian-speaking minority living in the Baltic States would physically exit—in other words, leave for Russia. With full EU membership in 2004, and access to a single EU labour market, followed by Schengen membership in 2007, the citizens of the Baltic States could freely exit the Baltics. Outward migration suddenly became easy. This meant an option to exit for a 'better' life with a possibility to move to higher-income, more developed EU member states, or to other regions of the world for that matter.

Because of these new exit options, using voice perhaps became less likely, according to the theory. Expressing voice—attempting to change domestic policies—would be possible, but the effects of doing so were uncertain at best. Citizens of the Baltic States were unaccustomed to opposing authority. Expressing voice became even less viable following the onset of the financial crisis in 2008, given the outside pressure from foreign bank owners as well as the EU, which sought to protect the euro area from domino effects should the Baltics opt for currency depreciation and a lesser degree of fiscal austerity. (Depreciation was a possibility since all three Baltic States had their own currency at that period and adopted the euro only after the end of the crisis period: Estonia in 2011, Latvia in 2014 and Lithuania in 2015.

With much greater availability of exit for the Baltic people, provided by access to the common EU labour market and Schengen, the less likely it was that voice would be used to attempt to force home governments to consider policy change. Many Baltic citizens chose to 'vote with their feet' (see Table 10.1), effectively walking away from the problem rather than protesting against the policies of a national government that was also under pressure from foreign interests. From 1 January 2008 to 1 January 2012, Latvia lost 8.5% of its population and Lithuania even more (9.8%). These were mostly young people. Why would they want to wait for the recovery of an economy on a downward spiral, exacerbated by the impact of austerity and of fixed exchange-rate policies?

According to the IMF World Economic Outlook database, the Baltic States had collectively about 7.8m. inhabitants at independence in 1991. By 2016 their population had declined to about 6.1m. inhabitants (International Monetary Fund 2017). Figure 10.1 below shows a steady decline in the population of all three Baltic States, most dramatically in Latvia and Lithuania.

Table 10.1 Population change from 1 January 2008 to 1 January 2012 in selected NB8 states

	Total population			*% change during 2008–2011 due to*		
	1 January 2008 (million)	1 January 2012 (million)	% change	Births	Deaths	Other (=migration)
Iceland	0.32	0.32	1.3	6.1	-2.5	-2.3
Latvia	2.27	2.04	-10.1	3.7	-5.3	-8.5
Lithuania	3.37	3.01	-10.7	4.2	-5.0	-9.8

Source: Darvas (2013).

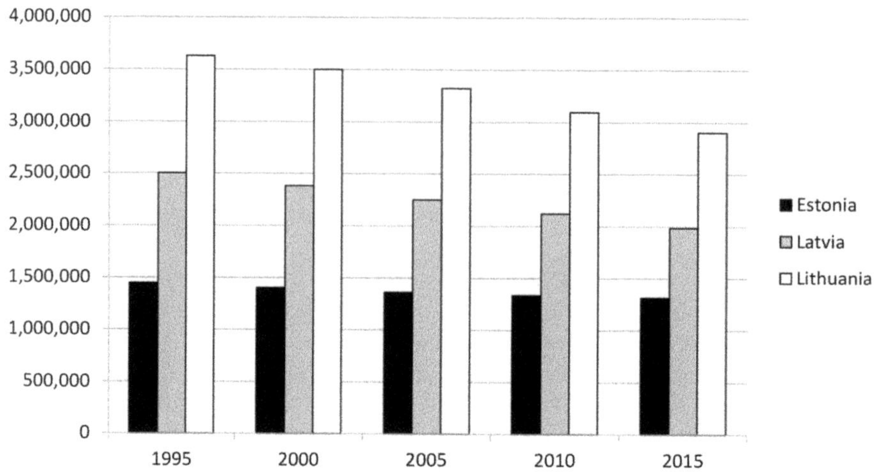

Figure 10.1 Population trends in the Baltic States 1995–2015
Source: International Monetary Fund (2017).

A recent IMF study confirmed that those exiting the Baltic States during this period are mostly young skilled or highly-skilled people who are unlikely to return (Atoyan et al. 2016). The resulting brain drain has adversely affected Baltic competiveness and long-term growth potential (Hilmarsson 2018). It is possible that the older segments of the population—who are less likely to find jobs in other EU countries—would exit mentally, i.e. remain but refrain from using their voice. Many of them were used to hardship anyway. Unemployment within this segment of the population is often labelled by international organizations, such as the IMF, as 'structural unemployment'. The older, Soviet-educated, generation did not have the right skills for the new free market economy, which imposed long spells of unemployment upon them. The younger generation, lacking experience, would also be victims of structural unemployment. They, too, did not belong in the new economy.

Furthermore, even after independence from the Soviet Union, Baltic political leaders may have been reluctant to express voice vis-à-vis larger states and international organizations. During times of crisis, when small, newly-independent countries like the Baltic States seek the assistance of the international community, the influence of their domestic authorities in a large union with larger more powerful member states is questionable. Used to living within a totalitarian union, they were now within a bureaucratic union dominated by larger and richer countries and unelected technocrats. They would depend on the Scandinavian countries, especially Sweden, to keep their banking system going and powerful states in the EU, most notably Germany and France, for their security.

Post-crisis recovery and performance

The economic performance of the Baltic States since the global economic crisis of the late 2000s has been mixed. Currently their gross domestic product (GDP) is growing, but at a rate too slow to allow any significant convergence with the richer Nordic countries or the older EU-15[2] member states in the foreseeable future (See Figures 10.2 and 10.3). None of the Baltic States have managed to regain their pre-crisis employment levels (see Figure 10.4) in spite of large outbound migration and shrinking populations (See Table 10.1 and Figures 10.1 and 10.6). The brain drain resulting from outward migration has reduced Baltic competitiveness and prospects for longer-term economic growth. Emigration has exacerbated the shortage of high-skilled labour, while an ageing population will result in higher social spending, further increasing the challenge from demographic changes.

One could argue that post-crisis unemployment in the Baltics was structural in origin. However, that is disputed. High though unemployment rates are, one could only imagine the effect on Baltic labour markets had large numbers of the region's young and educated population not exited/emigrated to countries such as Germany, the United Kingdom, Ireland and the Scandinavian bloc. The exit of skilled labour has also had structural implications for Baltic labour markets, as Sippola 2013 points out: 'Emigration is drastically shaping the Baltic labor market, since masses of skilled laborers are leaving their home countries, making it difficult for firms to maintain their skills base' (Sippola 2013, p. 459).

Some observers have asked why, in response to this exodus, the Baltic States have not yet taken more credible steps towards strengthening their social and education systems and presenting their citizens (especially their young people) with more attractive living conditions.. These steps could hardly meet with objections from any of the richer, larger and more powerful EU member states. As Sippola (2013) points out: 'The anti-socialist political climate in the post-Soviet Baltic [S]tates has left its imprint in the evolution of

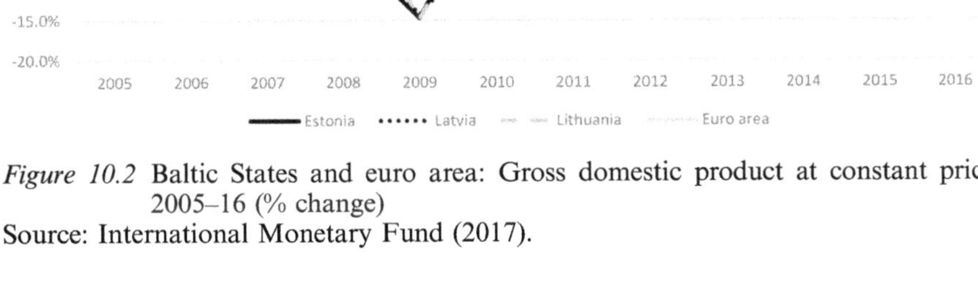

Figure 10.2 Baltic States and euro area: Gross domestic product at constant prices 2005–16 (% change)
Source: International Monetary Fund (2017).

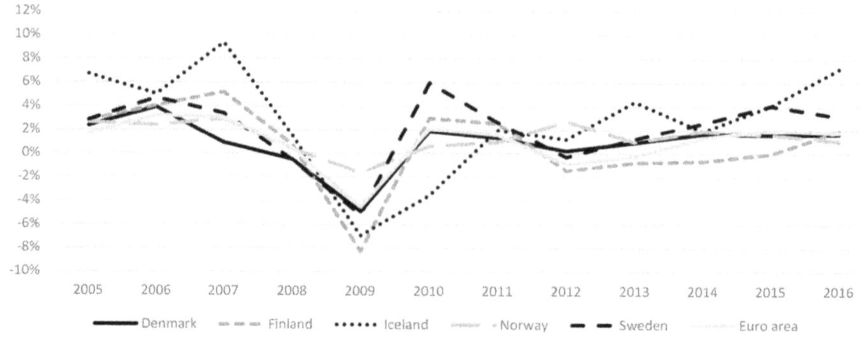

Figure 10.3 Nordic countries and euro area: Gross domestic product at constant prices 2005–16 (% change)

Source: International Monetary Fund (2017).

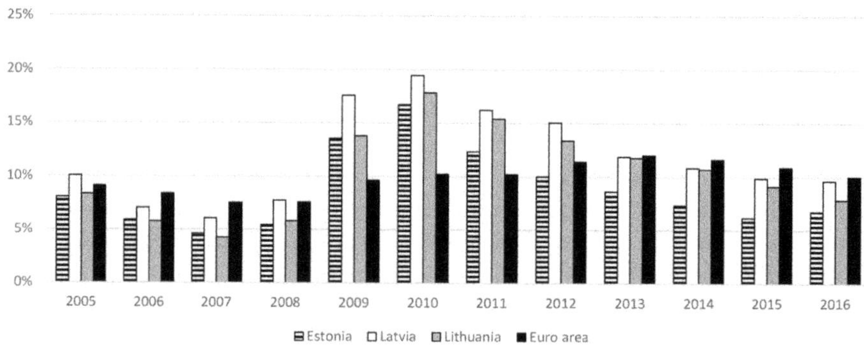

Figure 10.4 Baltic States and euro area: Unemployment rate 2005–16 (% of total labour force)

Source: International Monetary Fund (2017).

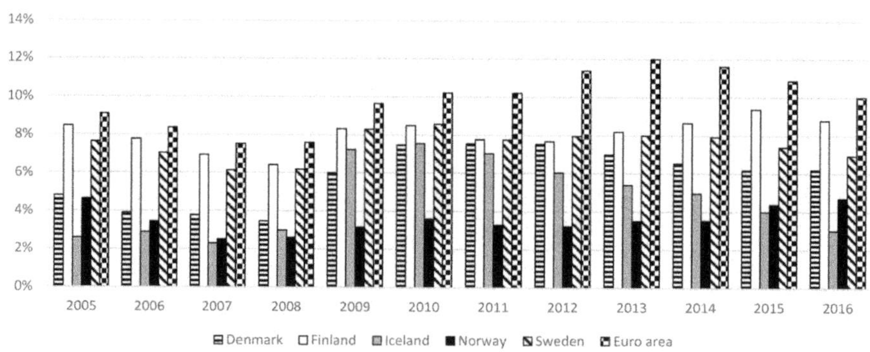

Figure 10.5 Nordic countries and euro area: Unemployment rate 2005–16 (% of total labour force)

Source: International Monetary Fund (2017).

the welfare regime in these countries' (Sippola 2013, p. 454). Specifically, it has been asked how Estonia, for example, avoid strikes and riots during the 2008 crisis—why did Estonians not take to the streets? 'Nobody would take to the streets flying the red flag', said Jürgen Ligi, Estonia's then Minister of Finance, in an interview with *The Economist* in 2010 (The Economist 2010). Toomas Ilves, Estonia's former president, suggested another factor: 'Maybe it's our peasant mentality' (*The Economist* 2010). This remark of Ilves' also refers to the third concept cited by Hirschman (1970), namely loyalty. It could be argued that long periods of Soviet occupation have left their mark on the mentality of many citizens of the Baltic States, making them unusually 'loyal' and submissive both to government policies (even if the latter are perceived as going against their own citizens' interests) and to powerful outside forces, such as larger, richer states and international organizations. Thus, Baltic political systems and governments survived the 2008-09 crisis under circumstances which would probably have led to their downfall in many other countries, including the Nordics.

An additional factor contributing to the preference of older Baltic citizens to stay put and consent is the relative absence, during the Soviet era, of any culture of labour mobility. Usually, people could not even consider living elsewhere; they would also be denied cross-border movement to the West. Consequently, those older Baltic citizens who had worked under the Soviet regime may not have a great desire to move to find work. In the post-Soviet era and after EU accession, these workers are also more likely to be part of the relatively high structural unemployment in the Baltic States along with the young and inexperienced, who also often cannot find work.

Thus, during the Soviet era, neither exit nor voice (or protest) was a viable option for citizens of the Baltic States. The EU opened up the exit option with its single labour market. With democracy, voice also became an option: however, it has been used only rarely. Firstly, the polities of the Baltic States are not accustomed to protest, and secondly, they constitute small states in the context of the EU, and might thus feel relatively powerless to protest against EU policies—or, indeed, against programmes proposed by the IMF or the Scandinavian banks. Indeed, the region now represented by the Baltic States has, over the centuries, been attacked or occupied on all sides: from the north (by the Scandinavian countries), from the east (Russia/the Soviet Union), and the south (Germany). Finland has been influential in Estonia and Poland in Lithuania, while the largest Russian-speaking minorities live in Latvia and Estonia. Historically these are fragile states, which have constantly struggled for survival. One can perhaps speak of an exit from the Soviet Union to the EU and then a mental exit within the EU, willing to accept whatever is demanded in exchange for the perception of greater security.

The Baltic politicians would be submissive, as in the case of Latvia, where an emergency rescue package was put together in December 2008 at an airport in a foreign country.[3] In this case the creditor country was Sweden. This arrangement would diplomatically be considered highly unusual, at least for a fully independent state that would normally be expected to want to negotiate such packages in its own capital or at a minimum in a third country that had no conflict of interest regarding the final deal.

Long-term unemployment represents a serious problem for the Baltics (see Figure 10.4), with the implications for affected workers including: a loss of self-esteem; increasing difficulty in finding work because of an erosion of skills; poverty; damage to health; material deprivation and social exclusion; and with governments having to bear the cost of supporting the long-term unemployed. In Europe the Nordic countries have the lowest rates of long-term unemployment, whereas the former Soviet Bloc countries—including the Baltic States—have the highest. In 2016 unemployment in Iceland was 3% while in Latvia it was 9.6%.

Unemployment is widely acknowledged to be the worst failure of the free market. It is the greatest source of inefficiency and a major cause of inequality (Stiglitz 2013). Among the dangers of long-term unemployment is that the longer a person is out of work, the less likely it is that potential employers will see them as being a serious contender for employment. The result is what is called hysteresis—the lagging effects of past economic events on future ones. Those who are unemployed gradually adjust to a lower standard of living; they also find it increasingly hard to get work and may lose interest in returning to the labour market. When looking at the breakdown of long-term unemployment, it seems that, while older people are more likely to be victims of long-term unemployment, there is an increasing (and worrying) number of young people across the EU who are falling into the long-term unemployment bracket.[4]

In short it can be argued that, when the 2008/09 financial crisis struck, Baltic host governments behaved in a submissive manner, accepting austerity programmes and rescue packages with little real negotiation and focusing on keeping the exchange rate fixed: this principally benefited foreign banks, the EU, and those local Baltic citizens who had borrowed in euro.

In contrast to its customary role of advocating neoliberal policies, the IMF found itself, in the case of Latvia, expressing concern about the austerity programme to be adopted and recommending devaluation of the lat to increase Latvia's competitiveness. Indeed, the exchange rate was the only stable economic variable in the Baltics during the 2008/09 crisis[5]. Many variables relating to human well-being showed a sharp decline in the years immediately following the crisis. None the less, Latvia has claimed victory, not only on the basis of GDP growth, which in any event has now slowed and remains insufficient for convergence, but also by reference to a reduction in unemployment, which, however, remains relatively high compared with both Estonia and Lithuania (see Figure 10.4). Lower unemployment is a welcome development in Latvia, but we need to keep in mind that a large share of that decline is due to persistent outward emigration dominated by educated and younger people (Atoyan et al. 2016).

As shown in Table 10.1, Iceland, Latvia and Lithuania were hit very hard by emigration during the 2008/09 crisis. According to Darvas (2013) 8.5% of Latvians chose to exit the country between 1 January 2008 and 1 January 2012. An even larger proportion of people, (9.8%), left Lithuania during the same period. By comparison, 2.3% left Iceland. According to one survey, only 20% of the emigrants who left Latvia during the crisis reported any intention of coming back within five years (Blanchard et al. 2013, p. 30). Those who left Latvia and Lithuania tended to be younger people with a university education. Once settled down in high-income countries, they may not be willing to return to lower salaries and weak social welfare systems at home.

Iceland has over the decades faced periods of outward migration of its people, but experience shows that a large share of these return when the economy recovers. In other words, flows have been circular. Iceland's per capita income is high in the EU context, so the incentives to return during periods of normal economic activity are clearer than in the case of the Baltics, where per capita income remains below the EU average and where the largely permanent departure of younger and more educated workers may indeed be costly for those who remain and pay taxes in their home country. Outward migration has reduced unemployment in the Baltics but is likely to have a negative impact on long-term growth, and full recovery will take a long time.

Social and economic justice

Like all other countries, the Baltic States face opportunities and threats in their external environment. However, internal strengths and weaknesses also need urgent attention and action.

After achieving independence from the Soviet Union in the early 1990s, the Baltics saw opportunities in an integrated Europe with access to the common market: they also saw that they could benefit from being better integrated globally through World Trade Organization membership. European integration was to bring prosperity and could have also brought a higher degree of social justice, which the richer European countries, most notably the Nordics, are well known for. EU membership would also bring more security, as would NATO membership. But there are also threats. In an integrated world economic, social, political and security issues are all interlinked. There is co-operation, but also competition and the possibility of exploitation.

Even after EU accession, Baltic sovereignty continues to be kept under a steady pressure by Russia. Growing uncertainty about the US commitment to NATO under the presidency of Donald Trump does not improve the Baltic security profile. In fact, both Russia (since its occupation of the Crimean region of Ukraine in 2014) and the USA have become more unpredictable. The ongoing debt crisis in the euro area, with its troubled financial sector, slow economic growth and relatively high unemployment, is a further source of instability.

Given the complex and unpredictable external environment, it would seem sensible for the Baltics to assess their strengths and weaknesses internally to see what could be improved. Slow growth and continued security concerns are to a large degree an external problem. These can result in continued outward migration and escalate internal conflicts that weaken the political and economic sustainability of the Baltics as independent states. But there are also internal challenges that can be addressed by the Baltic governments themselves and that could result in increased cohesion within the borders of the Baltic States.

In fact, with regional and global challenges it would seem rational for the Baltic peoples to seek more local unity and to strengthen themselves within their borders, in order to be better prepared for outside challenges. Economic and social justice could help in this regard. More cohesion and a greater inclusivity could strengthen these countries in dealing with global challenges. However, the reality within the Baltic borders is that political strife and ethnic tensions are exacerbated by social and economic injustice.

GDP, GDP per capita and GDP growth are important indicators for measuring countries' overall economic performance. However, these do not tell us anything about how a country's income is divided among its citizens. Other indicators are available that can help in analysing income distribution, poverty and social exclusion. Here we consider the following indicators, as measured by Eurostat, the EU statistical office: the Gini coefficient; the income quintile share ratio; the at-risk-of-poverty rate; and, finally, the proportion of people at risk of poverty or social exclusion (for definitions, see Box 10.1).

10.1 Social Indicators and Income Distribution used by Eurostat, the statistical office of the European Union

Gini coefficient

The Gini index, or coefficient, is a statistical measure of distribution. It is often used as a gauge of economic inequality, measuring income distribution or among a population. The coefficient ranges from 0 (or 0%) to 1 (or 100%), with 0 representing perfect equality and 1 representing perfect inequality. A country in which every resident has the same income would have an income Gini coefficient of 0. A country in which one resident earned all the income, while everyone else earned nothing, would have an income Gini coefficient of 1.

Here the Gini coefficient is defined as the relationship of cumulative shares of the population, arranged according to the level of equivalized disposable income, to the cumulative share of the equivalized total disposable income received by them.

Wealth Gini coefficients tend to be much higher than those for income[6].

Income quintile share ratio

The ratio of total income received by the 20% of the population with the highest income (top quintile) to that received by the 20% of the population with the lowest income (lowest quintile). Income must be understood as equivalized disposable income[7].

At-risk-of-poverty rate

The at-risk-of-poverty rate is the share of people with an equivalized disposable income (after social transfers) below the at-risk-of-poverty threshold, which is set at 60% of the national median equivalized disposable income after social transfers. This indicator does not measure wealth or poverty, but low income in comparison to other residents in that country, which does not necessarily imply a low standard of living[8].

Proportion of people at risk of poverty or social exclusion

This indicator corresponds to the sum of persons who are at risk of poverty or severely materially deprived or living in households with very low work intensity. Persons are only counted once even if they are present in several sub-indicators. At risk of poverty are persons with an equivalized disposable income below the risk-of-poverty threshold, which is set at 60% of the national median equivalized disposable income (after social transfers). Material deprivation covers indicators relating to economic strain and durables. Severely materially deprived persons have living conditions severely constrained by a lack of resources. They experience at least four out of the nine following deprivation items in that they cannot afford: i) to pay rent, mortgage or utility bills, ii) to keep the home adequately warm, iii) to face unexpected expenses, iv) to eat meat, fish or a protein equivalent every second day, v) a week's holiday away from home, vi) a car, vii) a washing machine, viii) a colour TV, or ix) a telephone[9].

Incidence of material deprivation

This indicator is defined as the percentage of population with an enforced lack of at least three out of the nine material deprivation items (see the nine indicators listed above)[10].

Source: Eurostat 2017.

When measuring income equality/inequality, researchers frequently refer to the Gini coefficient and the income quintile share ratio. In terms of income distribution, using the Gini coefficient, the Baltics have more in common with countries such as Bulgaria and Romania than the Nordics (see Table 10.2

below). Both Bulgaria and Romania are much poorer and less developed than the Baltics, while the Nordics are much richer and more advanced economically and socially. But it is notable that transition countries such as the Czech Republic (Czechia), Slovakia and Slovenia, that are at a similar income per capita to the Baltics, have a much more equal income distribution than the Baltics. In fact, according to the Gini Coefficient, their income distribution is similar to that of the Nordic welfare states (see Table 10.2 below and for more detail Box 10.1).

According to the Gini coefficient, income distribution in the Baltics has fluctuated and if anything became more uneven during the crisis, especially in Estonia and Lithuania. Since EU accession and to date, one cannot see a clear trend towards a more equal income distribution among the Baltic States, which continue to rank among the lowest in the EU in terms of income inequality. In Bulgaria, income inequality worsened from 2004 until EU accession in 2007, then remained stable until 2014, when it deteriorated, with growing income inequality. It is worth noting that the Czech Republic, Slovakia and Slovenia have been more successful than the Baltics in ensuring social and economic justice as measured by this indicator. It is likely that distribution of wealth is even more uneven in the Baltics than income distribution, given the private capture of state assets post-Soviet Union.

The income quintile ratio in the Baltics tells a similar story. Despite some fluctuations, the ratio has not changed much to date since EU accession. Income inequality decreased in Estonia pre-crisis from 2004 to 2008, but increased again after 2011. In Latvia income inequality grew during the crisis years 2008–09. In Lithuania, income inequality fell between 2005 and 2007, but rose again during the crisis years from 2008–10.

Overall, the income quintile ratio shows similar results to the Gini coefficient. The Baltics resemble more closely countries like Bulgaria and Romania than other transition countries in Europe at a similar level of development and income such as the Czech Republic, Slovakia and Slovenia, or or the higher-income Nordics.

Other measures, too, shed light on poverty and social exclusion. Those referred to here are the at-risk-of-poverty rate, and the proportion of people at risk of poverty or social exclusion. The at-risk-of-poverty rate rose in all three Baltic States during the crisis, but much more drastically in Latvia than in Estonia and Lithuania. The at-risk-of-poverty rate then declined in all three countries but started growing again in 2011–13 and thereafter. This indicator shows little improvement in the Baltics since EU accession; in fact the situation is worse today in all three countries compared to 2005 (see Table 10.4 below).

After EU accession the proportion of the population at risk of poverty or social exclusion was declining in the Baltic States until the economic crisis struck in 2008, whereupon it rose again (see Table 10.5). By 2016 this ratio in Estonia had not yet declined below its 2004–05 levels, but in both Latvia and Lithuania the 2016 proportion was well below that recorded in 2004–05. On

Table 10.2 Selected EU countries: Gini coefficients/indices 2004–16

	2004	*2005*	*2006*	*2007*	*2008*	*2009*	*2010*	*2011*	*2012*	*2013*	*2014*	*2015*	*2016*
Baltics													
Estonia	37.4	34.1	33.1	33.4	30.9	31.4	31.3	31.9	32.5	32.9	35.6	34.8	32.7
Latvia	n.a.	36.2	38.9	35.4	37.5	37.5	35.9	35.1	35.7	35.2	35.5	35.4	34.5
Lithuania	n.a.	36.3	35.0	33.8	34.5	35.9	37.0	33.0	32.0	34.6	35.0	37.9	37.0
South-Eastern Europe													
Bulgaria	26.0	25.0	31.2	35.3	35.9	33.4	33.2	35.0	33.6	35.4	35.4	37.0	38.3
Romania	31.0	31.1	33.0	37.8	36.0	34.9	33.3	33.5	34.0	34.6	35.0	37.4	34.7
Central Europe													
Czech Republic	n.a.	26.0	25.3	25.3	24.7	25.1	24.9	25.2	24.9	24.6	25.1	25.0	25.1
Slovakia	n.a.	26.2	28.1	24.5	23.7	24.8	25.9	25.7	25.3	24.2	26.1	23.7	24.3
Slovenia	n.a.	23.8	23.7	23.2	23.4	22.7	23.8	23.8	23.7	24.4	25.0	24.5	24.4
Nordics													
Denmark	23.9	23.9	23.7	25.2	25.1	26.9	26.9	26.6	26.5	26.8	27.7	27.4	27.7
Finland	25.5	26.0	25.9	26.2	26.3	25.9	25.4	25.8	25.9	25.4	25.6	25.2	25.4
Iceland	24.1	25.1	26.3	28.0	27.3	29.6	25.7	23.6	24.0	24.0	22.7	23.6	n.a.
Norway	25.2	28.2	29.2	23.7	25.1	24.1	23.6	22.9	22.5	22.7	23.5	23.9	25.0
Sweden	23.0	23.4	24.0	23.4	24.0	24.8	24.1	24.4	24.8	24.9	25.4	26.7	27.6

Source: Eurostat (2017) and Statistics Iceland (2015).

Table 10.3 Selected EU countries: Income quintile share ratios 2004–16

	2004	*2005*	*2006*	*2007*	*2008*	*2009*	*2010*	*2011*	*2012*	*2013*	*2014*	*2015*	*2016*
Baltics													
Estonia	7.2	5.9	5.5	5.5	5.0	5.0	5.0	5.3	5.4	5.5	6.5	6.2	5.6
Latvia	n.a.	6.7	7.8	6.4	7.3	7.4	6.8	6.5	6.5	6.3	6.5	6.5	6.2
Lithuania	n.a.	6.9	6.3	5.9	5.9	6.4	7.3	5.8	5.3	6.1	6.1	7.5	7.1
South-Eastern Europe													
Bulgaria	4.0	3.7	5.1	7.0	6.5	5.9	5.9	6.5	6.1	6.6	6.8	7.1	7.9
Romania	4.8	4.9	5.3	7.8	7.0	6.7	6.0	6.2	6.6	6.8	7.2	8.3	7.2
Central Europe													
Czech Republic	-	3.7	3.5	3.5	3.4	3.5	3.5	3.5	3.5	3.4	3.5	3.5	3.5
Slovakia	-	3.9	4.1	3.5	3.4	3.6	3.8	3.8	3.7	3.6	3.9	3.5	3.6
Slovenia	-	3.4	3.4	3.3	3.4	3.2	3.4	3.5	3.4	3.6	3.7	3.6	3.6
Nordics													
Denmark	3.4	3.5	3.4	3.7	3.6	4.6	4.4	4.0	3.9	4.0	4.1	4.1	4.1
Finland	3.5	3.6	3.6	3.7	3.8	3.7	3.6	3.7	3.7	3.6	3.6	3.6	3.6
Iceland	3.4	3.5	3.7	3.9	3.8	4.2	3.6	3.3	3.4	3.4	3.1	3.4	-
Norway	3.6	4.1	4.8	3.5	3.7	3.5	3.4	3.3	3.2	3.3	3.4	3.5	3.7
Sweden	3.3	3.3	3.6	3.3	3.5	3.7	3.5	3.6	3.7	3.7	3.9	4.1	4.3

Source: Eurostat (2017) and Statistics Iceland (2015).

Table 10.4 Selected EU countries: At-risk-of-poverty rates 2004–16 (%)

Baltics	*2004*	*2005*	*2006*	*2007*	*2008*	*2009*	*2010*	*2011*	*2012*	*2013*	*2014*	*2015*	*2016*
Baltics													
Estonia	20.2	18.3	18.3	19.4	19.5	19.7	15.8	17.5	17.5	18.6	21.8	21.6	21.7
Latvia	n.a.	19.4	23.5	21.2	25.9	26.4	20.9	19.0	19.2	19.4	21.2	22.5	21.8
Lithuania	n.a.	20.5	20.0	19.1	20.0	20.3	20.5	19.2	18.6	20.6	19.1	22.2	21.9
South-Eastern Europe													
Bulgaria	15.0	14.0	18.4	22.0	21.4	21.8	20.7	22.2	21.2	21.0	21.8	22.0	22.9
Romania	18.0	-	-	24.8	22.3	22.4	21.1	22.3	22.9	23.0	25.1	25.4	25.3
Central Europe													
Czech Republic	-	10.4	9.9	9.6	9.0	8.6	9.0	9.8	9.6	8.6	9.7	9.7	9.7
Slovakia	-	13.3	11.6	10.6	10.9	11.0	12.0	13.0	13.2	12.8	12.6	12.3	12.7
Slovenia	-	12.2	11.6	11.5	12.3	11.3	12.7	13.6	13.5	14.5	14.5	14.3	13.9
Nordics													
Denmark	10.9	11.8	11.7	11.7	11.8	13.1	13.3	12.1	12.0	11.9	12.1	12.2	11.9
Finland	11.0	11.7	12.6	13.0	13.6	13.8	13.1	13.7	13.2	11.8	12.8	12.4	11.6
Iceland	10.0	9.7	9.6	10.1	10.1	10.2	9.8	9.2	7.9	9.3	7.9	9.6	-
Norway	10.8	11.4	12.3	11.9	11.4	11.7	11.2	10.5	10.0	10.9	10.9	11.9	12.2
Sweden	11.3	9.5	12.3	10.5	12.2	13.3	12.9	14.0	14.1	14.8	15.1	16.3	16.2

Source: Eurostat (2017) and Statistics Iceland (2015).

Table 10.5 Selected EU countries: Proportion of population at risk of poverty or social exclusion 2004–16 (%)

	2004	*2005*	*2006*	*2007*	*2008*	*2009*	*2010*	*2011*	*2012*	*2013*	*2014*	*2015*	*2016*
Baltics													
Estonia	26.3	25.9	22.0	22.0	21.8	23.4	21.7	23.1	23.4	23.5	26.0	24.2	24.4
Latvia	n.a.	46.3	42.2	35.1	34.2	37.9	38.2	40.1	36.2	35.1	32.7	30.9	28.5
Lithuania	n.a.	41.0	35.9	28.7	27.6	29.6	34.0	33.1	32.5	30.8	27.3	29.3	30.1
South-Eastern Europe													
Bulgaria	-	-	61.3	60.7	44.8	46.2	49.2	49.1	49.3	48.0	40.1	41.3	40.4
Romania	-	-	-	45.9	44.2	43.1	41.4	40.3	43.2	41.9	40.3	37.4	38.8
Central Europe													
Czech Republic	-	19.6	18.0	15.8	15.3	14.0	14.4	15.3	15.4	14.6	14.8	14.0	13.3
Slovakia	-	32.0	26.7	21.3	20.6	19.6	20.6	20.6	20.5	19.8	18.4	18.4	18.1
Slovenia	-	18.5	17.1	17.1	18.5	17.1	18.3	19.3	19.6	20.4	20.4	19.2	18.4
Nordics													
Denmark	16.5	17.2	16.7	16.8	16.3	17.6	18.3	18.9	17.5	18.3	17.9	17.7	16.7
Finland	17.2	17.2	17.1	17.4	17.4	16.9	16.9	17.9	17.2	16.0	17.3	16.8	16.6
Iceland	13.7	13.3	12.5	13.0	11.8	11.6	13.7	13.7	12.7	13.0	11.2	13.0	-
Norway	15.8	16.2	16.9	16.5	15.0	15.2	14.9	14.5	13.7	14.1	13.5	15.0	15.3
Sweden	16.9	14.4	16.3	13.9	14.9	15.9	15.0	16.1	15.6	16.4	16.9	18.6	18.3

Source: Eurostat (2017) and Statistics Iceland (2015).

the whole, the Baltics are also performing better than the poorer South-Eastern European countries of Romania and Bulgaria, both of which have, however, shown improvements since their EU accession in 2007—especially in the case of Bulgaria. As before, the Czech Republic, Slovakia and Slovenia have performed much better in terms of this indicator than the Baltics and are, given their income level, surprisingly close to the much richer and more advanced economies of the Nordics.

Given the slow rate of change of income inequality in the Baltics, and the relatively high rates of poverty and social exclusion among their populations, it is perhaps unsurprising to observe that political strife and social tensions exist within those countries. Although the problems measured by those indicators are not the only potential sources of instability within each country, inequality and poverty do not help promote unity against external challenges within Baltic borders. Economic and social exclusion are likely to add to ethnic tensions, especially in Latvia. Social and economic injustice results in higher levels of political risk for those who want to engage in the Baltics, and can reduce foreign investment. With the exit option, made available by the Baltics' participation in the EU common labour market, outward migration and depopulation is a likely result, especially among the young and skilled, resulting in a more rapidly ageing population. The young are likely to vote with their feet (exit), while the older generation is more likely to remain in the country but exit mentally, without protest (voice), as has been the case since the onset of the financial crisis of 2008. All the Baltic States have to contend with shrinking populations, while the population of each Nordic country is growing, as Figure 10.6 shows.

Given persisting tensions with Russia, uncertainty as to US support for NATO, and the ongoing euro crisis, the Baltics should seek ways to strengthen themselves within their borders. They can consider the policies of the other transition countries mentioned in this chapter or the Nordic model and see what steps could be taken towards greater social and economic justice

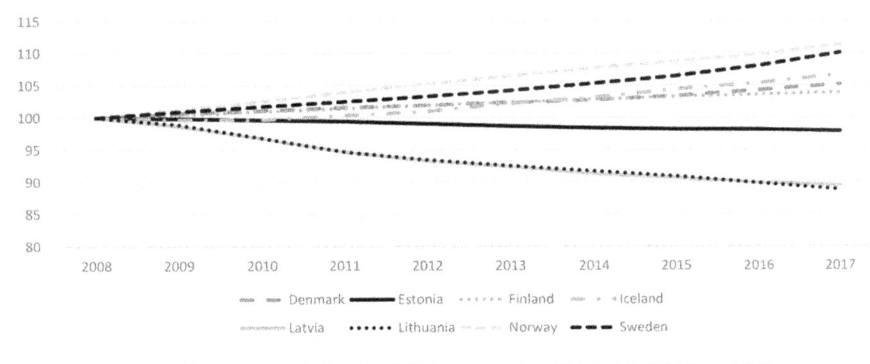

Figure 10.6 Population trends in the NB8 countries 2008–17 (2008 = 100)
Source: International Monetary Fund (2017).

to help make them more inclusive societies, more prepared to present a united front speaking with one voice to the outside world. They should also aim to achieve a greater degree of economic sustainability and improve their security profile. The Baltics cannot afford to adopt the Nordic model any time soon, nor is it argued that they should. Nevertheless, more inclusive societies could contribute to increased prosperity and stability in the Baltics.

Post-crisis, an IMF policy note recommends measures in the Baltics such as improving institutions, boosting job creation, modernizing education and encouraging return migration (Atoyan et al. 2016). However, during the 2008/09 financial crisis, institutions were weakened and austerity killed jobs, while schools and hospitals were closed. All these factors led to massive outward migration. The IMF notes that the exit of young and skilled people is largely permanent and its suggestions sound like buying an insurance policy for damage already done. A better course of action for the Baltics, with EU support, would be to develop policies that could prevent further demographic damage and reverse the one-way outward migration of some of the most talented Baltic citizens.

Notes

1 The eurozone is synonymous with the euro area.

2 The EU-15 member states (which constituted the EU from 1995 until enlargement in 2004) are: Austria, Belgium, Denmark, Finland, France, Germany, Greece, Ireland, Italy, Luxembourg, the Netherlands, Portugal, Spain, Sweden and the United Kingdom.

3 See https://piie.com/publications/chapters_preview/6024/03iie6024.pdf, pp. 45–46.

4 See also www.baltic-course.com/eng/analytics/?doc=129359.

5 What is stability when the only thing stable is the exchange rate? This question was posed by Thorbjörn Becker, Director of the Stockholm Institute of Transition Economics (SITE) at the Stockholm School of Economics (Becker 2008).

6 See further: http://ec.europa.eu/eurostat/tgm/table.do?tab=table&init=1&language=en&pcode=tessi190&plugin=1.

7 See further: http://ec.europa.eu/eurostat/tgm/table.do?tab=table&init=1&language=en&pcode=tsdsc260&plugin=1.

8 See further: http://ec.europa.eu/eurostat/tgm/table.do?tab=table&init=1&plugin=1&pcode=tespm010&language=en.

9 See further: http://ec.europa.eu/eurostat/web/products-datasets/-/t2020_50&lang=en.

10 See further. http://ec.europa.eu/eurostat/tgm/table.do?tab=table&init=1&language=en&pcode=tessi082&plugin=1.

References

Atoyan, R., Christiansen, L., Dizioli, A., Ebeke, C., Ilahi, N., Ilyina, A., Mehrez, G., Qu, H., Raei, F., Rhee, A. and Zakharova, D. (2016). Emigration and Its Economic Impact on Eastern Europe. *IMF Staff Discussion Note*, July 2016. SDN/16/07. Available at: www.imf.org/external/pubs/ft/sdn/2016/sdn1607.pdf (Accessed on 24 December 2017).

Becker, T. (n.d.). Latvia's Options—Internal versus External Devaluation. Available at: www.hhs.se/contentassets/558fa19998a247258a3cc96b82a239bf/latvias_options_internal_vs_external_devaluation.pdf (Accessed on 4 December 2017).

Blanchard, O. J., Griffiths, M. and Gruss, B. (2013). '*Boom, Bust, Recovery: Forensics of the Latvia Crisis*'. Final Conference Draft to be presented at the Fall 2013 Brookings Panel on Economic Activity, 19–20 September 2013. Available at: www.brookings.edu/wp-content/uploads/2016/07/2013b_blanchard_latvia_crisis (Accessed on 11 November 2017).

Darvas, Z. (2013). *Where does the youth exodus come from?* Available at: www.bruegel.org/nc/blog/detail/article/1103-where-does-the-youth-exodus-come-from/ (Accessed on 7 November 2017).

The Economist (2010). 'Baltic bet: Why fiscally prudent Estonia wants to join the troubled euro'. Available at: www.economist.com/node/17800259 (Accessed on 17 November 2017).

Eurostat (2017). *Database*. Available at: http://ec.europa.eu/eurostat/data/database.

Hansen, M. (2015). 'Baltic states' advice to Greece: "Do as we did"', *Deutsche Welle*, 20 July 2015. Available at: www.dw.com/en/baltic-states-advice-to-greece-do-as-we-did/a-18591847 (Accessed on 8 December 2017).

Hilmarsson, H. Þ. (2018). *Economic Austerity and Outward Migration*, Social Europe. Available at: www.socialeurope.eu/economic-austerity-outward-migration (Accessed on 20 January 2018).

Hirschman, A. O. (1970). *Exit, Voice and Loyalty: Responses to Decline in Firms, Organizations, and States*. Cambridge, MA and London: Harvard University Press.

Hirschman, A. O. (1993). 'Exit, Voice, and the Fate of the German Democratic Republic: An Essay in Conceptual History', *World Politics*, 45(2): pp. 173–202.

International Monetary Fund (2017). *World Economic Outlook Database*. Available at: www.imf.org/external/pubs/ft/weo/2017/02/weodata/index.aspx.

Krugman, P. (2011). 'Can Europe Be Saved?' *New York Times Magazine*. Available at: www.nytimes.com/2011/01/16/magazine/16Europe-t.html (Accessed on 20 January 2018).

Sippola, M. (2013). 'The Awkward Choices Facing the Baltic Worker: Exit or Loyalty', *Journal of Baltic Studies*, Vol. 44, Issue 4.

Statistics Iceland (2015). *Risk of poverty and income distribution 2014*. Available at: https://hagstofa.is/utgafur/nanar-um-utgafu?id=55055 (Accessed on 20 January 2017).

Stiglitz, J. E. (2013). *The Price of Inequality—How Today's Divided Society Endangers Our Future*. New York and London: W. W. Norton & Company.

11 The extreme cases of Iceland and Latvia during the global economic and financial crisis[1]

Two small countries in the Nordic-Baltic region, Iceland and Latvia, were exceptionally hard-hit by the 2008/09 global economic and financial crisis. Iceland was the first country to be affected, but the Latvian economy suffered more from its effects. Both countries received international attention for their responses to the crisis, which were classified as success stories by the International Monetary Fund (IMF). However, their responses were different in terms of both economic and social policies. As discussed in earlier chapters of this book, Icelandic economic and social policies are influenced by the Nordic welfare model, while Latvia is more neoliberal or Anglo-Saxon in its approaches. It is therefore interesting to compare their policy responses as well as policy outcomes some 10 years after the crisis struck.

These small countries, each of which was exposed to global turbulence, are extreme cases and, although at different levels of development, can make an interesting comparator case. Both countries were influenced by the action (and inaction) of larger countries as well as global and regional institutions. The level of European integration is different in each case, and politically these countries have a highly distinct history and culture. Iceland had a locally-owned banking system, while Latvia's banking system was mostly in foreign ownership. Geography also comes into play: Latvia shares a long eastern border with Russia, which has attendant security implications, while Iceland is distant from other countries, surrounded by the Atlantic Ocean, which has protected Iceland from threats from other powerful nations over the centuries.

In terms of fiscal adjustment, the governments of both countries implemented painful budget cuts, although the front-loaded fiscal austerity programme in Latvia was much more radical. Iceland ran larger fiscal deficits and for a longer time than Latvia did. This could be expected, given that Iceland is a welfare state with stronger automatic stabilizers than Latvia. Iceland, as a non-European Union (EU) member state, was also under less external pressure to balance its budget than Latvia, an EU member state subject to the Maastricht deficit criteria which restricted its budget deficit to no more than 3% of gross domestic product (GDP).

In terms of exchange rate policy, the response was quite different. Latvia maintained a fixed exchange rate, with its local currency, the lat, pegged to the euro, an EU condition for adoption of the euro, which materialized in 2014. In contrast, the Icelandic króna depreciated sharply and the government introduced a policy of capital controls[2]. Latvia received extensive international assistance during the crisis to rescue its mostly foreign-owned banking system (with the notable exception of the collapse of Latvian-owned Parex Banka, which was nationalized in late 2008) while Iceland, with its local banking system, was isolated, with 'friendly' nations hesitating to get involved and some being hostile, even going to the extreme of treating the country as a terrorist state[3]. Some 85% of the Icelandic banking system collapsed over a period of just a few days.

As mentioned above, although Iceland and Latvia were both badly affected by the economic crisis of 2008/09, each has its own distinct history and culture and they are at different stages of development, both economically and socially. Iceland has been a European Free Trade Association (EFTA) member state since 1970, having had access to the EU internal market via the European Economic Area agreement since 1994, while Latvia has been an EU member state since 2004, joining the euro area some five years after the crisis, in 2014. According to World Bank classifications, Iceland is a high-income country, with a welfare programme similar to other Nordic countries, and while Latvia has also recently achieved high-income status, its GDP was just US $14,062 per capita in 2016 (International Monetary Fund 2017), compared with $59,629 per head in Iceland. Latvia is still in transition and—according to Eurostat data—poverty, social exclusion and income inequality remain concerns.

While the focus here is on Iceland and Latvia, the study could also be of relevance for other countries. Important lessons may be learned about the effects of different policy responses during times of crisis, including in the EU and the euro area. In fact, among the main reasons for new member states to seek membership in the EU has been its promise of economic prosperity. However, in the post-crisis period both the EU and the euro area have continued to experience rather slow economic growth and high unemployment, especially among young people. Poverty and social exclusion are increasing concerns within the EU and income inequality is alarming in some countries. High levels of long-term unemployment within the EU will without doubt reduce long-term growth in the area, but surprisingly little attention has been given to this matter so far. According to a recent IMF staff discussion note, emigration from Central, Eastern, and South-Eastern Europe has been unusually high, persistent, and dominated by educated and younger people (Atoyan et al. 2016). This trend includes the Baltics and is a concern for their long-term growth and prosperity.

Following the 2008/09 crisis, Iceland applied for EU membership, but a few years later decided to withdraw its application and stop accession negotiations with the EU; the negotiating team was dissolved (See, for example,

Hilmarsson 2016). The benefits of EU membership were in doubt, at least for the time being, and too many of the Icelandic population feel that the EU has not adequately dealt with its problems, including a still-vulnerable banking system where the strategy seems to have been to buy time. There also seems to be a tendency to keep imposing additional burdens on taxpayers to keep the financial sector going[4]. Besides, social problems continue to arise; for example, dismal prospects greet young people attempting to find jobs. This is especially true of Central and Eastern European transition countries, including the Baltics as well as countries in Southern Europe.

Sufficient time has passed—almost ten years, since the crisis first erupted—for observers to be able to see and analyse the outcomes from the different policy responses, in terms of both economic and social progress, and to identify what lessons can be learned, by Latvia and Iceland, but also by the EU and the countries of the euro area. Both Iceland and Latvia sought and received assistance from the IMF during the crisis. Iceland also received assistance from the Nordic countries, the Faroe Islands and Poland. Latvia received much broader assistance. As an EU member it approached the EU, and as an emerging market economy it could approach the World Bank and the European Bank for Reconstruction and Development (EBRD). Iceland, classed by the Organization for Economic Co-operation and Development (OECD) as a high-income country, could not have requested assistance from the World Bank or the EBRD. Like Iceland, Latvia also received assistance from the Nordic countries as well as from Estonia, the Czech Republic and Poland.

Iceland received financial assistance totalling €1,500m. from the Nordic central banks prior to the crisis. However, that assistance proved insufficient and all its largest banks, representing some 85% of its banking system, collapsed during the first days of the crisis. In Latvia the rescue of its mostly foreign-owned banking system was a key element in its recovery plan, with strong Nordic and EU involvement. Clearly, external parties and interests played a key role in determining the fate of the banking system in these two countries as well as in designing their recovery programmes. Nevertheless, it was widely claimed—by bilateral and multilateral partners, especially the IMF—that the governments of Latvia and Iceland enjoyed strong 'ownership' of their reform programmes. A few years after the financial crisis, the IMF organized conferences in both countries[5] labelling their programmes as successful. EU and Nordic interests were very active in determining what direction the Latvian economy should take post-crisis, but were much less concerned and showed less interest in the fate of Iceland, whose banking system was in local ownership.

This chapter aims to analyse the challenges faced and action taken by the governments of Iceland and Latvia during the 2008 crisis. To what extent was the response to the crisis the choice of the domestic governments in Iceland and Latvia in exercising strong government 'ownership'? To what extent were actions taken shaped by external actors, including economic interests, such as bank owners from other countries, and international organizations such as the IMF and the EU? Can anyone in retrospect claim that the policy outcomes have turned out to be favourable for those small states economically and socially?

With reference to the small states literature discussed earlier in this book, the question arises whether it is beneficial for small states to be members of multilateral institutions such as the EU—as is Latvia—when crisis strikes, since small states have limited resources and human capacity to deal with crisis situations. Are small states likely to receive support and assistance from international organizations should things go wrong domestically on terms that are favourable for them economically and socially? Can a small state experiencing a crisis benefit from being part of a group such as the Nordic-Baltic group, given that they can receive support from nations considered 'friendly'?

What does ownership mean for the International Monetary Fund? Some definitions

According to the IMF, strong ownership of a programme occurs 'when the government is actively engaged in designing the program, publicly communicates its support for the program, and implements it with conviction'.[6] A more formal IMF definition of ownership can be found in the 2001 IMF Board paper 'Strengthening Country Ownership of Fund-Supported Programs'. There, ownership 'is a willing assumption of responsibility for an agreed program of policies, by officials in a borrowing country who have the responsibility to formulate and carry out those policies, based on an understanding that the program is achievable and is in the country's own interest' (IMF 2001, p. 6). In the same report the IMF states that it 'generally advocates outward-looking and market-oriented reforms, seeks to minimize adverse social and environmental impacts, and insists upon certain standards of governance on matters pertinent on the use of Fund resources' (IMF 2001, p. 4).

Both Latvia and Iceland can be classified as outward-looking and market-oriented states. Both countries are also very open to external trade but, as to market orientation, Latvia is still in transition, with relatively weak welfare systems and a lack of clarity as to where it is heading with social safety nets. The IMF statement on minimizing adverse social impact is notable—especially for Latvia, given its neoliberal policies with relatively unequal income distribution. Iceland more closely resembles the so-called Nordic welfare state. Arguably, the Latvian approach is closer to the Anglo-Saxon model than the Nordic approach. On governance issues, Iceland has for a long time been perceived as a country with a low level of corruption. However, during the crisis serious cases surfaced, resulting in a number of bankers receiving prison sentences.[7] In contrast, Latvia has long been associated with corruption and 'state capture' (see Chapter 9) according to the World Bank.

A review of the extensive collection of IMF reports written on Iceland and Latvia during the 2008/09 crisis (which can be found on the organization's website) reveals frequent reference to 'ownership', often programme ownership (referring to reform programmes designed and implemented in these countries as a response to the crisis). But whose ownership is the IMF talking about?

In the first definition above, the IMF mentions 'the government', and in a more formal definition speaks of 'officials in a borrowing country'. Who are these officials? Are they the cabinet of ministers and the central bank president (who may or may not agree about the reform programme)? Does this categorization include, for example, higher political authorities who may take action to overrule the economic authorities—such as a president who, under the constitution as in the case of Iceland, can refuse to sign legislation and call for a national referendum challenging the cabinet and the parliament? Does this include the parliament or the majority of the parliament? What about regional authorities? What about interest groups or non-governmental organizations, and so on?

Often the IMF simply speaks of strong programme ownership without any clarification of exactly who the owners are. How does the IMF judge whether or not ownership of a programme exists? Frequently, lack of clarity and transparency are apparent when the term 'ownership' is used. Thus the concept of ownership can be used to describe commitment, but it can also be ambiguous when it is unclear who is committed. A review of IMF programmes, including the recent programmes in Latvia and Iceland, shows that ownership of a reform programme is frequently mentioned without any attempt at all to explain what ownership is and how the IMF perceives ownership. This statement can be used to legitimize actions that in reality have little support in a country. The risk arises, for example, that the authorities in a country may serve narrow interests, such as political or financial élites, rather than national interests.

When the IMF speaks of ownership it usually seems to mean some kind of government ownership, although it is not clear which players in the government the IMF considers in each case. And even if it is clear which part of the government is taking ownership of a programme, what does ownership imply?

At one extreme, the government could be expected to take responsibility for doing what the IMF insists that it does. At the other extreme, ownership could mean that the government takes the lead and designs its own policies and programmes so that the IMF only plays a supporting or advisory role. A compromise is also possible where ownership becomes a shared vision of the borrowing government and the IMF. This seems to be the understanding in the formal IMF definition referred to above, which mentions 'an agreed program of policies'.

In addition to problems in achieving consensus within governments and a shared vision with the IMF, the risk also arises that national authorities are influenced or even captured by strong outside interests.

A borrowing government may be dependent on other countries whose private sector has, for example, invested intensively in or has important trade relations with the borrowing country. Another risk relates to interference by other institutions, for example international financial institutions such as the World Bank or regional development banks, and supranational institutions such as the EU, of which the borrowing country is a member. The risk is especially high when the borrowing country is in great need of outside assistance from those institutions. When designing its programme, the borrowing country may be tempted to serve outside interests at the cost of serving its constituents. This is especially true of situations when the IMF is only providing part of a loan to a borrowing government to support a reform programme while third countries or other international organizations provide the bulk of the funding.

Crisis response and 'government ownership' in Iceland and Latvia

When the crisis struck Iceland and Latvia, the response in the two countries was very different. Regarding exchange-rate policy, Iceland had no real options other than to let its national currency depreciate sharply. Depreciation in nominal terms was about 50%. Its three largest banks, representing 85% of the banking system, collapsed in a few days. Limited fiscal space and insufficient reserves in the Central Bank of Iceland (CBI) meant that Iceland did not have the capacity to defend its banks and currency. Iceland was isolated and sufficient international assistance to defend its local currency could not be assembled except for assistance from other Nordic countries, which proved insufficient[8].

Latvia, on the other hand, opted for internal devaluation by attempting to impose sharp reductions in wages (mainly in the public sector) and prices. This response was consistent with one of its key goals at the time, namely the adoption of the euro[9]. Latvia's policy response was supported by a substantial international rescue package worth €7,500m, then equivalent to more than one-third of Latvia's GDP (see Table 11.1). This package was provided by the IMF, the EU, the EBRD, the World Bank, and bilaterally by countries, especially the Scandinavian countries, that had made large investments in the banking sector and had a strong interest in Latvia's recovery (see Table 11.1). Even one of the Baltic States, Estonia, offered assistance to Latvia. Latvia's future adoption of the euro required a peg to the euro and this international effort enabled Latvia to fulfil its commitments.

Iceland, a non-EU member state, could not rely on the EU as Latvia had been able to do. Moreover, Iceland, as a high-income OECD donor country, was not eligible for assistance from the World Bank or the EBRD. When the crisis struck, Latvia—with its EU membership and middle income status—had access to multilateral development banks (World Bank 2013a, 2013b and 2017). In addition, the foreign owners of the principal banks in Latvia (which

Table 11.1 Latvia's 2008 rescue package—Burden sharing

	Value (million euro)	*% of total*
EU	3,100	41.3
Nordic countries	1,800	24.0
IMF	1,700	22.7
World Bank and EBRD	500	6.7
Czech Republic, Poland and Estonia	400	5.3
Total	7,500	100.0

Source: International Monetary Fund (2013b).

Note: In Hungary the IMF provided 63% of the 2008 rescue package, and in Romania 65 %.

were mainly Swedish-owned) were not passive bystanders during the crisis: they protected their own interests. So did continental Nordic governments.

The sitting Latvian government claimed to have decided to maintain a fixed exchange-rate regime in Latvia, while the IMF initially suggested a 15% depreciation of the lat. The policy of keeping the exchange rate fixed was, however, clearly favoured by external interests, especially continental Nordic banks (mostly Swedish), which owned most of the Latvian banking system, and the EU. EU interests feared the effects of a large depreciation on the banking sector in the other Baltic States and the Scandinavian countries which could then spill over to other EU member states. Disorderly devaluation would have caused a Swedish banking crisis (Åslund and Dombrovskis 2011, p. 116). This is understandable, not only because of Swedish investments in the banking sector in the Baltic States, including Latvia, but also because of interlinkages between the Nordic banks that made them vulnerable, as will be discussed below. These vulnerabilities continued to exist in the post-crisis period.

In contrast, when the banks were privatized in Iceland, they were sold to local interests—or, more precisely, to local actors with political interests and connections. No foreign investment was made in the Icelandic banks, and no foreign banks were operating in Iceland when the crisis hit. This was fundamentally different from the situation in Latvia, where foreign investors became the owners of most of the banking system, except for Parex Banka and some other small local banks. Given the size of the banking system in Iceland, with total assets equivalent to more than nine times the country's GDP[10], the government had no choice other than to let the banks fail. Outside assistance could not be assembled. In Latvia the mostly foreign-owned banking system was rescued via a concerted international effort led by external interests. It is questionable whether the Latvian government had any real choice other than to rescue the banks if it wanted to keep good standing within the EU. Depreciation of the lat would clearly not have been in the interests of the euro area.

As discussed above, the IMF likes to speak of strong ownership of the reform programme in Iceland and Latvia. In the initial phases of the crisis there was hardly much ownership in Iceland as there was only one way that the government could proceed: with a sharp exchange rate depreciation and the collapse of the major banks. The government made desperate efforts to save the banks, but was isolated. This has been documented in detail in the 2010 report to the Alþingi (Althingi—parliament) by the Special Investigation Commission (2010). Latvian government ownership can also be questioned: as the IMF says, '[t]he European Commission was heavily involved in program design, especially in the fiscal and financial sectors' (IMF 2013b, p. 7). When discussing aggressive government cuts in the education and health sectors in Latvia during the crisis, Åslund and Dombrovskis state 'reform starts where the money ends' (Åslund and Dombrovskis 2011, p. 73). The policy was chosen because the flow of outside money had ended, not necessarily because the government or the people wanted to tread this path. The foreign-owned banks also had a strong voice and, as the IMF chief economist said in a conference paper, 'if your financial sector is largely composed of foreign subsidiaries, it is a good idea to be friends with the parent banks' (Blanchard et al. 2013, p. 33). And friends they were.

During the crisis, capital controls were introduced in Iceland, but not in Latvia. The decision to introduce capital controls was supported by the IMF, and thus also the EU, whose member states are represented on the IMF board of directors. These controls were introduced as a temporary measure, but they proved long-lasting, indeed not being removed until 2017. Capital controls helped prevent the Icelandic króna from depreciating any further than it already had. Nevertheless, the sharp depreciation in Iceland resulted in household and corporate balance sheet problems. Adjustment of corporate and household debt was introduced, with a large package of debt relief for households—questionable when considering the limited fiscal space available to policymakers. When such policies are implemented, 'free-riding' becomes a concern alongside what we might term moral hazard. Those who took heavy risks and borrowed excessively imposed costs indirectly on those who were more modest in their investments and borrowed little or nothing. Those who purchased more modest homes or rented a place to live were effectively punished.

The global reaction to Iceland's crisis

As argued above, the evidence strongly suggests that neither Iceland nor Latvia had a real choice when the crisis struck. Iceland could not save its banks and, in reality, had little international support. The report of the SIC to the Icelandic parliament documents in some detail the desperate attempt by the Government of Iceland (via the CBI) to assemble outside assistance.

According to the report, the Nordic central banks were contacted as well as major central banks such as the Bank of England, the European Central

Bank (ECB) and the US Federal Reserve. It was a natural move for the CBI to turn to the Bank of England for help, in the light of the large expansion of Icelandic banks in the United Kingdom. That request was turned down, however, and the SIC report shows[11] that the Bank of England and the Swedish central bank—the Riksbank—were closely co-ordinating their response to the CBI. Iceland could not expect much assistance from the ECB, given that Iceland is neither an EU nor a euro area member state. However, the substantial operations of Icelandic banks within the euro area, for example in the Netherlands, must have been a concern at the ECB.

It was also understandable that the CBI would turn to the US Federal Reserve for support. During the Cold War years, Iceland could count on support from the USA during critical times. Indeed, the USA was Iceland's strongest ally. But when the Cold War ended, US interest in Iceland sharply diminished. In fact, at the end of September 2008 the US Federal Reserve entered into a currency swap agreement with Sweden, Norway and Denmark, to which Iceland was not a party. At this point, the CBI was isolated and could only assemble limited support from the Nordic central banks. This proved insufficient either to defend the local currency from a sharp depreciation or to rescue the local banks. Only after Iceland's banking system had collapsed did sufficient outside support emerge—this time with assistance from the Nordic countries, but under IMF conditions.

It would appear that the Nordic countries never had a strong interest in saving the locally-owned Icelandic banking system, although the Icelandic authorities seem to have been naïve enough to believe so, at least for some time. Indeed, as documented in the SIC report[12]there seems to be a tendency among politicians in Iceland to believe that the Nordic countries can be counted upon as allies when crisis hits in Iceland.

Small states will often find it difficult to defend their own interest on the global stage. It is unlikely that the Nordic countries would choose to enter into a serious dispute with the UK in order to protect Iceland's interest, since their relationship with the UK is far more important strategically than their relationship with Iceland. Moreover, the Nordic central banks—especially the Riksbank—appear not to have held much faith in the CBI's handling of the situation. This became clear in a letter to the SIC from the Governor of the Riksbank, Stefan Ingves, after the collapse of the Icelandic banks. In this letter he states 'his opinion that unclear ownership and rapid expansion of the banks' balance sheets had caused a hazard which the Icelandic government had neither seemed to fully grasp, nor fully understand how to deal with by reducing the size of the banks' (Special Investigation Commission 2010, p. 109).

In retrospect, this global disinterest in Iceland was in a sense a blessing for the nation, although it may not have appeared so at the time these events were taking place. This meant that the local banks went into bankruptcy and were not rescued at a heavy cost to taxpayers, as has occurred in a number of

OECD countries, most notably in Ireland but also in Latvia, as will be discussed below.

Iceland's dispute with the UK and the Netherlands

During the period of overseas expansion of the country's three largest banks, the incumbent President of Iceland, Ólafur Ragnar Grímsson, played a key role in promoting them with high-profile speeches overseas (see Grímsson 2005, Grímsson 2006 and Hilmarsson 2013). He thus took an active role in fuelling their expansion.

After the banks fell, Grímsson also played an important role in the international debate over Iceland's sovereign responsibility for the liabilities of these private banks. When the Icelandic parliament agreed in December 2009 on a repayment scheme for the Icesave branded overseas savings accounts, the president activated a clause in the constitution that allowed him to call a public referendum in March 2010, at which the overwhelming majority of Icelanders rejected the proposed scheme. The parliament passed a revised settlement scheme in February 2011, with terms that were widely considered to be more favourable for Iceland. The president again invoked his constitutional right to call for a referendum, and again, in April, the nation rejected the deal, in an extraordinary series of political events.

In a speech after these events took place, the president stated the following:

> And when we faced the […] Icesave dispute in which the Governments of the United Kingdom and the Netherlands, supported by all EU governments and others, demanded that the ordinary people of Iceland—fishermen, farmers, teachers, nurses—should shoulder through their taxes the debts of a failed private bank—we had to choose between the financial interests as they were presented by the established leadership of Europe and the democratic will of the Icelandic nation and decided to allow democracy to prevail. Following the two referendums, in which the people overwhelmingly voted No, the economy started to recover, becoming healthier with each quarter. The financial doomsayers, whether experts or leaders, who advised strongly against the democratic will of the people turned out to be entirely wrong in their analysis and predictions; a result which certainly should serve as a challenge to many of the policies which are still being advocated and followed in many countries.
>
> (Grímsson 2013, pp. 5–6)

The president thus saw this not only as a dispute between a small country versus the UK and the Netherlands, but as a battle of a small nation for democracy against the whole EU establishment. It was clear that the new government, elected after the collapse of the banks, was not able to stand up to the UK and the Netherlands and feared EU pressure even more.

During this crisis the Icelandic constitution allowed the elected president to take action against what was widely perceived as an unfair and undemocratic deal, which had been forced on the Icelandic Government by external powers. Later, when the EFTA Court ruled on this case in favour of Iceland, Grímsson commented as follows: 'When the EFTA Court last month ruled that there was no legal basis for the case of Britain, the Netherlands and the EU against Iceland, it became clear that in addition to the democratic will of the people, justice and the rule of law was also on our side' (Grímsson 2013, p. 6). However, it can be argued that the president had behaved irresponsibly prior to the crisis, in his efforts to support ever-increasing cross-border banking expansion.

EU desperation and the Scandinavian rush to 'rescue' Latvia

As with Iceland, it also appears that Latvia had very little influence over its own policy response. As soon as the financial crisis erupted in late 2008, external actors took control, with a large rescue package (see Table 10.1). Unlike in Iceland, the possibility to let the banking system collapse was never an option. The Swedish Riksbank became in effect the Baltic central bank, and the Baltic rescue effort became a rescue effort for foreign banks.

The EU feared the domino effect of a banking collapse in Latvia and acted swiftly, overruling the IMF's initial advice of a 15% depreciation of the lat. There was no need for the Bank of Latvia to undertake a desperate campaign to generate interest within, and assemble assistance from, Scandinavia, as Iceland had done. As the former Latvian prime minister and his co-author have documented, 'the Swedish Riksbank and the Danish central bank offered a bridge loan to keep Latvia going until the IMF-EU-Nordic package was concluded' (Åslund and Dombrovskis 2011, p. 35). Nor did the Swedish government drag its feet in coming to Latvia's rescue: the 'Swedish Minister of Finance Anders Borg called the closest friends of Latvia to an emergency meeting at Arlanda airport in Stockholm on December 10' (Åslund and Dombrovskis 2011, p. 46). There was not only a strong concern that things could get out of control in Riga: additionally, as the incumbent Latvian prime minister documented, 'if multiple banks collapsed in all three Baltic Countries, the two Swedish banks, Swedbank and SEB, would be in serious trouble' (Åslund and Dombrovskis 2011, p. 53).

The Swedish Government was not impressed with the early discussion between the government of Latvia and the IMF about possible devaluation of the lat and, according to Åslund and Dombrovskis, the EU was activated to pressure the IMF on the matter. 'Swedish Prime Minister Fredrik Reinfeldt stated publicly: "We think that a clear signal of support from the EU would help them to achieve support from the IMF."' (Åslund and Dombrovskis 2011, p. 86).

Not all observers were impressed with these developments. One author commented:

> In Latvia, the neo-liberal insanity continues. The EU and IMF have told the government to borrow foreign currency to stabilize the exchange rate to help real estate debtors pay the foreign-currency mortgages taken out from Swedish and other banks to fuel its property bubble, raise taxes, and sharply cut back public spending on education, health care and other basic needs to 'absorb' income. Higher taxes are to lower import demand and also domestic prices, as if this automatically will make output more competitive in export markets.
>
> (Auerback 2009)

The overruled IMF commented as follows:

> The unequivocal commitment of the authorities, and of the other stakeholders to the exchange rate peg has determined their choice of program strategy. Though this commitment augurs well for program ownership, the authorities also recognize that their choice brings difficult consequences, including the need for fiscal tightening and the possibility that recession could be protracted.
>
> (International Monetary Fund 2008b)

The IMF recognized that the fixed exchange-rate policy represented good news for the euro area, but worse news for the most vulnerable Latvians, affected by the austerity programmes that followed.

The risks of Nordic-Baltic banking sector interconnectedness

As the incumbent Latvian prime minister and his co-author observed after the crisis hit Latvia, '[t]he Swedish Riksbank and the Financial Supervisory Authority (*Finansinspektionen*) should also have paid attention to the excessive exposure of the Swedish commercial banks to the Baltic economies, but they did nothing' (Åslund and Dombrovskis 2011 p. 29). It seemed that the Swedish authorities had failed in their role in the Baltic States, just as their sister institutions had failed in Iceland.

An IMF Working Paper, authored by Audun Grönn and Maria Wallin Fredholm and published in 2013, documented the risks and the still-obvious vulnerabilities caused by the interconnected Scandinavian and Baltic banks in the post-crisis period. Basically, the situation remained as before, in the shape of major interlinked trans-Nordic banking operations and the increasingly interconnecting nature of the financial systems in the Nordic-Baltic region, in turn dominated to a greater or lesser extent by the Nordic banks: in other words, a recipe for risk contagion. (Grönn and Fredholm 2013, p. 6).

A common pre-crisis problem both in Iceland and Latvia was that the housing bubble had to a large extent been funded by loans in euro (or other foreign currencies) taken out by people whose income was in local currency. Indeed, as Grönn and Fredholm state: 'Another characteristic is that many of these banks were exposed to a large share of unhedged borrowers, with income in domestic currency and loans in foreign currency'. (Grönn and Fredholm 2013, p. 6).

This is one key reason why some people, typically the élite, in Latvia shared a common interest with the foreign banks. They, like the foreign banks, feared the balance sheet effects of devaluation. As Grönn and Fredholm point out, risk—which is absent while the exchange rate remains fixed—may involve significant credit losses in the event of currency depreciation, adding that—because investors had failed properly to account for the likelihood of risks materializing in the Baltic States—funding remained available to Nordic parent banks at a low cost reflecting the risk to banking groups. In turn, according to Grönn and Fredholm, failure by the Nordic parent banks to adequately assess their own risk resulted in Baltic borrowers benefiting from lower-than-adequate interest rates, so that '[t]his inadequate risk management contributed to large capital flows to these countries as the Nordic banks underestimated the risks of exposure in the Baltic countries' (Grönn and Fredholm 2013, p. 7).

When commenting on Iceland they say:

> Before the crisis, Iceland's private sector had accumulated a relatively large share of FX-denominated debt as the tightening of monetary policy led to much higher interest rates on loans in Krona than in foreign currency. In addition to the macrofinancial risks posed by the FX-denominated debt, a large part of Icelandic household debt was also indexed to inflation. This exposed the financial sector to similar risks as the household balance sheets could be seriously impaired because of the rapid pass-through to the exchange rate.
>
> (Grönn and Fredholm 2013, p. 7)

In Iceland, the government could not defend the currency, and a sharp depreciation soon materialized. All three major banks fell, and many households faced financial hardship. Some loans were partly cancelled, some were declared illegal and the government had to implement plans to assist the most vulnerable households.

In Latvia, external forces kept the lat exchange rate at par with the euro. There was no way that Latvia could have kept the peg on its own account. In order to achieve this, harsh austerity measures were imposed in a country with an already weak welfare system and the most unequal income distribution in the EU, as will be discussed below. Grönn and Fredholm comment as follows: '… it was not until after the crisis had materialized that broader austerity measures were implemented and approved by the Latvian government in the general government budget for 2009. Fiscal tightening was a prior action set by the IMF, EU and bilateral lenders' (Grönn and Fredholm 2013, p. 7).

The former Latvian Prime Minister and his co-author state that 'Latvia also learned from the Swedish and Finnish banking and devaluation crisis in the early 1990s that banking collapses and devaluation should be avoided if possible' (Åslund and Dombrovskis 2011, p. 117). This comment sits uncomfortably alongside the fact that, unlike Latvia, both Finland and Sweden have strong welfare systems, and both allowed their currency to depreciate sharply during the 1990s crisis, which in both countries was followed by a period of strong export-led growth.

In a report published by the EU in 2008, Jonung et al. review the recovery of Finland and Sweden from 1993 to 2000. When commenting on Finland they state that 'the biggest macroeconomic change contributing to the recovery was the loosening of monetary policy, including the currency depreciation in the aftermath of the 1992 EMS [European Monetary System] crisis' (Jonung et al. 2008, p. 31). The cumulative depreciation of the markka was more than 30% and, according to Jonung et al., exports were the first component of GDP to recover. The effects of depreciation turned out to be long-lasting. Unemployment in Finland fell from 17% in 1994 to 10% in 2000, and to 6% in 2008. When commenting on Sweden, Jonung et al. state that '[t]he depreciation of the krona in November 1992 marked the culmination of the crisis and the beginning of the recovery in Sweden' (Jonung et al. 2008, p. 36). The large depreciation increased Swedish competitiveness. Economic growth turned positive in 1993, and exports were the major driving force behind the Swedish recovery.

It is hard to see what lessons Latvia learned from the crisis in Finland and Sweden, since both these countries depreciated their currency sharply, followed by export-led growth. This has also been the experience in Iceland. Finland and Sweden did not stick with a fixed exchange rate and implement austerity programmes, as did Latvia. However, austerity would not have been as intense in Finland and Sweden as in Latvia since both countries have strong welfare programmes and strong safety nets for the most vulnerable. Automatic stabilizers were allowed to run their course.

Economic growth and unemployment

During the crisis Latvia suffered the greatest fall in GDP of any country in the world: around 20.5% from 2008–10. Iceland was less affected, with GDP falling by 8.9% from 2008–10 (see Table 2.1 and Figures 10.2, 10.3 and 11.1). Prior to the crisis Latvia and Iceland had unusually large current account deficits, as discussed earlier in the book.

Imports declined by about 40% in Iceland and Latvia during the crisis and investment collapsed in both countries. Private consumption declined during the crisis but growth has resumed in both countries. Both cut their government budget, but public consumption adjusted more in Latvia than in Iceland (Darvas 2011). Iceland did not implement nearly as intensive an austerity programme as did Latvia.

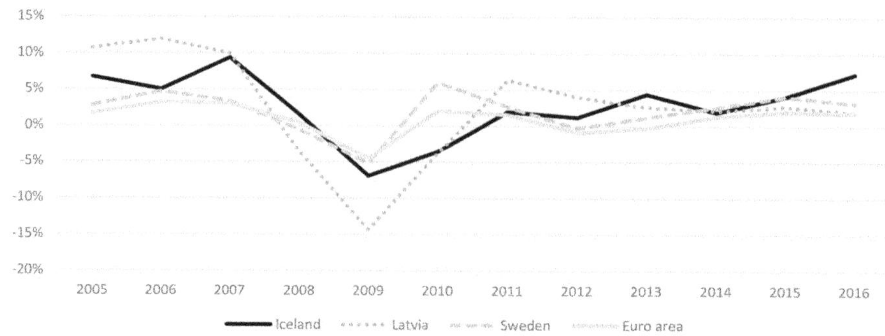

Figure 11.1 Iceland, Latvia, Sweden and euro area: Gross domestic product, constant prices 2005–16 (% change)
Source: International Monetary Fund (2017).

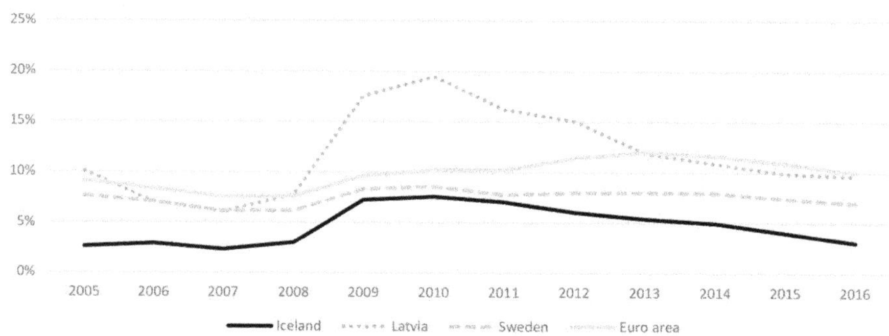

Figure 11.2 Iceland, Latvia, Sweden and euro area: Unemployment rate 2005–16 (% of total labour force)
Source: International Monetary Fund (2017).

Overall, economic adjustment involved a larger decrease in output, a larger increase in unemployment, and more outward emigration in Latvia than in Iceland (see Tables 2.1 and 2.2, and Figures 10.2, 10.3, 10.4, 10.5, 10.6, 11.2 and 11.3). The question arises whether an alternative strategy for Latvia could have achieved a better outcome: for example, depreciating the lat by around 15%, as suggested by the IMF. As Blanchard et al. have stated, in the post-crisis period nobody can give a definitive answer (Blanchard et al. 2013, p. 3). However, the experience of Finland and Sweden in the 1990s, discussed earlier in this book, shows that depreciation in those countries resulted in healthy export-led growth and a reduction in unemployment; as stated above, these countries avoided the imposition of austerity programmes with the high human cost that Latvia had to live with during the crisis and which continues in its aftermath (see Jonung et al. 2008). The adjustment in Iceland after the 2008/09 crisis far more closely resembles the adjustment in Sweden and Finland in the 1990s than the Latvian adjustment in 2008/09.

According to IMF data[13], by 2016 Latvia's GDP had still not recovered to its 2007 peak (measured at constant prices), but this was likely to be matched in 2017. Registered unemployment in Iceland is now about 3%, compared with 9.6% in Latvia. Both countries enjoy positive GDP growth rates. The GDP growth rate in 2016 was about 1.9% in Latvia, which was close to EU and euro area averages. In the same year the GDP growth rate for Iceland was 7.2%. Both countries have dramatically improved their current account balance and, according to IMF data, have maintained current account surpluses in 2016.

Social progress

In terms of unemployment, job losses have been much more dramatic in Latvia than in Iceland. Although the Latvian unemployment rate of 9.6% in 2016 was close to the euro area average, it was significantly higher than the country's pre-crisis unemployment rate of 6.1% in 2007. As the IMF noted in a report five years after the crisis, the labour market is improving in Latvia but unemployment, especially long-term unemployment, was still high (International Monetary Fund 2013c, p. 4)[14] and this remained the case in 2016. Iceland, with unemployment at 3% in 2016, was much closer to its pre-crisis low of 2.3% in 2007.

Many economists were critical of Latvia's reform programme during the crisis. Nobel Prize-winning economist Paul Krugman, for example, stated that '[t]hey have made a desert, and called it adjustment' (Krugman 2011). The former prime minister of Latvia, on the other hand, stated that '[t]he greatest pleasure in life is doing what people say you cannot do…'[15]. (Åslund and Dombrovskis 2011, p. 118). The question remains: what cost is the government prepared to impose on its people to adjust, and how is this likely to affect the social fabric and long-term growth in the country?

Latvia's claim to victory is to a large extent based on rates of GDP[16] growth and reductions in unemployment in the post-crisis period. It is true that, according to this measure, Latvia is on a path to recovery, and its GDP growth appears to be relatively healthy compared with other euro area countries, but growth performance has been dismal across both the EU and the euro area in the years since the crisis.

As in Latvia, recent data (2016) from the IMF put GDP growth in the other two Baltic States—Estonia and Lithuania—close to the EU and euro area averages. But the overall growth rate is disappointing if we consider these numbers in the context of pre-crisis growth rates, where Latvia was the hardest-hit country in the world and lost about 20.5% of its GDP between 2008 and 2010. The Baltics are also not in any convincing way catching up with the richer European countries, including the Nordics. Nevertheless, the return to a path of positive GDP growth is a welcome development.

Economic growth in Iceland in 2016 was much higher than in the Baltics or the other Nordics. Iceland is a very open economy with most of its exports going to the EU, which has recently experienced low GDP growth. But following the crisis-era depreciation of the króna the tourism industry has flourished, bringing in much-needed foreign-exchange revenue, which has proved vital for recovery.

Few would doubt the importance of economic growth, as measured by GDP, as an indicator of economic performance. However, the question remains whether this indicator is sufficient to support Latvia's claim to victory and to declare it a success story for other countries to follow.

Measures of economic performance and social progress

How good is GDP as an indicator of economic and social progress in a country? It may be worth reviewing statements that noteworthy economists and policymakers have made about the importance, as well as the limitations, of GDP as an indicator of economic development.

Paul Samuelson, for example, asserted that '[w]ithout measures of economic aggregates like GDP, policymakers would be adrift in a sea of unorganized data. The GDP and related data are like beacons that help policymakers steer the economy toward the key economic objectives' (Samuelson and Nordhaus 1995). It is understandable that economists should wish to employ a common measure of economic progress and development, but their views are diverse. The acknowledged creator of GDP, Nobel Prize-winning economist Simon Kuznets, also recognized its obvious limitations, stated in 1962 that '[t]he welfare of a nation can scarcely be inferred from a measurement of national income' (see European Commission 2013). More recently another Nobel laureate, Joseph Stiglitz, stated that '[n]o one would look just at a firm's revenues to assess how well it was doing. Far more relevant is the balance sheet, which shows assets and liability. That is also true for a country' (Stiglitz 2005). Human capital is normally not included in company balance sheets, yet it is critical, both to a company's profitability and a country's economic growth.

Policymakers have also commented on GDP and its derivatives as measures of economic development. For example, Robert McNamara, a former president of the World Bank, commented that '[p]rogress measured by a single measuring rod, the GNP, has contributed significantly to exacerbate the inequalities of income distribution' (European Commission 2013). McNamara was focusing on developing countries in his work at the World Bank. The Baltics are transition economies, and there is a risk in overemphasizing the importance of GDP, GDP growth and GDP per capita without adequately considering how income is shared within an economy. Former President of France Nicolas Sarkozy (who played an important role in policy- and decision-making within the EU both prior to and after the economic crisis) once stated that '[n]othing is more destructive than the gap between people's perceptions of their own day-to-day economic well-being and what politicians and statisticians are telling them about the economy' (Sarkozy 2009).

Going 'beyond' GDP when measuring 'success'

In the post-crisis period there has been a movement to go 'beyond' GDP when measuring progress within the EU. Given the highly uneven developments in the EU in terms of economic and social progress, it is understandable that the EU wants a more comprehensive picture of status within the Union. During the crisis, the EU has also performed poorly in terms of GDP growth, especially the older EU–15 member states[17]. What story would other indicators tell about the EU's economic and social progress?

The Commission on the Measurement of Economic Performance and Social Progress issued a report in 2009 (Stiglitz, Sen and Fitoussi 2009)[18]. Arguably, the global economic and financial crisis has reinforced the need for additional indicators to assess the economic and social situation throughout the world, in particular poverty and social exclusion, risks and sustainability. GDP per capita and its growth over time also do not tell us how economic benefits are shared within a society: 'A 2008 Eurobarometer poll showed that more than two thirds of EU citizens feel that social, environmental and economic indicators should be used equally to evaluate progress. Only just under one-sixth prefer evaluation based mostly on economic indicators' (Commission of the European Communities 2009).

Poverty, social exclusion and income inequality in Latvia and Iceland

While work continues on the basis of the Commission on the Measurement of Economic Performance and Social Progress's 2009 report, and new indicators are developed and introduced, it is worthwhile to revisit some of the indicators currently published by Eurostat, in order to assess how post-crisis Iceland and Latvia are performing in the context of social progress. (For the relevant tables, please see Chapter 10).

Between 2004 and 2016 the proportion of people at risk of poverty or social exclusion, which in Iceland was the lowest—or among the lowest—in Europe, in Latvia was among the highest (see Table 10.5). Although it had improved in the run-up to the crisis, decreasing from 46.3% of the population in 2005 to 34.2% in 2008, the Latvian rate deteriorated again thereafter, rising to 40.1% in 2011 before falling to 28.5% in 2016. Countries with similar income levels to Latvia, such as the Czech Republic (Czechia), Slovakia and Slovenia, show ratios over the 2004–16 period which are closer to those of the Nordic countries. Indeed, the Baltics, especially Latvia and Lithuania, perform relatively poorly according to this indicator, with ratios only exceeded by the South-East European states of Bulgaria and Romania. The proportion of people at risk of poverty or social exclusion in Iceland was 13.0% in 2015, compared with 30.9% in Latvia.

When focusing on the at-risk-of-poverty rate, the proportion was also lowest in 2015 in Iceland, at 9.6% compared with 22.5% in Latvia. Again,

Iceland and Latvia should arguably not be compared on this indicator because of their different income levels. Latvia is on the margin between an upper middle- and a high-income country—according to World Bank classifications—whereas Iceland is a high-income OECD country. However, the Czech Republic, a country with a similar income level to Latvia, has one of the lowest ratios in the EU, not only in terms of the ratio for the proportion of people at risk of poverty and social exclusion, discussed above, but also in terms of the at-risk-of-poverty rate. Slovakia and Slovenia also perform much better than Latvia in terms of this indicator, with rates surprisingly close to those of the richer Nordics. (The income threshold below which an individual is considered to be at risk of poverty is defined as 60% of median income in each country.)

Moreover, when we consider income distribution according to the Gini index and the income quintile share ratio, the Czech Republic, Slovakia and Slovenia are among the EU countries with the most even income distribution—again not far below the Nordics (see Tables 10.2 and 10.3). The Baltics, on the other hand, have highly uneven income distribution, with rates close to those of Romania and Bulgaria. In particular, Latvia's distribution of prosperity as measured by the Gini coefficient is among the most unequal in the EU.

In an IMF report written in 2013 the following sentence appears: 'the Latvian authorities do believe that the current degree of inequality is unacceptable and the high level of poverty, tracing back to the collapse of the Soviet Union, should be reduced' (International Monetary Fund 2013c, p. 2). Latvia's performance on the four accounts shown in Tables 10.2 to 10.5, measuring poverty, social exclusion and income equality, must be considered poor. Latvia has been an independent country for more than 25 years (since 1991) and a member of the EU for 14 years (since 2004). Its policymakers must address the issues of poverty, social exclusion and income equality for Latvia's economic progress to be regarded as successful.

According to the EU's— *Europe 2020* report, published in 2012, a high level of tax is imposed on low-income earners in Latvia, while youth unemployment is high and some 40% of the population is at risk of poverty or social exclusion—one of the highest rates in the EU (European Commission 2012). The 2012 Latvia Competitiveness Report argued that 'Latvia's high income inequality, is an indicator highlighting the presence of underlying competitiveness weaknesses that not only drive inequality but also negatively affect productivity' (Cunska et al. 2013, p. 17).

In terms of the indicators considered by the EU that measure social progress, Latvia seems to have more in common with Bulgaria and Romania than the Czech Republic and Slovakia, especially as regards income distribution. This is not a favourable outcome for Latvia, given that those countries only have about half of Latvia's per capita income and are the poorest countries in the EU.

An important question remains: why would the EU desire to diminish Latvia still further in terms of social progress indicators, by insisting on strict fiscal austerity in the aftermath of the financial crisis? Aggravating what is already a serious social crisis in Latvia will only further divide the nation. Given this poor record, it is appropriate to question how the social cohesion funds that Latvia has received (since well before its accession to the EU) have been utilized. This should not be regarded solely as a Latvian failure, but also an EU failure. Nor can the current situation be attributed to the legacy of the former Soviet Union. The latter collapsed more than 25 years ago and there is a need for Latvians to form some shared vision of how they intend to bring the nation together. Despite undeniable progress in modernizing, and in achieving stability, Latvia now needs to become a society that is more just and where wealth and income are shared, not captured by corrupt élites..

Emigration

While lower unemployment is a welcome development in Latvia, it needs to be borne in mind that emigration has mitigated unemployment to a much more significant extent there than in Iceland. According to Darvas (2013), 8.5% of Latvians left the country between 1 January 2008 and 1 January 2012, compared with 2.3% of Icelanders (see Table 10.1). According to a post-crisis survey, only 20% of the emigrants who left Latvia during the crisis report an intention of returning within five years (Blanchard et al. 2013, p. 30). Those who have left tend to be younger Latvians with a university education—in other words, the segment of the population most likely to reform the economy.

An IMF Staff Discussion Note from 2016 confirms that emigration from Central, Eastern, and South-Eastern Europe has been unusually high, persistent and dominated by educated young people (Atoyan et al. 2016). Emigration has led to positive outcomes for migrants themselves, while receiving highly educated and skilled people has likely benefited the receiving countries in the EU, and possible the EU as a whole. But there are negative externalities for countries like Latvia and all the Baltics in terms of loss of competitiveness, adversely affecting growth and slowing per capita income convergence. The IMF report notes that the effects have been particularly strong in the Baltic States. Migration from the Baltics, dominated as it is by educated, younger people, appears to be permanent, with limited return migration resulting in far-reaching effects on output and productivity. As the IMF note states: 'emigration has aggravated already negative demographic trends in the Baltics' (Atoyan et al. 2016, p. 8) Furthermore, the impact of highly-skilled emigration on skill shortages is particularly acute in the Baltics, while the ageing of the population left behind could put pressure on pension and health spending (Atoyan et al. 2016, p. 8).

Iceland has seen an exodus of people at times of economic difficulty, but a large share of those people return when the economy recovers. Icelandic per capita income is well above the EU average. Cross-border flows of people can be beneficial for countries as long as they are circular, with people returning with more education and new experience. But a one-way exodus is damaging for long-term growth. In Latvia the largely permanent departure of younger and more educated workers may indeed be costly for those who stay, while those who leave may have few incentives to return if Latvia's per capita income remains far below the EU average.

According to the IMF's World Economic Outlook database, the total population of the Baltic States was about 7.8m. people close to their independence in 1991. As of 2017 the total population of the Baltics was about 6.1m. (International Monetary Fund 2017). In contrast, the total population of Sweden was about 8.6m. when the Baltic States became independent but in 2017 was just under 10.2m. At independence, the total Baltic population was thus equivalent to about 90% of the Swedish population—but by 2017 was equivalent to only 60%. Figure 11.3 below shows that since the onset of the financial crisis in 2008 the Swedish population has grown by some 10%, while that of Iceland has increased by 7%. At the same time, the population of Latvia has declined by about 11%.

Have the reform programmes in Iceland and Latvia been successful?

Both Iceland and Latvia were exceptionally hard-hit by the 2008/09 crisis, but followed very different paths in selecting their response. The actions of these two small countries received international attention and continue to be debated.

In terms of GDP, both countries are on a growth path. Iceland currently enjoys stronger GDP growth than Latvia. Taking GDP at constant prices, in 2015 Iceland surpassed its pre-crisis (2008) peak, but by 2016 Latvia had not yet managed to equal its 2007 pre-crisis peak. In Iceland unemployment is about 3%—only about one-third of the 9.6% recorded in Latvia, which is about the same as average unemployment in the EU.

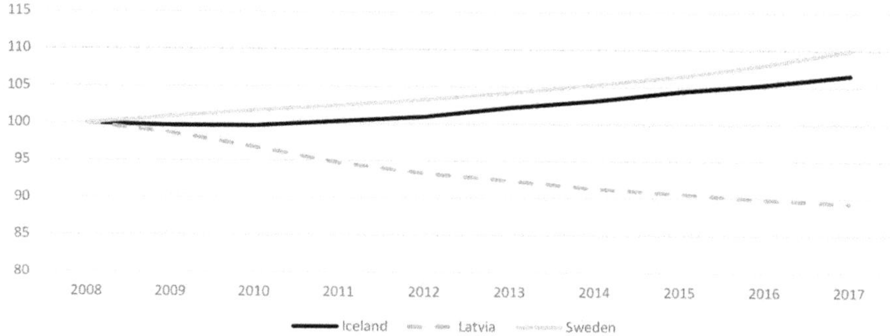

Figure 11.3 Iceland, Latvia, Sweden and euro area: Population growth 2008–17 (2008 = 100)

Source: International Monetary Fund (2017).

In terms of GDP growth and level of unemployment, Iceland has been successful in surmounting the crisis. GDP growth is high and the unemployment rate low by European and global standards. Iceland also performs well in terms of the indicators of social progress reviewed in this chapter. Latvia has returned to economic growth, and unemployment has been reduced, though it still remains high. Latvia's recovery has been presented by its own government as a success story and, to some extent, as a model for other countries to follow. However, in terms of social indicators and measures of income inequality that the EU measures and publishes, Latvia compares rather poorly with Iceland and also with countries at a similar income level to itself, such as the Czech Republic, Slovakia and Slovenia. In fact, in terms of social progress Latvia has more in common with the upper-middle-income economies of Romania and Bulgaria, where per capita incomes are only about half that of Latvia. Under those circumstances one can say that although Latvia has recorded some economic successes, the human cost remains too high for the country to be regarded as an outright success within the EU, or a model for the rest of the world to follow. Judging success on a single measure—GDP growth—is too narrow. The effects of the Latvian austerity programme, while promoted as a significant achievement by former Prime Minister Dombrovskis, the erstwhile Government and international organizations—specifically the IMF, have held back social progress in the country. Since independence was re-established, the population of Latvia has slumped from 2.68 m. in 1992 to 1.97m. in 2016. This appears largely to be due to emigration by younger, educated people, as confirmed by the recent IMF study discussed in this chapter. Such significant and apparently permanent migration is likely to have negative effects on long-term growth and slow Latvia's prospects for catching up with richer European countries such as the Nordics.

Iceland and Latvia were both severely affected by the crisis, though their policy responses differed: in Latvia's case with a fixed exchange rate, and in Iceland with a flexible exchange rate and large depreciation. Both countries adjusted and made sacrifices, implementing painful budget cuts, although Iceland ran larger fiscal deficits and for a longer time to stimulate the economy. Iceland is enjoying GDP growth well beyond the EU and the euro area, while unemployment has dropped. Latvia's GDP growth in 2016 was similar to the EU and euro area average; the same applies to unemployment, which appears to be long-term and is still a concern in Latvia, despite large-scale emigration. The austerity programme in Latvia has had damaging effects on the social fabric of the country; a burden has been placed on future generations and many of the youngest, brightest and best-educated have left the country. Iceland certainly experienced outward migration during the crisis but at much lower levels than Latvia. Migration in Iceland is more circular than in Latvia, with people returning to Iceland post-crisis.

Did Latvia and Iceland 'own' their reform programmes? When the crisis struck in Iceland, the country's government tried to assemble external assistance to rescue its three largest banks. That plan was clearly 'owned' by the incumbent government and the financial élite, and was carried out via the Central Bank of Iceland, which contacted the Nordic central banks, as well as major central banks elsewhere in the world, such as the Bank of England, the ECB and the US Federal Reserve. However, the government failed to assemble support, and the Icelandic banks collapsed in just a few days. This was followed by a sharp depreciation of the króna. Clearly this was not a path chosen by the incumbent government, but in retrospect it can be said that the Icelandic nation was fortunate that its severely ailing banking system was not rescued at the taxpayers' expense. Other small countries, like Ireland, whose governments did rescue their banks, appear to be paying a high price, with a heavy burden placed on future generations. The reforms that took place in Iceland were implemented under IMF conditions with financial support from the Nordic countries. These reforms have resulted in a resounding recovery. Economic growth is strong, at 7.2% in 2016, given the relatively slow growth in the EU, which remains Iceland's most important trading partner. Had the incumbent government been able to force taxpayers to bail out the banks, the situation in Iceland would be much worse than it is today. During the Icesave dispute, the new government twice agreed to a settlement with the Netherlands and the UK. This proposed settlement was 'owned' by the cabinet and by the majority in parliament. In both cases, the president of Iceland called for a referendum, and in both cases the nation rejected the government's agreement. The fall of the banks and the depreciation of the króna soon led to export-led growth and reduced unemployment. Had the previous government succeeded in saving the Icelandic banks, and had the new government succeeded in agreeing on a repayment scheme with the Netherlands and the UK, Iceland's overall recovery would at best have been slowed for years. Bank rescue was rejected by foreign governments, and the Icesave settlement was rejected by the nation: taken together, those rejections created fiscal space to defend the welfare system in Iceland.

In Latvia, however, it seems clear that external forces took control to ensure that Latvia could keep the peg with the euro. Of course, some Latvians favoured a fixed exchange rate, especially those who had borrowed in euro but had income in lats. However, when the IMF—in co-operation with the government of Latvia—worked out a scenario for a modest devaluation, both were effectively sidelined by the EU and the Swedish Government. The Swedish banks, which dominated the banking system in Latvia and throughout the Baltic States, feared a domino effect, not only in the Baltic States but also in Scandinavia, which has a banking system that was, and still is, dangerously interconnected. The Swedish banks were too concerned over the impact of devaluation to let the government of Latvia devalue. The EU, with a serious problem on its hands in the euro area, was concerned over the potential regional spill-over effects of devaluation in Latvia. Thus Latvia implemented an austerity programme at the cost, as it turned out, of the most vulnerable members of its society. The human costs appear to be high, as problems of poverty, social exclusion and income inequality are more visible in Latvia as a consequence of policy choices whose main goal was to serve the euro area. This reform programme may have had the ownership of political élites but was hardly owned by the majority of the Latvian population, who still remain poor, at least by European standards. After the crisis, the former Latvian prime minister became an EC Commissioner for the Euro and Social Dialogue, a clear signal that the EU considered Latvia's response to the crisis a success and a case to follow for poorer and weaker member states.

Notes

1 An earlier version of this chapter was presented by the author at the Baltic and Scandinavian Studies conference at Yale University on 15 March 2014. The author benefited from questions asked and comments by participants during the conference. Since then the author has discussed the cases of those small countries with students at universities in all three Baltic States, again benefiting from their questions and comments.

2 While Iceland is not a member of the EU it is part of the European Economic Area, where labour, goods, services and capital are to flow freely. Capital controls are inconsistent with this policy, but in the case of Iceland the international community through the IMF, and thus the EU, accepted capital controls in Iceland. These controls proved long-lasting and were mostly removed in 2017.

3 The Faroe Islands, Poland and Russia were the only countries that supported Iceland from the beginning. The Scandinavian countries initially hesitated to become involved. The UK was hostile, using anti-terrorism legislation against Iceland. Iceland's dispute with the UK and the Netherlands, which originated in the collapse of the Icesave online savings brand, may have influenced the Scandinavian countries. The government of Iceland probably overestimated potential support from central banks in the Scandinavian countries, which were more likely to give priority to considering their own economic and political interests in the UK and in the Netherlands than to support Iceland during a period of crisis and uncertainty. In fact, the Report of the Special Investigation Commission (2010), section 4.5.6.2., documents communications between the Central Bank of Sweden and the Bank of England that show the close relationship between those two institutions when the Central Bank of Iceland was isolated.

4 In 2008 a government bailout of six leading Irish banks was agreed; the cost to taxpayers was widely estimated at around €40,000m. by 2015. (See further: www.bbc.co.uk/news/world-europe-30834738.

5 The conference in Iceland was in 2011 and the conference in Latvia was in 2012.

6 According to an email from Daria V. Zakharova of the IMF received on 16 December 2013.

7 See further: www.bloomberg.com/news/features/2016-03-31/welcome-to-iceland-where-bad-bankers-go-to-prison and http://icelandmag.is/article/26-bankers-already-sentenced-a-combined-74-years-prison.

8 This is well documented in the Special Investigation Commission (SIC) report delivered to the Althingi on 12 April 2010. See e.g. chapter 4.5.6.2. (Special Investigation Commission 2010).

9 Latvia adopted the euro in January 2014.

10 According to the IMF the consolidated assets of the three main Icelandic banks increased from 100% of GDP in 2004 to 923% at the end of 2007, reflecting

expansion overseas. By the end of 2007 almost 50% of the three banks' assets were held abroad (IMF 2008a, p. 11).

11 See www.rna.is/media/skjol/RNAvefurKafli21Enska.pdf, p. 96, for example.

12 See www.rna.is/media/skjol/RNAvefurKafli21Enska.pdf.

13 See IMF World Economic Outlook Database: www.imf.org/external/pubs/ft/weo/2017/02/weodata/index.aspx.

14 It remains unclear how far unemployment needs to adjust to reach the natural rate of unemployment in Latvia. According to Blanchard et al., writing in 2013, output had not yet reached its potential, thus unemployment was not back to the natural rate. However, it may not have been very far off it (Blanchard et al. 2013, p. 3). The question remains: how can a country with a low minimum wage, weak trade unions, limited unemployment insurance and employment protection have such a high natural rate of unemployment?

15 Here, Åslund and Dombrovskis are citing the English economist and journalist Walter Bagehot.

16 Gross domestic product, abbreviated as GDP, is the most widely used measure of a country's overall economic health and development. As an aggregate measure of production, GDP is equal to the sum of the gross value added of all resident institutional units (i.e. industries) engaged in production, plus any taxes, and minus any subsidies, on products not included in the value of their outputs. Gross value added is the difference between output and intermediate consumption. See, further, for example, Eurostat: http://epp.eurostat.ec.europa.eu/statistics_explained/index.php/Glossary:Gross_domestic_product_(GDP).

17 Austria, Belgium, Denmark, Finland, France, Germany, Greece, Ireland, Italy, Luxembourg, the Netherlands, Portugal, Spain, Sweden and the UK.

18 See http://ec.europa.eu/eurostat/documents/118025/118123/Fitoussi+Commission+report. The commission included Professor Joseph E. Stiglitz, Chair, Columbia University, Professor Amartya Sen, Chair Adviser, Harvard University, and Professor Jean-Paul Fitoussi, Co-ordinator of the Commission, Institut d'études politiques de Paris.

References

Åslund, A., and Dombrovskis, V., (2011). *How Latvia Came Through the Financial Crisis.* Washington, DC: Peterson Institute for International Economics.

Atoyan, R., Christiansen, L., Dizioli, A., Ebeke, C., Ilahi, N., Ilyina, A., Mehrez, G., Qu, H., Raei, F., Rhee, A., and Zakharova, D., (2016). *Emigration and Its Economic Impact on Eastern Europe.* IMF Staff Discussion Note, July 2016. SDN/*16/07*. Available at: www.imf.org/external/pubs/ft/sdn/2016/sdn1607.pdf (Accessed on 24 December 2017).

Auerback, M. (2009). *In Latvia, the neo-liberal insanity continues.* Credit Writedowns. Available at: www.creditwritedowns.com/2009/10/latvia-the-insanity-continues.html (Accessed on 8 January 2018).

Blanchard, O. J., Griffiths, M. and Gruss, B. (2013). *Boom, Bust, Recovery: Forensics of the Latvia Crisis.*'Final Conference Draft to be presented at the Fall 2013 Brookings Panel on Economic Activity, 19–20 September 2013. Available at: www.scribd.com/document/205371312/Boom-Bust-Recovery-Forensics-of-the-Latvia-Crisis (Accessed on 11 November 2017).

Cunska, Z., Ketels, C., Paalzow, A. and Vanags, A. (2013). *Latvia Competitiveness Report.* Stockholm School of Economics in Riga/Baltic International Centre for

Economic Policy Studies. www.biceps.org/assets/docs/LCR2013 (Accessed on 5 September 2017).

Darvas, Z. (2011). *A tale of three countries: recovery after banking crises.* Bruegel Policy Contribution (No. 2011/19). Available at: www.bruegel.org/publications/publication-detail/publication/663-a-tale-of-three-countries-recovery-after-banking-crises/ (Accessed on 7 September 2017).

Darvas, Z. (2013). *Where does the youth exodus come from?* Available at: www.bruegel.org/nc/blog/detail/article/1103-where-does-the-youth-exodus-come-from/ (Accessed on 7 November 2017).

European Commission (2009). *GDP and beyond—Measuring progress in a changing world.* Communication from the Commission to the Council and the European Parliament. Available at: https://ec.europa.eu/eurostat/cros/system/files/06_GDP%20and%20beyond.pdf (Accessed on 1 December 2017).

European Commission (2012). *Europe 2020.* Available at: http://ec.europa.eu/europe2020/europe-2020-in-your-country/latvija/country-specific-recommendations/index_en.htm (Accessed on 7 December 2017).

European Commission (2013a). *President of the World Bank Mr Robert McNamara on GDP and social equity in 1973.* Available at: http://ec.europa.eu/environment/beyond_gdp/key_quotes_en.html (Accessed on 7 November 2017).

European Commission (2013b). *Simon Kuznets on GDP and well-being in 1934.* Available at: http://ec.europa.eu/environment/beyond_gdp/key_quotes_en.html (Accessed on 7 November 2017).

Eurostat (2017). *Database.* Available at: http://ec.europa.eu/eurostat/data/database.

Grímsson, O. R. (2005). '*How to succeed in modern business: Lessons from the Icelandic voyage*'. Speech by the President of Iceland Ólafur Ragnar Grímsson at the Walbrook Club, London, 3 May 2005.

Grímsson, O. R. (2006). '*Icelandic ventures: Can the success continue?*' Speech by the President of Iceland Ólafur Ragnar Grímsson at the Kaupthing Seminar, Helsinki, 24 May 2010.

Grímsson, O. R. (2013). '*A Clean Energy Economy Lesson From Iceland.*' Speech by the President of Iceland Ólafur Ragnar Grímsson at a meeting of OECD Ambassadors, Paris, 27 February 2013. Available at: www.oecd.org/iceland/a-clean-energy-economy-lessons-from-iceland.htm (Accessed on 7 March 2017).

Grönn, A. and Fredholm, M. W. (2013). *Baltic and Icelandic experiences of capital flows and capital flow measures* (IMF Working Paper WP/13/242). Washington, DC: International Monetary Fund.

Hilmarsson, H. Þ. (2013). 'Small states and big banks—the case of Iceland'. *Baltic Journal of Economics* (1), pp. 31–48. Available at: www.biceps.org/assets/docs/bje/bje2013_no1/Policy_paper_2 (Accessed on 7 September 2017).

Hilmarsson, H. Þ. (2016). 'Iceland and the Challenge of European Integration: Is European Union Membership Feasible?' In Lino Briguglio (ed.) *Small States and the European Union. Europa Economic Perspectives.* London: Routledge.

International Monetary Fund (2001). *Strengthening Country Ownership of Fund-Supported Programs.* Available at: www.imf.org/external/np/pdr/cond/2001/eng/strength/120501.htm (Accessed on 3 January 2017).

International Monetary Fund (2008a). *Iceland: Financial System Stability Assessment—Update.* Available at: www.imf.org/external/pubs/ft/scr/2008/cr08368.pdf (Accessed on 5 August 2017).

International Monetary Fund (2008b). *IMF Executive Board Approves €1.68 Billion (US$2.35 Billion) Stand-By Arrangement for Latvia.* Available at: www.imf.org/external/np/sec/pr/2008/pr08345.htm (Accessed on 5 November 2017).

International Monetary Fund (2013a). *World Economic Outlook (WEO)—Transitions and Tensions, October 2013.* Available at: www.imf.org/external/pubs/ft/weo/2013/02/ (Accessed on 7 November 2017).

International Monetary Fund (2013b). *IMF Country Report No. 13/30. Republic of Latvia: Ex Post Evaluation of Exceptional Access Under the 2008 Stand-By Arrangement; Public Information Notice on the Executive Board Discussion; and Statement by the Executive Director for the Republic of Latvia.* Available at: www.imf.org/external/pubs/ft/scr/2013/cr1330.pdf (Accessed on 7 March 2017).

International Monetary Fund (2013c). *IMF Country Report No. 13/28. Republic of Latvia 2012 Article IV Consultation and Second Post-program Monitoring Discussions.* Available at: www.imf.org/external/pubs/ft/scr/2013/cr1328.pdf (Accessed on 11 November 2017).

International Monetary Fund (2017). *World Economic Outlook Database. Available at:* www.imf.org/external/pubs/ft/weo/2017/02/weodata/index.aspx.

Jonung, L., Kiander, J. and VaritaP. (2008). *The great financial crisis in Finland and Sweden—The dynamics of boom, burst and recovery, 1985–2000* (No. 350). Directorate General Economic and Financial Affairs (DG ECFIN), European Commission. Available at: http://ec.europa.eu/economy_finance/publications/publication13551_en.pdf (Accessed on 8 February 2017).

Krugman, P. (2011). 'They Have Made A Desert, And Called It Adjustment'. *New York Times*, 7 December 2011. Available at: http://krugman.blogs.nytimes.com/2011/12/07/they-have-made-a-desert-and-called-it-adjustment/ (Accessed on 7 June 2017).

Samuelson, P. and Nordhaus, W. (1995). *Economics.* 15th edn. New York: McGraw-Hill.

Sarkozy, N. (2009). French president Nicolas Sarkozy at the unveiling of the Stiglitz Report in Paris on 14 September 2009. Available at: http://ec.europa.eu/environment/beyond_gdp/key_quotes_en.html (Accessed on 16 June 2018).

Special Investigation Commission (2010). *Report of the Special Investigation Commission (SIC)* to the Alþingi, 12 April 2010. Available at: www.rna.is/eldri-nefndir/addragandi-og-orsakir-falls-islensku-bankanna-2008/skyrsla-nefndarinnar/english/ (Accessed on 7 February 2017).

Statistics Iceland (2015). *Risk of poverty and income distribution 2014.* Available at: https://hagstofa.is/utgafur/nanar-um-utgafu?id=55055 (Accessed on 20 January 2017).

Stiglitz, J. E. (2005). 'Growth may be everything, but it's not the only thing.' *Foreign Affairs*, November/December 2005 Issue. Available at: www.foreignaffairs.com/articles/61208/joseph-e-stiglitz/the-ethical-economist (Accessed on 2 December 2017).

Stiglitz, J. E., Sen, A. and Fitoussi, J.-P. (2009). *Report by the Commission on the Measurement of Economic Performance of Social Progress.* Available at: http://ec.europa.eu/eurostat/documents/118025/118123/Fitoussi+Commission+report (Accessed on 11 November 2017).

World Bank (2013a). *Doing Business 2014. Understanding Regulations for Small and Medium-Size Enterprises.* Available at: www.doingbusiness.org/reports/global-reports/doing-business-2014 (Accessed on 6 April 2014).

World Bank (2013b). *E11 Regular Economic Report*, Issue 27, June 2013. Available at: www.worldbank.org/content/dam/Worldbank/document/eca/eu11-rev-report-jun-2013.pdf (Accessed on 1 November 2017).

World Bank (2017). *Doing Business 2018. Reforming to Create Jobs.* Available at: www.doingbusiness.org/reports/global-reports/doing-business-2018 (Accessed on 7 December 2017).

12 The Nordic–Baltic region: successes, failures, lessons learned and future challenges

This chapter seeks to highlight the successes and failures of the Nordic countries and Baltic States, the lessons learned from their experience of the 2008/09 economic crisis, and future challenges. The internal strengths and weaknesses of these countries are assessed as well as external opportunities and threats. The potential for Nordic-Baltic co-operation is discussed as these countries are linked via trade, investment and mobility of labour, in addition to a shared common history.

The participation of the Nordic-Baltic group in European integration has implications for this group of countries economically and politically, as well as for security. We have noted the different approaches within the group towards European integration. These include what we may term 'hard-core' European Union (EU) and euro area member states (Finland and the Baltics), 'reluctant' EU member states that do not participate in the monetary union (Denmark and Sweden) and finally 'outsiders', with access to the common market via a European Free Trade Association (EFTA)/European Economic Area (EEA)[1] agreement without EU membership (Iceland and Norway). Can this diverse group co-operate and become more influential by doing so?

Besides, events unfolding in their environment, such as Brexit, can affect the Nordic-Baltic countries. In the extreme case that the United Kingdom should disintegrate, an independent Scotland wishing to maintain access to the single market could potentially co-operate more closely with the Nordic-Baltic group via an EFTA/EEA agreement. Internal issues also relate to what kind of societies the Baltics are likely to become. Will they remain neoliberal societies, resembling the Anglo-Saxon model, or will they move closer to the more inclusive Nordic model? Strong external forces affect the Nordic-Baltic group, and especially the three Baltic States. These include most notably the behaviour of Russia towards them, the commitment by the USA to defending them, and developments in the EU, especially the euro area crisis. Given the present external challenges facing the Baltic States, which are largely beyond their control, they could in the near future seek increased internal cohesion, and more inclusive societies. Strengthening those countries within their borders might be especially important with an external environment that is so unpredictable.

In the introduction to this book, the following questions were asked:

- How did the Nordic countries and the Baltic States respond to the 2008/09 global crisis, and what are the economic and social post-crisis consequences?
- How did banking, investment and trade linkages affect the crisis response in the Nordic-Baltic region?
- How did the Baltic States respond to the 2008/09 crisis, compared to the crisis response in Finland and Sweden in the 1990s?
- How have the welfare and tax systems in the Baltic States developed in recent years compared to the Nordic welfare systems?
- How are the austerity programmes implemented in the Baltic States, and the associated human costs, likely to affect long-term growth potential in the Baltic States?
- What are the opportunities and the challenges of economic integration in the Nordic-Baltic region, given the different levels of involvement of those countries in EU institutions and systems, including financial sector integration?

Those questions have been answered in the previous chapters, but the arguments are summarized below, along with further discussion about successes, failures, lessons learned from the 2008/09 crisis, and the nature of future challenges for the Nordic-Baltic region.

Crisis response, and the economic and social post-crisis consequences

The 2008/09 global economic and financial crisis was a serious setback for the Baltic States and their subsequent recovery has been difficult. Achieving convergence with richer European countries, including the Nordic group, remains challenging. These challenges have economic, social, political and security dimensions. For the Nordics, the crisis was more of a typical advanced economy downturn, except in Iceland and, perhaps, in Finland. The Nordics as welfare states have much stronger automatic stabilizers to counteract a crisis and also to help in speeding up recovery. The Baltics are both poorer and more vulnerable, with uneven income and wealth distribution aggravating the problem.

The pre-crisis fixed exchange-rate policy and post-crisis adoption of the euro have been costly for the Baltic States. Once they had forgone the possibility of adjusting interest rates and exchange rates, the need for fiscal discipline became much greater, resulting in austerity programmes during the 2008/09 crisis that could hardly have been implemented anywhere else in the developed world, including in the Nordics, without considerable protest. Latvia should, for example, have been allowed to devalue during the 2008/09

Table 12.1 Baltic States: Strengths, weaknesses, opportunities and threats

	Helpful	*Harmful*
Internal	Strengths • The Baltics have made a transition from republics of the Soviet Union to independent modern states • Post-crisis have emerged as stable economies with relatively low public debt • Relatively well educated and competitive human capital	Weaknesses • Ethnic divisions—tensions with Russian minority[2], especially in Estonia and Latvia • Income and wealth inequality, poverty and social exclusion • Flat or regressive tax systems • Low tax on property • Austerity policies • Corruption • Relatively high unemployment; youth unemployment a concern • Lost human capital due to outward migration • Need to increase military expenditure to keep up with commitments to the North Atlantic Treaty Organization (NATO), but at the same time need to increase social expenditure • Political strife, ethnic divisions and increased political risks for investors
External	Opportunities • Central location in Europe with links to the Nordics and mainland central Europe as well as east-west links with Russia • EU membership: access to single market, goods, services, labour and capital • Security with both NATO and euro area membership • The Baltics could strengthen their international status by increasing development co-operation contributions to less advantaged transition countries such as Belarus, Georgia, Moldova and Ukraine[3]	Threats • Russia threatens Baltic sovereignty • Uncertain US commitment to NATO and the Baltics • US military presence in Europe greatly reduced since the fall of the Soviet Union and independence of the Baltic States • EU fiscal policies at regional and national level contribute to stagnation • Euro area crisis • Financial sector dominated by a single country—Sweden. Financial sector interlinkages with continental Nordics remain a risk • Vulnerable when dealing with larger richer states and international organizations • External threats most notably related to Russia; uncertainty in the USA and euro area crisis increase political risks in the Baltics

Source: Constructed by the author.

Table 12.2 Nordic countries: Strengths, weaknesses, opportunities and threats

	Helpful	*Harmful*
Internal	Strengths • The Nordics are high-income welfare states with relatively even income distribution • Relatively strong social safety nets, low levels of poverty and social exclusion • Progressive tax systems • Stable, prosperous economies • Relatively low public debt • Well-educated, competitive human capital • Relatively low levels of corruption • Vibrant private sector	Weaknesses • Relatively high private debt • Relatively high taxes
External	Opportunities • The Nordics have access to the single EU market but with different levels of integration. Iceland and Norway via EFTA/EEA membership, Sweden, Denmark and Finland via EU membership. Continued access to the common market is critical for their future economic growth. • Have their own currencies except Finland, a euro area member state. Denmark has a peg with the euro. Domestic currency allows for more flexible monetary policy. • Respected internationally. The continental Nordics, especially Denmark, Norway and Sweden, contribute generously to international development co-operation, which increases their influence in institutions such as the World Bank, the International Monetary Fund (IMF) and the United Nations as well as regional development institutions.	Threats • Lack of common approach in European integration complicates co-operation • Uncertain US commitment to NATO. Denmark, Iceland and Norway are member states but Finland and Sweden are not. Sweden, and especially Finland, with its eastern Russian borders, rely on co-operation with NATO. • US military presence in Europe is greatly reduced since the fall of the Soviet Union and the military base in Iceland has been closed down. • EU fiscal policies have contributed to stagnation in Nordic EU member states. • The euro area crisis is a source of uncertainty and slows down growth in the Nordic region. • Financial interlinkages among the continental Nordics and with the Baltics are a threat to the Nordic-Baltic region and potentially the euro area. • Sweden largely owns the banks in the Baltics but does not participate in EU banking union; this may lead to co-ordination and supervision problems.

Source: Constructed by the author.

crisis and still adopt the euro. While the Baltic States were able to implement severe austerity, that 'success' can hardly be labelled as a blessing for the Baltic peoples and has not resulted in a brighter future for these countries in terms of strong convergence or increased social justice. On the contrary, the results are devastating, with long-lasting consequences, especially because of outward migration that largely appears to be permanent. The social indicators discussed in the book show that uneven income distribution, poverty and social exclusion remain a problem in the Baltics, compared not only to the richer Nordics but also to countries at similar income levels, such as the Czech Republic, Slovakia and Slovenia. In this regard, the Baltics more closely resemble Bulgaria and Romania in terms of social progress.

Fortunately, growth seems to be picking up in the Baltics. It remains to be seen whether gains in gross domestic product (GDP) growth will lead to accelerated progress towards convergence with the Nordics or other prosperous EU member states. By 2016, Latvia had still not attained its pre-crisis (2007) level of GDP, measured in terms of constant prices. Estonia surpassed its 2007 GDP only in 2016 and Lithuania in 2014. In contrast, Norway attained its 2008 pre-crisis GDP peak in 2012, with Sweden also reaching its 2007 pre-crisis GDP peak in 2012. By 2016, Finland—the only Nordic country to adopt the euro—had not yet equalled its pre-crisis (2008) peak GDP value.

The Baltic fixed exchange-rate policies are yet another confirmation of the unworkability of internal devaluation as a crisis solution. The economic crisis in Greece brought mass protests to the streets as many citizens lacked the means to adequately support their families. The crisis in the Baltics did not result in massive or long-lived protests, unless mass migration from those countries can be viewed as protest (in the shape of 'voting with one's feet'). Many energetic and educated, primarily young, Baltic citizens lost hope and faith in the future of their countries and felt better off leaving countries that were moving away from prosperity, with continued or increased social injustice and economic inequality. Of course, outward migration from the Baltics could have been expected following the collapse of the Soviet Union, but government policies in the Baltics aggravated the problem.

The consequences of Nordic-Baltic interlinkages

Prior to the 2008/09 crisis, all three Baltic States experienced large current account deficits, massive external private-sector borrowing and then a sudden stop in capital inflows when the crisis hit. A sudden stop, in this context, means a sudden slowdown in external capital inflows into the Baltic economies, and a corresponding sharp reversal from large current account deficits into smaller deficits or small surpluses. The sudden stop in the case of the Baltics was mainly due to foreign banks (Scandinavian, mainly Swedish in ownership) that became risk-averse and sharply decreased their lending to those countries. Sudden stops are usually followed by a sharp contraction in

GDP, private spending and credit to the private sector, along with real exchange rate depreciation. In the case of the Baltics, exchange depreciation was not allowed and their governments implemented internal devaluation and fiscal austerity. Unfortunately, this policy formula is not a ticket to rapid economic recovery, nor does it lead to prosperity. The immediate result in the Baltic States was a sharp decline in GDP, accompanied by very high unemployment and a desperate social crisis characterized by more economic inequality than can be seen in most countries in the EEA, even compared with countries at a similar per capita income level.

Other challenges relate to the integration of the Baltic States into regional and global economic and political structures. EU membership, the determination of the Baltics to join the euro area, as well as interlinkages with the Scandinavian countries, especially financial sector interlinkages, have had profound effects on the Baltics. Economic integration can bring great benefits, including access to the common EU market, foreign investment and more stability. But integration comes at a cost. It can constrain the ability of the Baltics to respond in a way that is in their best long-term interests. This is especially true when regional integration into EU structures allows richer and larger nations to impose costs on smaller and less prosperous nations such as the Baltics during times of crisis. Mistakes in the financial sector resulting from the actions of irrational and irresponsible borrowers in the Baltics, as well as foreign bank lenders, are mostly imposed on borrowers in smaller and poorer countries, while lenders from larger, more prosperous countries are bailed out. In this sad scenario the EU becomes an agent of foreign banks and larger, richer countries.

The crisis in Sweden and Finland in the 1990s

The Baltics had little choice during the 2008/09 crisis other than to implement policies that suited the Swedish bank owners and were demanded by the EU as a condition for euro area admission. This meant fixed exchange rates and far-reaching austerity programmes. Sweden itself did not implement such policies during its financial crisis in 1992. Neither did Finland. In both countries the currencies depreciated and, ever since, Sweden's Riksbank—the longest-established central bank in the world—has kept its exchange rate floating with an inflation target. Automatic stabilizers were allowed to run their course in Sweden. Baltic-style austerity was not implemented. Indeed, such austerity would almost certainly have led to serious civil unrest in Sweden as well as in any other Nordic welfare state, giving rise in some quarters to accusations of the application of a double standard.

Tax and welfare systems and the consequences of austerity

While the Nordics tend to operate progressive tax systems that make their income distribution more even and allow their governments more room to address social problems, the Baltic States tend to have a flat, regressive tax system that results in the poor disproportionately bearing the burden during an economic slump compared to the rich[4]. During a crisis, when social programmes are cut, this is likely to result in damage to the social fabric and in permanent outbound migration that slows long-term growth and income convergence with richer EU countries. Less damage occurs in countries such as the Nordics so long as automatic stabilizers are allowed to run their course, as indeed occurred during the crisis in the 1990s.

The Baltic States already face a lost decade in terms of economic growth. Unemployment remains rather high in spite of outbound migration. The effects of lost human capital, due to erosion of skills and migration, can be long-lasting. Austerity policies and continued social inequality contributed to massive outward migration during the crisis and prevented circular migration flows in the aftermath. The massive exit of a better-skilled younger generation is especially worrisome. It could take decades to recover from this loss. Indeed, it may be more realistic to speak of a lost quarter of a century, rather than the lost decade already described.

Some of the challenges and failures that the Baltics are currently facing relate to domestic policies, including an extreme free-market orthodoxy that is unusual within the EU, let alone within the Nordic countries. Cohesion and solidarity are lacking domestically; corruption remains a problem; and tensions with the Russian minorities, especially in Latvia and Estonia, only make matters worse. Besides, those tensions increase political risk and insecurity in the Baltic States.

External challenges including further economic integration

In the Baltic States, economic prosperity as well as social and political stability remain uncertain. They have security concerns and are constantly fighting for survival. Tensions with Russia threaten Baltic sovereignty and keep them under steady pressure; an unpredictable USA weakens NATO; the euro area crisis along with austerity, economic stagnation and social inequality undermine domestic cohesion in the Baltics. It also remains to be seen how Brexit and the possible disintegration of the UK will affect the Nordic-Baltic region.

In the midst of this, the Nordic model has been successful, whereas wealth and income inequality in the Baltics is unsustainable. The Nordic countries face challenges in keeping up the quality of their welfare systems while maintaining control over their cost, but compared to other European countries they are clear leaders in terms of GDP per capita, income distribution, social services and democracy.

The geographical area occupied by the present-day Baltic States has had a turbulent past. Throughout the centuries the region has been overrun by larger, powerful countries from all directions, including German and Soviet invasions during the Second World War, followed by Soviet occupation until 1991. An unstable Russia is a security concern and tensions with Russian minorities, especially in Latvia and Estonia, make the political situation complex and possibly explosive. The eastern borders that Estonia and Latvia have with Russia, as well as Lithuania's western border with Kaliningrad Oblast, remain a significant concern. The recent Russian invasion in Ukraine and the uncertainty of US commitment to NATO, along with the drastic scaling-down of the US military presence in Europe since the fall of the Soviet Union, have not improved the security profile of the Baltics or indeed other European countries looking to the USA to serve as guarantor of peace in the region.

While the process of European integration continues, it is the opinion of this author that that process must become safer, with the risks and rewards of integration and interlinkages being shared more fairly. Following the collapse of the Soviet Union, the transition from planned to market economy was necessary, but economic and social inequality within the Baltic States remains a threat to the growth and well-being of those countries. This should be a concern, not only for the Baltics, but also for Europe—most notably, the EU and euro area member states and the Nordic countries. EU integration was meant to result in convergence, not divergence, and prosperity, not despair.

Weighing the successes and failures of the Baltic States, arguably the Baltics have succeeded in becoming modern states, especially compared to other former Soviet republics. They are now well integrated into European and global structures, which in turn can bring stability and security. Although they have often benefited from this co-operation, there are also side-effects from Baltic integration, discussed in this book, to be dealt with in the future.

After the pre-crisis economic boom, post-crisis growth is rather slow for emerging economies that are still in transition. Unemployment remains high and income inequality is among the highest within the EEA. Emigration from the Baltic States remains worrisome and has reached levels that threaten not only reproduction of their populations but also the sustainability of their weak social security systems, not to mention further economic development[5]. This is not what one expected from the pre-crisis 'Baltic tigers'. While integration with European institutional structures can bring benefits such as stability and security, it can also be an obstacle, with the Baltics needing to adjust to supranational structures and yield to the interests of other, more powerful countries in Europe. The benefits of European integration have come at a very high cost for the Baltics, especially in human terms, which is bound to diminish their long-term growth prospects—economically as well as in terms of increased social injustice, which can certainly result in political instability. Security is also a concern, with a weak EU and euro area, and with NATO lacking a certain commitment of support from the USA.

It is notable that entering the EU was initially to be a ticket for growth and benefits for potential member countries. Now that the benefits are no longer clear, the EU has used what amounts to threats, in order to keep the group together. This has been seen most clearly during early dialogue between EU and UK leaders over Brexit. The message is evident: If you attempt to leave the EU, the consequences will be dire.

Countries such as the Baltics, faced by numerous external threats related to shared borders with Russia, an unpredictable USA, and a euro area crisis, can hardly afford serious divisions and strife within their own borders. While these countries have limited effects on external challenges, they can strengthen themselves internally and become more inclusive societies, as their Nordic partners have done.

While cross-border financial sector co-operation can be beneficial in the Nordic-Baltic region, excessive interlinkage across the Nordic region and into the Baltic region is dangerous for both groups of countries. The fact that Sweden, the dominant owner of the Baltic banks, does not participate in EU banking union, and the adoption of the euro by all three Baltic States poses serious challenges for the region, not least the issue of bank supervision. More diverse ownership of the Baltic banking sector could help reduce the risk of a future recurrence of catastrophic events such as those that unfolded during the 2008/09 crisis.

12.1 Successes, failures and challenges for the Baltic States

Successes

Are now modern states and probably more advanced than any other former Soviet republics.

Have managed to become EU and subsequently euro area member states with access to the EU common market, a common currency and perhaps more economic stability.

Are now NATO member states which, with EU and euro area membership, provides more security.

Are well integrated regionally and globally via membership of institutions such as the European Investment Bank, the European Bank for Reconstruction and Development (EBRD), the World Bank and the IMF. Estonia and Latvia are now members of the Organisation for Economic Co-operation and Development.

Failures

Implemented fixed exchange-rate policies and severe fiscal austerity programmes during and after the 2008/09 crisis, resulting in low economic growth and high unemployment.

EU and euro area membership became a straitjacket for the Baltics, leaving few economic options to respond to the 2008/09 crisis consistent with the long-term interest of their citizens.

Have since independence implemented free market policies with weak welfare systems and high levels of economic and social inequality.

Have suffered massive, apparently mainly permanent, migration of their citizens to richer neighbouring countries.

Have not been able to manage risks related to financial interlinkages with other countries, including banking interlinkages with Sweden.

Economic and social convergence with richer EU countries is slow and fragile, with no clear path for catching up economically and socially.

Corruption remains a problem.

Challenges

Become more inclusive societies; reduce income and wealth inequality.

Strengthen welfare systems during a period of population ageing, aggravated by the outbound migration of a large share of their younger and most skilled citizens.

Introduce more progressive tax policies and higher property taxes.

Continue fighting corruption.

Increase competitiveness with increased contributions to investment in education and infrastructure.

Reduce banking interlinkages with the continental Nordics.

Strengthen capacity in dealing with international organizations and take advantage of Nordic co-operation when possible and beneficial.

Take an active part in reforming the euro area to become more accommodating for transition countries striving for economic and social conversion within Europe. This includes the European Central Bank (ECB) broadening its focus from a narrow inflation target to giving higher priority to reducing unemployment, boosting economic growth and promoting financial stability.

Strengthen development co-operation with less advanced transition countries in Europe and Central Asia.

Strengthen security with increased cohesion within borders during times of external challenges, including instability in Russia, uncertain US military support and diminished presence in Europe, and euro area crisis.

Lessons learned

Some important policy lessons can be learned from the 2008/09 economic and financial crisis in the Baltic States about EU membership, euro adoption, interlinkages with the continental Nordic countries (especially financial sector interlinkages), free market policies, as well as consequences of fiscal discipline and austerity programmes.

• *Need for more balanced and sustainable economic growth—not asset bubbles driven by cross-border capital inflows. Need to strengthen the tradable sector.* Pre-crisis GDP growth in the Baltic States was primarily driven by capital inflows, mainly from the continental Nordics (especially Sweden), fuelling domestic demand and creating a series of vulnerabilities, inflating the non-tradable sector, and ultimately becoming unsustainable. Under those circumstances, the Baltic States did not retain sufficient focus on exports. This growth pattern created a series of vulnerabilities including: (i) high current account deficits and rising private-sector debt, (ii) significant real exchange-rate appreciation[6]—as the profitability of the non-tradable sector surged, exports became less competitive and less attractive, (iii) continued growth became dependent on the continuation of strong cross-border capital inflows from the continental Nordics.

During the crisis, a slowdown of foreign credit inflows from the continental Nordics was enough to disrupt demand in the non-tradable sector, which had become the main engine of growth in the Baltics. Cross-country differences clearly show the benefits of seeking more balanced growth. In contrast to most, a few central European countries, including the Czech Republic, Poland and Slovakia, preserved a balanced and trade-oriented growth pattern, which provided a cushion during the crisis (Bakker and Gulde-Wolf 2012, p. 279). In the future, the Baltics need to consider policy frameworks to avoid renewed bubbles. They, along with emerging Europe, need to strive for growth that relies more on the tradable sector.

Additionally, as Bakker and Gulde-Wolf (2012) state in their discussion on emerging Europe:

> The credit booms revealed the need for better supervisory policies and more effective coordination of home and host supervisors. In the future, more effective supervisory intervention will be needed so that risks associated with credit growth and sectoral loan concentration can be addressed by higher capital and liquidity ratios. Cooperation of home authorities that supervise cross-border banking groups is essential to give such measures teeth. Reducing lending in foreign currency to unhedged households will also be an important measure to safeguard financial stability and avoid real estate bubbles.
>
> (Bakker and Gulde-Wolf 2012, p. 280)

During the crisis, foreign-currency lending from the continental Nordics became a serious problem for the Baltics, which have now adopted the euro. Thus, currency risk has now been eliminated as long as loans are made in euro. But as for supervision, it is important to emphasize the role of local policymakers and the responsibility of foreign banks and their home countries, as well as international organizations. Sweden, which remains the main owner of Baltic banks, does not participate in EU banking union: a situation that can create complications for the co-ordination and supervision of banks in the Baltics.

Measures to ensure more balanced and sustainable economic growth should also include structural reforms, for example in education, including vocational training and measures that bolster investment and the business climate. Fighting corruption is also important. According to the World Bank *Doing Business* report (World Bank 2017), the Baltics perform well but their human capital base deteriorated during the crisis, with austerity programmes cutting funding for both education and health programmes. A large share of their most highly skilled young citizens appears to have left permanently (Atoyan et al. 2016). Attracting foreign investment is important, especially projects that benefit the trade-oriented sector. Such investment would support growth and technology transfer and help contribute to improving labour-force skills in the Baltics. As Bakker and Gulde-Wolf (2012) point out, 'In the Czech and Slovak republics, growth during the boom was much more balanced, credit growth more restrained, and current account deficits small—and exports have been playing an important role' (Bakker and Gulde-Wolf 2012, p. 281).

- *Take measures to limit credit growth*. Rapid credit growth can result not only in unbalanced economic growth but also in future problem loans that complicate economic recovery during downturns. Building safeguards against excessive credit growth requires combining macro-economic and supervisory measures. Effective co-ordination of home and host supervisors is essential if cross-border banking groups are important, as in the case of the Baltic States and the Nordic countries[7]. The fact that the continental Nordic bank owners, except Finland, are outside the euro area, whereas Finland and the Baltic States are all euro area member states, only makes co-ordination and supervision more complicated. Furthermore, during periods of rapid credit growth, credit quality is likely to suffer. Countries with the highest credit growth experience the largest increase in non-performing loans. According to Bakker and Gulde-Wolf (2012) and the European Bank for Reconstruction and Development (2009), the size of the pre-crisis credit boom better explains the depth of recession than any other variable. Countries with very rapid credit growth experienced a much deeper recession than countries where credit growth remained more moderate.

Financial systems dominated by foreign-owned banks are not very responsive to domestic liquidity conditions, as funding can be provided by the foreign parent from abroad. The continental Nordic banks provided loans to the Baltics as if the risk there was comparable with that in the Nordics. They behaved irresponsibly and irrationally but when hit were able to impose the costs of their behaviour on a Baltic public facing austerity as a consequence. Austerity was supported by the domestic Baltic authorities. Better co-operation between home and host supervisors could bring greater success in controlling credit growth through prudential measures. But co-ordination between the continental Nordics which, except for Finland, are outside the euro area and do not participate in the banking union, can prove complex in the future.

Pre-crisis government debt was low in the Baltics, much lower than in the Nordics, but increased substantially during the crisis in spite of austerity to fund rescue efforts for foreign banks. Government debt as a percentage of GDP in Estonia is currently very low but in Latvia and Lithuania is similar to government debt in Denmark, Norway and Sweden. All the Nordics and the Baltics have much lower government debt than the average in either the euro area or the EU (see Tables 2.5 and 2.7).

Pre-crisis private-sector debt grew dramatically in all three Baltics, but began to decrease in all countries in 2010 or 2011. Pre-crisis private debt also grew in the Nordics, but started to decrease in Sweden and Denmark in 2010, though remaining stable in Finland. The Nordics have much higher private-sector debt than the Baltics, which continues to be a concern especially because of continental Nordic-Baltic banking interlinkages (see Tables 2.6 and 2.8).

• *The fixed exchange-rate policy implemented in the Baltics has not served them well: the Nordics, except Finland, keep their own currency.* Recent empirical evidence from emerging Europe shows that in countries with fixed exchange rates, credit booms are hardest to stop because, as the economy heats up and inflation rises, real interest rates decline, further fuelling demand. It is striking that the strongest credit growth during the boom years took place in countries with fixed exchange-rate regimes, including the Baltic States, but also Bulgaria, Montenegro, and Ukraine, which all experienced annual credit growth of at least 10% of GDP (see Figure 25.2 in Bakker and Gulde-Wolf 2012, p. 282). Pre-crisis real interest rates became highly negative in the Baltics, further encouraging borrowing in the real estate sector. Baltic people, especially the élites, were to a large extent borrowing in foreign currencies and were in fact paid to borrow for housing via negative real interest rates—and did so aggressively. For them, this was rational behaviour, as long as the exchange rate remained fixed. The negative real interest rate was like a subsidy for those receiving loans.

Recent empirical evidence also shows that emerging countries in Europe with flexible exchange rates can dampen booms by letting the nominal exchange rate appreciate. Such an appreciation helps prevent overheating of the economy and lowers inflation by reducing import prices, which keep real interest rates higher. Many of the countries that avoided a credit boom, including the Czech Republic, Poland and Slovakia, operated flexible exchange-rate regimes and saw a substantial appreciation of their nominal exchange rates during the boom years (Bakker and Gulde-Wolf 2012, p. 282). As we have discussed, it is also notable that Sweden, with strong financial-sector interest in the Baltics, including Latvia, demanded a fixed exchange rate in Latvia during the 2008/09 crisis, whereas during its own banking crisis in 1992 Sweden had abandoned its fixed exchange rate policy, also sharply devaluing its own currency, and has kept a floating exchange rate ever since.

The Baltics are already euro area member states, so that abandoning the euro would not be a simple task, nor does this book recommend it. However, the euro area remains in crisis and its architecture is flawed. It is also important to keep in mind that entering the euro area was not only an economic question for the Baltic States. Security presumably played a prominent role in the final decision. Nevertheless, regarding the Nordic-Baltic region, empirical evidence shows that countries with their own currency and a more flexible exchange rate regime, such as Iceland, Norway and Sweden, have been more successful recently in terms of GDP growth and low unemployment than the Baltic States. Signs of pre-crisis convergence—for example from 2005 to 2007, when the Baltic 'tiger' economies were growing at around 10% a year—are not clear, with rather slow growth post-crisis. If GDP growth in the Baltics was close to 10% annually, their economies would more than double in size every 10 years, but at the current growth rate they can barely keep up with the richer Nordic countries.

- *Take measures to discourage lending in foreign currencies.* The pre-crisis surge in foreign currency borrowing in the Baltic States created credit risks for banks that were mostly in foreign ownership. Due to external pressures, macroeconomic policy options during the crisis in the Baltics were limited to austerity, while devaluation was off the table. A devaluation of the currencies of the Baltic States would have adversely affected the portfolio of the continental Nordic banks. This would not only be a concern in their home countries but also for other EU member states, not to mention the wider euro area. During the boom years, when fixed exchange rates were in place, the risks associated with foreign-currency lending appear not to have been taken seriously. The continental Nordics and the EU were able to save the banks with fixed exchange rates and austerity programmes, but Sweden—the main bank owner in the Baltics—enjoys a flexible exchange rate with inflation targets. Poland was much more careful to discourage lending in foreign currencies, as discussed earlier in this book (see for example, Allington and McCombie 2016). Countries with local currencies can learn from the Baltic experience, but the Baltics—now euro area countries—no longer face this risk unless they borrow in currencies other than the euro.
- *Fiscal austerity during the 2008/09 crisis and the post-crisis period was damaging for long-term growth and has contributed to massive and largely permanent outbound migration of skilled young people from the Baltic States*

The pre-crisis rate of public expenditure growth in the Baltic States was reasonably prudent, with fiscal balances at surplus or close to balance. However, with booming GDP, fiscal surpluses are needed. This is among the key lessons which were learned from the 2008/09 crisis. The Baltic States have followed orthodox capitalism since independence was re-established in 1991, with flat-rate taxes and weak welfare systems. Income distribution is highly uneven, compared not only to the Nordic countries but also to emerging European countries at a similar income level, such as the Czech Republic, Slovakia and Slovenia. This needs to change: on the expenditure side the Baltics should give priority to human capital development, especially education, training and research. This can help the Baltics to improve their productivity and make them more able to compete with richer EU and euro-area member states as well as advanced high-income countries in other regions. Likewise, improved health services are urgently needed.

On the income side, the tax system should be more progressive and tax on capital and land should be increased. The flat income-tax system has not served the Baltics well and only increases income inequality. The austerity implemented in the Baltics during and after the crisis had a damaging effect on human capital and contributed to a massive exit of Baltic citizens to other countries. The external assistance which the Baltics received during the 2008/09 crisis appears to have been a bailout for foreign banks, but not to alleviate the severe human and demographic crisis that followed.

Estonia never ran a fiscal deficit above the Maastricht criteria (not exceeding 3% of GDP) during the crisis, but Latvia did from 2008 to 2011 and Lithuania from 2008 to 2012. The only continental Nordic countries where fiscal deficits exceeded the Maastricht criteria were Denmark in 2012 (-3.5%) and Finland in 2014 (-3.2%). Iceland, however, which was hit very hard, ran large deficits from 2008 to 2012 due to the use of automatic stabilizers as well as fiscal stimulus (see Table 2.4).

Challenges

Some of the imbalances that characterized much of emerging Europe, including the Baltics, prior to the 2008/09 crisis have unwound. However, other pre-crisis vulnerabilities remain, while new vulnerabilities have emerged, some as a result of the crisis.

The challenges for small countries, and the possible conflicts of interest in their dealings with international organizations and larger, more powerful states, have become more visible and need to be addressed. Partnerships with other countries and international organizations are important, but the costs and benefits must be assessed when important actions are taken under external pressure. The Baltics should take action that is in the interest of their own people. The democracies in the Baltic States are still maturing and Baltic citizens tend to be passive and emigrate rather than protest against unwelcome policies, poor governance and incidences of corruption.

It makes perfect sense for the Nordics and the Baltics to co-operate within Europe when possible, as their peoples are in many ways like-minded, but their different approaches to European integration and different levels of integration and development may mean that common pathways could be hard to find. There can even be conflicts of interest, as discussed, for example when what could have been well-intended cross-border financial sector engagement turned into a nightmare for both groups—the Baltic States and the continental Nordic countries.

The fall of the Berlin Wall in 1989 may have been seen as a victory for capitalism and proof that markets can work well and efficiently in many countries, including the Baltic States. Under those circumstances, countries formerly under communist rule might be tempted to move to extremes with orthodox neoliberalism. But we now know that markets can be unstable and that free market policies have not served the Baltic States well. The Baltics have not, for example, invested sufficiently in human capital and still suffer from corruption.

Communism failed when the Berlin Wall fell, but free market policies have done long-term damage to the social fabric of the Baltics which will have long-term effects on their economic performance. The demographic challenge they face is daunting after the outbound migration of young, skilled citizens.

The Baltic States can learn from the Nordic model, which has produced favourable economic and social outcomes in mature and inclusive societies. This was not always so, and there were many bumps on the road for the Nordics, but those countries are seen by many as leading globally in economic performance and social justice. This is not to say that the Baltics should become like the Nordics in every respect. But looking at the Nordic experience to see what lessons may be learned and applied in the Baltics makes sense.

On the economic front, the Baltic States have returned to GDP growth and unemployment has declined. Nevertheless, GDP growth is rather low for emerging economies that have the ambition to converge with the richer EU member states. The Baltics have barely recovered pre-crisis GDP levels, if one corrects GDP for inflation. Unemployment remains higher than before the crisis, in spite of massive migration. Youth unemployment remains a serious concern.

Current account deficits in the Baltic States have come down and inflation has receded. Private sector consolidated debt as a percentage of GDP has declined in all countries and is lower than in Nordic countries such as Denmark and Sweden. Whereas a large percentage of loans taken out of the (mostly foreign-owned) banks in the Baltics in the run-up to the economic crisis were in foreign currencies, the Baltics maintained fixed exchange rates throughout the pre-crisis period and adopted the euro after the crisis. Public finances are significantly weaker than in the pre-crisis period (2005 to 2007). This crisis made clear that policymakers need to reconsider how best to achieve lasting convergence. Quick convergence may not always be the best approach. A comprehensive approach is called for, in which policies in a broad range of areas may need to be adjusted to achieve the desired goals. Key components of a policy agenda for resilient convergence include:

- *Policies to contain domestic consumption, strengthen domestic saving, scale up government revenues and invest in human capital.* These would include tax policy, pension plans, and fiscal savings when possible. Supporting measures include developing domestic debt markets, encouraging private savings and fostering the emergence of institutional investors for the efficient allocation of savings[8]. The Baltics could introduce progressive income tax[9] and higher property taxes, which could help scale up government revenues needed for investment in human capital and action to make the Baltics more inclusive societies with more even income distribution. In this regard they could learn from the Nordics. Countries facing external uncertainty can take measures to strengthen cohesion within their borders.

- *Policies to discourage foreign debt in favour of foreign investment.* Relevant measures include all structural efforts to increase the attractiveness of the Baltics for investment. The Baltics have a relatively good business and investment climate, according to the World Bank *Doing Business* reports (World Bank 2017), but they need to take action that encourages the younger and better-educated Baltic population to remain within their own countries and those who have left to return. Without access to a competitive and more productive labour force, foreign investors will be discouraged from investing in the Baltics. There is nothing wrong with young Baltic citizens seeking cross-border experience as long as the flow of people is circular rather than a one-way exit with few returning. At present the migration seems permanent (Atoyan et al. 2016).
- *Action to reduce dependence on foreign banks and avoid excessive cross-border banking interlinkages.* When the 2008/09 crisis hit, most domestic borrowing had been from foreign-owned banks and in foreign currencies. This made the Baltics vulnerable and limited their policy options, given outside pressure from foreign bank owners and their home governments—which are also larger states—as well as the EU in its efforts to protect the euro area. Rescue packages for weaker countries often involve bailing out Western banks from stronger and richer countries: arguably, the Greek bailouts are primarily for the benefit of German and French banks. In the Baltics the aim of the rescue packages was to bail out continental Nordic—mainly Swedish—banks. The Baltics have now adopted the euro and in the future will not face the same risks related to exchange mismatches as they did during the 2008/09 crisis, unless loans are taken in currencies other than the euro. Over time the Baltics should be able to develop their own banking system and increase the share of domestic banks in their financial sector. This is not to say that foreign banks should not operate in the Baltics. Measures supported by regulatory and prudential steps should be taken to discourage excessive foreign borrowing by banks, including from parent banks. The fact that Sweden is not participating in the EU banking union remains a concern.
- *Measures to support broader-based, more shared growth and inclusive societies.* Pre-crisis, the Baltics focused on high GDP growth and were labelled 'Baltic tigers'. But it is not enough to focus on GDP, GDP growth or GDP per capita. Growth needs to be more widely shared. The Baltics have about the most unequal income distribution in the EU. In more mature democracies, the 2008/09 austerity programmes would have resulted in political instability, but in the Baltics this has resulted in massive outbound migration, undermining the future of those countries as viable states. In most other EU countries, such drastic austerity

measures would have sparked labour unrest and social disorder. Increasing the flexibility of the workforce through appropriate schooling will increase the resilience of economies and allow for a smoother shift from the once-booming property and financial sectors to other activities. Similarly, steps to prevent unbalanced growth concentrated in a few sectors—including, for example, through strict adherence to sectoral exposure limits in lending—will help avoid the re-emergence of bubbles in narrow parts of the economy, especially in housing. An open and competitive environment fostered by deregulation of product and service markets will support the overall economic environment and allow the efficient reallocation of resources in response to changing economic opportunities (Bakker and Gulde-Wolf 2012). Measures should be taken to invest in human capital, including strengthening the education and healthcare systems. Measures to fight remaining poverty and reduce income inequality are urgent. Progressive tax as well as higher taxes on capital and land could help fairer, more sustainable burden-sharing in the Baltic States.

- The Baltic States must be more independent and firmer in their dealings with international organizations, especially the EU and larger countries, to protect their own interests. It has been argued in this book that the crisis response in the Baltic States was not in the best long-term interests of the Baltic States and their peoples. The EU defended its own interests in its efforts to avoid domino effects in its banking sector, while the continental Nordics (primarily Sweden) protected their own banks from possible collapse. International organizations defend their own interests and cannot be regarded as neutral during a crisis, while larger, richer and more powerful states can be expected first and foremost to defend their own interests during times of crisis. While the Baltic States should build healthy partnerships with other countries, including their Nordic neighbours, they should be more firm in defending the interests of their own people during a crisis and better consider the long-term effects of their actions. This is especially important when a clear conflict of interest exists as between the Baltics vis-à-vis international organizations and larger, more powerful states. At the same time, the Baltics should build coalitions with other states internationally, including the Nordic countries, when it serves their interests and is mutually beneficial for the Nordic-Baltic group as a whole. The Baltics should also be more willing to support other weaker countries in their transition via their bilateral development co-operation programmes (Hilmarsson 2011). This would typically apply to less advanced transition countries such as Belarus, Georgia, Moldova and Ukraine. While their contributions are small in a global context, even a modest engagement will strengthen their bargaining position vis-à-vis international organizations. Civil contributions should be preferred to military engagement.

- *More independence in security, improved relations with Russia and strong Nordic-Baltic co-operation.* While the EU and euro area membership as well as NATO are key to Baltic security, overreliance on those institutions should be avoided. After the collapse of the Soviet Union, the USA dramatically scaled down its military presence in Europe—indeed, US commitment to NATO is now being questioned by none other than the incumbent US President, Donald Trump. The Baltics must strengthen their own defence forces, but also do what is possible to build a healthier, more stable relationship with Russia. The Baltics can to some extent serve as a diplomatic bridge between Russia and the traditional Western countries. This is critical, given that all the Baltic States have borders with Russia and have large numbers of Russians residing in their country, especially in Latvia and Estonia. Nordic-Baltic co-operation remains of the utmost importance for the Baltics, as it has been throughout their transition to democracy and a market economy. During times of tense relations with Russia, uncertainty in the USA and crisis in the euro area, the Baltics should do all they can to become more socially just and more inclusive societies. This is necessary but will be challenging, especially as they are also called upon to increase their military contributions to NATO. Increased social justice within Baltic borders is likely to improve their security profile.

Challenges related to EU membership: a dysfunctional euro area?

Certain challenges within the EU and euro area will affect the Baltics, including the Stability and Growth Pact, a common currency without a fiscal union and banking union, actions of the ECB and its narrow policy target. Those issues and future challenges will be discussed below:

- *Flaws in the Stability and Growth Pact (SGP).* According to the SGP (European Commission 2017)[10], euro area member states should aim for a balanced fiscal budget[11]. It is not clear why the budget should be in balance as it would hardly be imprudent for countries to run a small budget deficit as long as they are enjoying sustained long-term GDP growth. If countries run a fiscal deficit this should, according to the 1992 Maastricht Treaty (which details the euro area convergence criteria), amount to no more than 3% of GDP and total debt to not more than 60% of GDP. The rationale behind this criterion is rather unclear, but it is notable that a 60% debt-to-GDP ratio was close to that of Germany in 1992. It is questionable if this is suitable for emerging countries like the Baltic States, especially during the early years of transition, that, for example, need to invest in human capital and infrastructure to become competitive. It is also questionable whether this maximum allowable budget deficit would always enable a country to let its automatic fiscal stabilizers come into play during a recession. This could be crucial in a monetary union such as the EU's economic and monetary union[12], because member states have already given up their right to pursue an independent monetary policy and they cannot use interest rates or the exchange rate as an instrument of economic policy. When France and Germany were in breach of the SGP excessive deficit criteria, they did not pay fines. This shows that large states within the euro area are in a strong position to manipulate the system when it suits them to do so. The consequences of the financial crisis have made the limitation of the SGP even clearer and translate into straitjacketing for emerging countries such as the Baltics. The combination of strict fiscal discipline and a fixed exchange rate has not proved so far to be a formula for economic growth in the euro area. In the post-crisis period, it is more like a formula for stagnation with low growth and high long-term unemployment, especially among the young.

- *A common currency without a fiscal union and banking union.* Without a banking union, including deposit insurance, money within the euro area will flow from poorer countries to richer countries, for example, from Spanish banks to German banks. The fact that national governments stand behind banks makes them vulnerable in poorer countries. We have seen this, for example, in Greece, Italy, Portugal, and Spain. If money flows from those poorer countries to richer European countries, this means that less capital will be available to lend to businesses and individuals in those disadvantaged countries. In turn, this creates a vicious circle that is hard to break, resulting in lower GDP growth and higher unemployment.

A fiscal union would need to ensure that money flows into depressed areas. This works in the USA with its federal government system, though it is not likely to work equally well in the EU, with different countries, each with their own independent fiscal policies. Moreover, transferring funds from one country to another in Europe would often be difficult to justify politically. Germany, the main economic engine within the euro area, is against fiscal stimulus and continues to be very concerned about inflation. The EU is not seen as a transfer union. There is little trust and high concern about the risks associated with moral hazard. European bonds have been suggested as government bonds issued in euros jointly by the 19 euro area countries. European bonds are debt investments whereby an investor loans a certain amount of money, for a certain amount of time, at a certain interest rate, to the euro area as a whole, which then forwards the money to individual governments. European bonds have been suggested as a way to tackle the European sovereign debt crisis as indebted states could borrow new funds on better conditions since they are supported by the rating of non-crisis states. Because European bonds would allow already highly-indebted states access to cheaper credit, thanks to the strength of other euro area economies, they are controversial, and may suffer from the free-rider problem. Tax harmonization is also an issue to consider within the EU and emergency assistance to crisis countries has sometimes been considered illegitimate given the low levels of taxation in some countries for companies or wealthy individuals (Bénassy-Quéré et al. 2014). This concern would certainly apply to the Baltic States.

- *The European Central Bank and the narrow policy target.* The ECB has an inflation target, whereas the US Federal Reserve has an inflation target but also targets unemployment, growth and financial stability. The ECB's narrow target limits its mandate. The EU and the euro area have been suffering from high unemployment and low growth for a decade. Unemployment is especially high among the young. Some economists speak of a lost decade for Europe, but the loss is much greater than that, given the damage to the social fabric so far. There is an urgent need for the euro area member states to reconsider this narrow policy and it is notable that the USA, which is often assumed to be more market-oriented than Europe, in this case has a broader and more humane policy than the euro area countries have chosen. Instead of convergence within the euro area, diversions are the outcome. The euro has created a condition for a crisis, not growth and prosperity.

Notes

1 See further; www.efta.int/eea/eea-agreement.
2 See endnote discussion in Preface.
3 See also Hilmarsson 2011.
4 At the time of writing in early 2018 Latvia was taking steps toward a progressive personal income tax.
5 For comprehensive discussion about migration from the Baltic States, see Mihails Hazans (2016) http://link.springer.com/chapter/10.1007%2F978-3-662-45320-9_13.
6 The IMF, for example, recommended a 15% devaluation in Latvia when the crisis struck.
7 See also Bakker and Gulde-Wolf 2012.
8 See also Bakker and Gulde-Wolf 2012.
9 As Stiglitz (2013, p. xxxiii) has pointed out, countries with less progressive taxation have more inequality. At the time of writing in early 2018, Latvia is taking steps towards a progressive income tax.
10 For more detail see http://europa.eu/rapid/press-release_MEMO-15-3221_en.htm.
11 It is understandable that individuals need to balance their budget over a lifetime as their life naturally comes to an end at some point. Nations, however, can go on forever running a deficit as long as their economy continues to grow over the long run.
12 See further: https://ec.europa.eu/info/business-economy-euro/economic-and-fiscal-policy-coordination/economic-and-monetary-union_en.

References

Allington, N. F., and McCombie, J. S. (2016). 'An Eastern European Perspective on the Recent Financial Crisis and an Examination of Poland's Exceptionalism.' In

P. Arestis and M. Sawyer (eds) *Emerging Economies During and After the Great Recession*, Houndmills, Basingstoke: Palgrave Macmillan, pp. 195–231.

Atoyan, R., Christiansen, L., Dizioli, A., Ebeke, C., Ilahi, N., Ilyina, A., Mehrez, G., Qu, H., Raei, F., Rhee, A. and Zakharova, D. (2016). *Emigration and Its Economic Impact on Eastern Europe*. IMF Staff Discussion Note, July 2016. SDN/*16/07*. Available at: www.imf.org/external/pubs/ft/sdn/2016/sdn1607.pdf (Accessed on 24 December 2017).

Bakker, B. B. and Gulde-Wolf, A. M. (2012). 'Lessons and Renewed Challenges'. In B. B. Bakker and C. A. Klingen, *How Emerging Europe Came Through the 2008/09 Crisis: An Account by the Staff of the IMF's European Department*. Washington, DC: International Monetary Fund. Available at: www.imf.org/en/Publications/Books/Issues/2016/12/31/How-Emerging-Europe-Came-Through-the-2008-09-Crisis-An-Account-by-the-Staff-of-the-IMF-s-25765 (Accessed on 12 December 2017).

Bénassy-Quéré, A., Trannoy, A. and Wolff, G. (2014). *Tax Harmonisation in Europe: Moving Forward*. Available at: http://bruegel.org/wp-content/uploads/imported/publications/cae-note014-en.pdf (Accessed on 15 November 2017).

European Bank for Reconstruction and Development (2009). *Transition Report 2009: Transition in Crisis?* London. Available at: www.ebrd.com/downloads/research/transition/TR09.pdf (Accessed on 12 September 2017).

European Commission (2017). *Fact Sheet—Commission issues guidance to encourage structural reforms and investment*. Available at: http://europa.eu/rapid/press-release_MEMO-15-3221_en.htm (Accessed on 12 January 2017).

Eurostat (2017). *Database*. Available at: http://ec.europa.eu/eurostat/data/database.

Hazans, M. (2016). 'Migration Experience of the Baltic Countries in the Context of Economic Crisis', in M. Kahanec and K. F. Zimmermann (eds), *Labor Migration, EU Enlargement, and the Great Recession*. Berlin—Heidelberg: Springer, p. 297–344.

Hilmarsson, H. (2011). 'How can the Baltic States as Non-DAC donors best contribute to international development cooperation?' *Baltic Journal of Economics*, Vol. 11 (2), pp. 27–40.

International Monetary Fund (2017). *World Economic Outlook Database*. Available at: www.imf.org/external/pubs/ft/weo/2017/02/weodata/index.aspx.

Stiglitz, J. E. (2013). The Price of Inequality—How Today's Divided Society Endangers Our Future. New York and London: W. W. Norton & Company.

World Bank (2017). *Doing Business 2018. Reforming to Create Jobs*. Available at: www.doingbusiness.org/reports/global-reports/doing-business-2018 (Accessed on 7 December 2017).

13 The Nordic countries and the Baltic States—the need for further research

This book has attempted to answer the questions stated in the introductory chapter and restated in the concluding chapter. Answering those questions also raises other questions that call for further research. Among those issues and questions are the following:

Why did the Baltics adopt neoliberal policies post-independence, and what policy mix could help make them more inclusive?

Firstly, as the book has discussed, the Baltic States turned to neoliberal economic, welfare and tax policies after regaining independence from the Soviet Union, in turn contributing to uneven income and wealth distribution by European Union (EU) standards. Further research is needed to fully understand why the Baltics chose this path rather than considering gradual steps towards the Nordic model that includes more Keynesian fiscal policies, progressive tax systems on income as well as higher tax on property and wealth, and relatively strong safety nets to assist the most vulnerable members of society and create more inclusive societies. The Baltics adopted neoliberal policies in spite of the fact that they received development assistance from the continental Nordic countries immediately after reclaiming their independence from the Soviet Union, including policy advice and ongoing technical assistance. Furthermore, EU member states, whose 'club' the Baltics were determined to join, have a greater tendency than some other major economies (most notably the USA) to provide social support for their citizens. In fact, as this book has noted, Baltic economic and welfare policies as well as their tax systems appear to be more Anglo-Saxon in origin than Nordic or European. How is this likely to develop in the upcoming years or decades? Future research is also needed to better understand if and how the presence of a Russian-speaking minority may affect decisions in the Baltics regarding economic and welfare policies. The Baltics remain divided societies internally, which makes public policy decisions more complicated. The Nordic societies have more homogeneous populations, which makes social cohesion easier. To what extent have a lack of trust in politicians, weak public institutions and corruption affected the policy stance on redistribution in the Baltics? It takes years at best, or decades, to develop the institutions that handle welfare and tax issues comparable to those in the Nordics or some of the richer EU member states, so the process in the Baltics would need to be gradual—all the more necessary as the per capita income in the Baltics remains below the EU average. The failure of the Soviet Union to provide collective benefits may have contributed to limited interest in provision of government services in the Baltics. A free market stance was chosen, as a result of which the Baltics moved from one extreme to another, instead of choosing a third way, embracing capitalism and free markets as the Nordics have done while also taking measures to promote social justice and inclusive societies. Free market policies, including privatization, were favoured by the Baltic élite, as these provided avenues to capture public assets and public income in the vacuum created by the fall of the Soviet Union. Further research is needed to identify a policy mix favourable to more sustainable, more inclusive development in the Baltics.

How can the Baltics promote business development and better share the benefits?

In the post-independence period the Baltics appear to have made efforts to create a low-tax business-friendly environment that could encourage foreign direct investment (FDI), which in turn could become a key source of economic growth and prosperity in the region and facilitate technical transformation. In Estonia, the US Chicago school of economics influenced policymakers, at least an early prime minister, as documented in Chapter 9 (Laar 2005). According to the World Bank's *Doing Business* reports, performance in the Baltics is good and, according to the indicators examined, the Baltics tend to offer a favourable business and investment climate (World Bank 2017). Furthermore, income and property taxes for businesses are low, favouring business development. However, the loss of human capital as a consequence of outward migration post-independence has resulted in a scarcity of qualified staff for businesses in the Baltics. Income differences between the EU-15[1] countries and newer EU member states were always likely to result in outward migration. However, further research is needed to better understand to what extent the austerity policies implemented in the Baltics during the 2008/09 crisis aggravated this 'brain drain', and what measures can be taken to alleviate the problem in the post-crisis period. Internal divisions in the Baltics as well as external security threats affect the business and investment climate in the region. Geopolitical tensions (such as those which arose from the Russian annexation of Crimea from Ukraine in 2014) have adversely affected the risk profile of the Baltics, reducing FDI and growth. Further research is needed to identify business development in the Baltics that is more inclusive and whose benefits are better shared among citizens.

How can the Baltics become more democratic and achieve more circular flows of people instead of showing a tendency to one-way exodus?

In contrast to the continental Nordics, democratic processes have not always been used in making decisions on European integration in the Baltics. In particular, the Baltics did not use referendums to decide on euro area membership. Rather, this decision was left to the political élites. As discussed in Chapter 4, Norway twice rejected EU membership in public referendums and could thus not adopt the euro, while in Denmark and Sweden euro area membership was rejected. It is not known with any certainty if euro area membership enjoyed broad public support in the Baltics or if it was primarily supported by the Baltic élite. Baltic democracy is still fragile and traditions of democratic decision-making are still developing. During the Soviet era people could not protest (voice concerns) and they could not migrate to other countries (exit) as the border was closed. However, EU membership made voice possible. And being part of a common labour market makes exit possible. Instead of voicing concerns, many Baltic citizens chose the exit option, resulting in massive migration from the Baltics which is still ongoing, aggravated by the 2008/09 crisis and post-crisis developments. Further research is needed to analyse this problem and to identify mitigation measures encouraging more circular flows of people in and out of the Baltics instead of the mostly one-way exodus seen so far. This could include more democratic decision-making, creating more inclusive societies.

What can the Baltics do to improve cohesion within their borders in order to improve their internal security during a time of growing external uncertainty?

The Baltic quest for EU membership was largely driven by the quest for growth and prosperity. But—as argued in this book—for the Baltics and Finland, membership of the EU and subsequently the euro area were not only influenced by economic factors. Security concerns played an important role. Joining the euro area is in a way making European powers such as Germany and France responsible for Baltic security. Borders with Russia—which has eastern borders with Finland, Estonia and Latvia, as well as Lithuania's border with Kaliningrad—represent a constant threat to sovereignty for these countries. To some extent, the Baltics can be considered prisoners of geography. This is very different from Iceland, whose location in the middle of the Atlantic Ocean has sheltered the country for centuries. Further research is needed to see what the Baltic States can do to improve cohesion within their borders in order to improve their internal security during a time of growing external uncertainty.

How can small states reduce their vulnerability in their dealings with international organizations?

As the book discusses, multilateral co-operation is often considered important for small states and can potentially provide them with shelter from larger, more powerful states. But as the book argues, small states can also be vulnerable when dealing with powerful organizations such as the EU, the European Central Bank (ECB) and the International Monetary Fund (IMF). Further research is needed to identify measures for small states to reduce their vulnerability in their dealings with international organizations.

The Nordics have been very active in international development co-operation. How can the Baltics contribute more to development most notably in less advanced transition countries?

The Baltic States can to some extent be considered free riders in international organizations, receiving funds from the EU and protection from the North Atlantic Treaty Organization (NATO) without contributing much to their respective budgets. Their contributions to international development co-operation remain small. This was understandable during the early years of their development after reclaiming independence. In contrast, the continental Nordics are large contributors in the field of development co-operation. How can the Baltics increase their credibility internationally and by doing so become more influential in international organizations? Further research is needed to better understand how small states such as the Baltics can also participate in international organizations as contributors, in particular to policy reforms in less advanced transition countries (see for example Hilmarsson 2011).

How do foreign banks (mostly Nordic in the case of the Baltic States) influence the policy stance of governments as well as international organizations?

It has been argued in the book that Nordic-Baltic banking interlinkages influenced Baltic exchange rate policy during the 2008/09 crisis. A fixed exchange-rate policy in the Baltics was also an EU condition for euro area membership. In fact, as pointed out, the only stable economic variable in the Baltics during the 2008/09 crisis was the exchange rate (Becker 2009). During the rescue of foreign banks in Latvia, private debt became public debt. In addition to the banks' ability to influence the exchange-rate policy of the Baltic governments, further research is needed to better understand to what extent the banks influenced the policy stance of their home governments (in this case the continental Nordic governments) as well as international organizations, most notably the EU and the ECB.

How can the Baltics better diversify the ownership of their banking sector to reduce cross-border Nordic-Baltic vulnerabilities?

At independence the Baltics imported their banking sector from the continental Nordics. Why did Sweden become so dominant in the Baltic banking systems? Why did international organizations such as the EU, the IMF and the World Bank not step in with a clear signal to the government that financial sector dominance by a single country could be dangerous for both home and host countries as well as for the EU and the euro area? Further research is needed to better understand how the Swedish banks succeeded in achieving dominance and what methods were used. Further research is also needed to identify steps that can be taken to better diversify the financial sector in the Baltics and reduce Nordic-Baltic banking interlinkages and current cross-border banking vulnerabilities in the region.

How can the Baltics develop a more vibrant export sector?

How has a fixed exchange-rate policy post-independence affected the export sector, welfare systems and long-term growth in the Baltics? How did it influence the exodus of young and educated people from the Baltics? Were the Baltic currencies overvalued when the euro was adopted in spite of internal devaluation prior to euro adoption? What sectors, including goods and services, have export potential? Further research is needed to explain why the export sector in the Baltics remains so underdeveloped a quarter of century following independence and 10 years after the onset of the economic crisis, and how much exchange-rate policy has contributed to this weakness. Further research is also needed to better understand what steps can be taken to strengthen the tradable sector in the Baltics. What export strategy can be most effective among the Baltic States, and how can they best use their location and access to the EU single market to build a vibrant export sector? Small countries can be successful exporters, as the Nordics, including Iceland, have shown.

What level of global integration serves the long-term interest of the Baltics?

How does Sweden see the Baltics, given its past imperial status in the Nordic-Baltic region? Is the Nordic-Baltic region seen as a Swedish area of influence, threatened by an unstable Russia? Sweden and the Nordic countries have been supporters of Baltic integration in Western economic and political structures including the EU, the euro area and NATO. The Russian annexation of Crimea from Ukraine shows how important this integration is for Baltic independence. Uncertain US commitment to NATO only makes EU integration more important for Baltic security. Further research is needed to analyse what level of European and global integration serves the long-term interest of the Baltics.

How can small states benefit from international organizations, obtain shelter and avoid vulnerabilities?

International organizations cannot be viewed as neutral advisors on economic policy. Larger states tend to dominate those organizations. The Baltics have long battled corruption within their own borders but may in the future be faced with battling corruption within EU institutions that can adversely affect them. Why would a powerful international organization or a large state want to be benevolent supporters of a small state? Circumstances can make small states winners or victims, depending on circumstances and time. Shelter provided by international organizations can be a blessing and a curse for small states. Further analysis is needed in order to better determine how international organizations can become more neutral in their actions and so that power can be better shared among smaller and larger countries.

What policy mix, most notably in fiscal policy, is most suitable for small transition countries within the EU?

The current economic formula of a fixed exchange rate and fiscal discipline can be a straitjacket for transition countries such as the Baltics. Euro area exit is hardly feasible at the present moment but more flexibility in fiscal policies should be possible within the EU and euro area. In fact, the rationale for the current fiscal policy stance in the EU is not well grounded in economic theory. Economic policy—especially monetary policy—in the EU is mostly determined by technocrats with little democratic influence from elected representatives. Further research is needed on what policies are more suitable for transition countries wishing to catch up with richer EU member states.

Note

1 The EU-15 countries are: Austria, Belgium, Denmark, Finland, France, Germany, Greece, Ireland, Italy, Luxembourg, the Netherlands, Portugal, Spain, Sweden and the United Kingdom.

References

Becker, T. (2009). *IMF and Latvia—Why Going for Third Best?* Available at: www.researchgate.net/publication/266339036_IMF_and_Latvia-why_going_for_third_best (Accessed on 12 November 2017).

Hilmarsson, H. (2011). 'How can the Baltic States as Non-DAC donors best contribute to international development cooperation?' *Baltic Journal of Economics*, Vol. 11 (2), pp. 27–40.

Laar, M. (2005). 'Walking on Water: How to Do It.' *The Brussels Journal*. Available at: www.brusselsjournal.com/node/202 (Accessed on 23 October 2017).

World Bank (2017). *Doing Business 2018. Reforming to Create Jobs.* Available at: www.doingbusiness.org/reports/global-reports/doing-business-2018 (Accessed on 7 December 2017).

Index

Note: Page numbers in *italics* and **bold** denote references to Figures and Tables, respectively.

For Product Safety Concerns and Information please contact our EU representative GPSR@taylorandfrancis.com
Taylor & Francis Verlag GmbH, Kaufingerstraße 24, 80331 München, Germany

www.ingramcontent.com/pod-product-compliance
Ingram Content Group UK Ltd.
Pitfield, Milton Keynes, MK11 3LW, UK
UKHW022020180926
475701UK00005B/951
9780367901264